WE CAME
TO
REBUILD
NEW
ORLEANS

CHRISTOPHER E. MANNING

WE CAME
TO
REBUILD
NEW
ORLEANS

STORIES OF
THE HURRICANE
KATRINA
VOLUNTEERS

LOUISIANA STATE UNIVERSITY PRESS × BATON ROUGE

Published by Louisiana State University Press
lsupress.org

LSU Press Paperback Original

Designer: Kaelin Chappell Broaddus
Typefaces: Sentinel, text; Acumin Pro and Lacquer, display

Cover photo (background): *Plywood over Doorway,* by StevertS / Adobe Stock.

Library of Congress Cataloging-in-Publication Data

Names: Manning, Christopher E., author.
Title: We came to rebuild New Orleans : stories of the Hurricane Katrina
   volunteers / Christopher E. Manning.
Description: Baton Rouge : Louisiana State University Press, [2025] |
   Includes bibliographical references and index.
Identifiers: LCCN 2024034689 (print) | LCCN 2024034690 (ebook) | ISBN
   978-0-8071-8202-4 (paperback) | ISBN 978-0-8071-8417-2 (pdf) | ISBN
   978-0-8071-8416-5 (epub)
Subjects: LCSH: Hurricane Katrina, 2005. | Disaster relief—Louisiana—New
   Orleans—Case studies. | Volunteer workers in social
   service—Louisiana—New Orleans—Case studies. |
   Voluntarism—Louisiana—New Orleans—Case studies.
Classification: LCC HV636 2005.N4 M26 2025 (print) | LCC HV636 2005.N4
   (ebook) | DDC 363.34/9220976090511—dc23/eng/20250331
LC record available at https://lccn.loc.gov/2024034689
LC ebook record available at https://lccn.loc.gov/2024034690

CONTENTS

CONTENTS

8. Motivation

THE MAKING OF A
LONG-TERM VOLUNTEER

9. A Thousand Points of Light?

THE LIMITATIONS OF NONPROFITS IN
ADDRESSING DISASTER RECOVERY

Conclusion

INTEGRATING NONPROFITS INTO
A BROAD RECOVERY EFFORT

ACKNOWLEDGMENTS

I would like to extend my heartfelt gratitude to Loyola University Chicago and the University of Southern California for their support. A research support grant from Loyola significantly contributed to the realization of this project in its early stages, while USC provided a generous research budget for me, despite my role as a university administrator; these funds were instrumental to completing this endeavor. To the dedicated grad students of my Oral History Methods and Theory class at Loyola University, who conducted numerous interviews for the project, I offer my sincere appreciation. Your hard work deepened our historical knowledge, and your keen insights into oral history as a field gave this book its ultimate form. A special acknowledgment goes to Christopher Woodward, my editor, whose invaluable guidance proved indispensable during the final round of revisions. To my wife, Katherine Wood, I extend my profound gratitude for her unwavering patience, steadfast support, and endless encouragement throughout this journey. Last but certainly not least, I am grateful to my daughter, Simone, whose presence is a constant source of inspiration and joy. Kate and Simone, the two of you are the ground beneath my feet and the sun that lights my world.

WE CAME
TO
REBUILD
NEW
ORLEANS

Introduction

We came to rebuild New Orleans, but New Orleans rebuilt us.

—Scott Porot, Operation Helping Hands

In more than six years, Operation Helping Hands accomplished a
critically important task, enabling people like Ms. Thomas to finally
return to homes that are whole. Operation Helping Hands and other
groups that have taken on that work—Habitat for Humanity, the St.
Bernard Project, Rebuilding Together New Orleans, and others—have
made a significant difference in the lives of those they've helped
and in the life of the larger community. That won't be forgotten.

—Scott Threlkeld, *New Orleans Times-Picayune*

It was a balmy, pleasant Monday afternoon in New Orleans in the spring of
2008—a great day to be outside. Yet my colleagues and I were exasperated.
The day before, our group of four faculty and staff from Loyola University
Chicago had driven fourteen hours to New Orleans to do Hurricane Katrina recovery work during a spring break immersion project. We arrived
late Sunday evening at Loyola University New Orleans, where a bleary-
eyed volunteer coordinator led us to a set of well-used dorm rooms on the
edge of campus. Stiffness from the drive and the alleged "beds" notwith-
standing, we awoke the next day excited to begin our contribution to the
recovery effort. Indeed, over the previous two years, Loyola Chicago had
welcomed many students from Loyola New Orleans who had fled the hurricane and ultimately stayed in Chicago. Hearing those students' stories of
evacuating the city had given us a deep desire to make a difference.

Earlier that morning, around 7:30 a.m., we had arrived at the old St.
Raymond Catholic Church and School that then housed the central operations center of Operation Helping Hands (OHH) on Paris Avenue. Dozens

1

of short-term volunteers like us were gathered in small, somewhat nervous, somewhat enthusiastic groups here and there around the parking lot. Most appeared to be college aged, with a few youngish seniors who were perhaps in their sixties; volunteers like those in our group, arrayed across our thirties and forties, were rare. As we waited, several confident-looking young people wearing construction boots, paint-spattered pants, and OHH shirts strode into the headquarters—obtaining their assignments, assembling tools, and shepherding volunteer crews to their projects. After a half-hour, a clean-shaven young man with spiky hair and a laid-back demeanor introduced himself to us as Adrian Manriquez. He informed us that we would be doing some painting that day. It was not exactly the dramatic, feel-good work we had anticipated, like gutting or building a house, but we figured we would get the chance to rebuild a home later that week.

As we drove across town in our OHH van, we frequently spotted other volunteers conspicuously marked by the t-shirts of the organizations they worked with: Common Ground Relief, Operation Nehemiah, Mennonite Disaster Services, and scores and scores of AmeriCorps volunteers. This army of helpers deployed across the city appeared to be everywhere. We arrived at the home we were going to paint around 8:30 a.m., all of us ready and eager to get to work. But there was one problem: the owner was not there.

We waited in the front yard talking to each other, trying to remain cheerful for about an hour until a couple of people we could not see well drove up to the curb and spoke with Adrian. He came over to us to announce that he and the owner would make a run to the paint store and return soon. So, we waited again.

Adrian returned around 11:30. We waited expectantly as he walked over, only to be told that the owner was still deciding on the color and might be a while. This provoked a lot of grumbling and troubled looks. We complained that we had already been there for three hours and were not doing much good just sitting around. Adrian listened calmly and said he understood why we were upset at having to wait a few hours to get started. But, he explained, the woman who owned this house had been waiting almost three years for it to be rebuilt. Much of the process had been out of her control, and the paint was her first real choice for her home since the process had

2

begun. He then asked us if we could be a little more patient. We all shame-
facedly agreed that we could.

Ultimately, it took us far longer to paint the house than we had expected,
which I have come to believe is a familiar story among many eager short-
term volunteers. We then spent the last couple of days of our trip stripping
lead-contaminated paint from the home of a senior Katrina survivor who
could not afford to pay for the work.

Nevertheless, that moment on our first day of work, when a young man
barely out of college gave emotional support to a Katrina survivor while
gently reminding middle-aged professionals to have some grace, made me
aware of a genuine phenomenon. All that week, I watched in admiration
as any number of young people like Adrian guided volunteers from across
the country into action in the hot, difficult, and unglamorous work of rebuilding and repainting homes. Yet I also felt some wariness when I saw
the confusion of the morning muster at OHH headquarters, the haphazard
proliferation of volunteers throughout the city, and our own collection of
middle-aged higher education professionals wearing Tyvek suits and res-
pirators getting a five-minute lesson on removing lead paint.

These observations motivated this oral history project. Using more than
120 hours of interviews with fifty Katrina recovery leaders and staffers
involved in housing, criminal justice reform, legal aid, and wetlands restoration, this book seeks to understand what characteristics led people to
dedicate a significant portion of their lives (six months or longer) to the
recovery and whether using nonprofit volunteer labor was the most effective method to achieve recovery of this scale. These stories reveal that
long-term volunteers, not to be confused with the astronomically larger
cohort of short-term volunteers who numbered well over one million, possessed characteristics—most significantly, a history of activism or civic engagement—that scholars correlate to high volunteering rates under normal
circumstances. Additionally, our interviews indicate that using volunteer
labor scattered across hundreds of decentralized nonprofit organizations
is a poor strategy for recovering from a catastrophe of this scale.[1] Indeed,

1. Although I come to this second conclusion through an analysis of interviewees from a
range of charitable organizations, several other scholars reached the same conclusion primarily from the analysis of radical grassroots efforts. See Benham, "Birth of the Clinic," 69–

in future disasters, a government-coordinated and intentional integration of the nonprofit sector into the recovery process would yield improved outcomes. Meanwhile, charitable organizations could enhance their impact by resisting the extreme pressures for immediate action and giving more attention instead to volunteer preparation and organizing volunteer efforts in ways that empower the local population.

There is little disagreement that the real catastrophe was not caused by the storm but rather by human-made causes such as the destruction of the wetlands, which had historically acted as a natural barrier against hurricanes headed toward New Orleans; the cresting of the government-built levees, which had been improperly constructed; and to some extent global warming, which many argue contributes to a higher number of hurricanes of greater intensity.[2] The storm and subsequent flooding affected an area of more than 93,000 square miles, displaced 770,000 people, and killed 1,833 people, most of whom were senior citizens. With more than 118 million cubic yards covered in wreckage and 300,000 homes rendered unlivable, the recovery cost was over $250 billion. Meanwhile, much of New Orleans's economy collapsed, with one-third of the Port of New Orleans destroyed, suffering $100 million in damages; in addition, 113 offshore oil rigs were ruined, and tourism declined from 10.1 million visits in 2004 to 3.7 million in 2006.[3]

With 80 percent of New Orleans covered in floodwater, the city's financial, political, physical, and even natural infrastructure lay ruined. Of New

79; Berra, Leibenthal, and Incite!, "To Render Ourselves Visible," 31–47; Flaherty et al., *Floodlines*, 266; Salam, "Below the Water Line," ix–xviii; Luft, "Looking for Common Ground," 19.

2. For clarity, this study considers the circumstances surrounding Katrina's impact in New Orleans a catastrophe, rather than a disaster. According to E. L. Quarantelli, catastrophes possess five characteristics that distinguish them from disasters: (1) Virtually all the community's infrastructure is negatively affected; the breaking of the levees in New Orleans flooded eighty percent of the city, rendering even multistory buildings inoperable and precluding New Orleans's emergency providers from giving assistance; (2) the impact of the event hinders local leaders from acting in their official capacity not only during the event but also well into the relief period; (3) nearby communities are experiencing the same event and cannot provide assistance; (4) virtually all regular community activities are curtailed or stopped; and (5) the media constructs a narrative around the event to a greater extent than they do in the case of disasters. Quarantelli, "Catastrophes Are Different."

3. Sexton, "Obscurity of Black Suffering," 122; Lapham, "Slum Clearance," 8; Amadeo, "Hurricane Katrina: Facts, Damage and Costs"; Sayre, "New Orleans Port."

Orleans's many trouble spots, the displacement of its citizens due to the destruction of their homes attracted the most scrutiny, and volunteerism, as noted in the epigraph, quickly emerged as a principal strategy to address the desperate need to rebuild homes. This situation came to pass because of the failures of the homeowner's insurance industry and the limitations posed by government's reliance on neoliberal strategies to guide the recovery process.

First, insurance companies failed to support Katrina survivors. They rejected claims for damages caused by the hurricane, arguing that such claims were not covered by traditional home or hurricane insurance but rather by flood insurance. For example, journalists Leslie Eaton and Joseph B. Treaster reported on the experiences of Maxine Cassine and Emile Labat, whose policies of $100,000 and $300,000 paid out only $41,000 and $16,000, respectively. Eaton and Treaster noted, "Every neighborhood is full of horror stories about insurance companies that reneged on their promises, offered only pennies on the dollar in settlements, dribbled out payments, low-balled the costs of repairs, dropped long-time customers and sharply increased the price of coverage."[4] By 2007, Louisianans had filed more than six thousand insurance lawsuits with the U.S. District Court and submitted more than four thousand formal Katrina-related complaints to the Louisiana Department of Insurance. That year, the state of Louisiana estimated that, on average, each homeowner received approximately $5,700 less than they should have, leaving a $900 million shortfall to be covered by the government.[5]

Unfortunately, the government-sponsored and neoliberal-inspired Road Home Program was administered with unprecedented incompetence in its first two years by ICF International, a for-profit company.[6] Louisiana granted ICF International a $756 million contract in 2006 to distribute federal funds to homeowners affected by Hurricane Katrina. ICF had no prior experience managing a housing project of this size, having had government contracts in the previous four years totaling only $23.6 million. *New Orleans Times-Picayune* reporter David Hammer noted that "ICF

4. Eaton and Treaster, "Insurance Woes," Schneider, *Renew New Orleans,* 4.
5. Southeast Louisiana Legal Services, "Katrina Stories"; Kerley, "Katrina Victims"; Eaton and Treaster, "Insurance Woes"; Schneider, *Renew New Orleans,* 4.
6. Adams, *Markets of Sorrow,* loc 1449.

parlayed its Road Home experience into lucrative deals elsewhere. At the end of 2005, it held $227 million in contracts. It immediately quadrupled that by inking the Road Home deal, then went public a few months later. In the past year alone [2008], it won more than $500 million in contracts involving such agencies as the National Institutes of Health, the Environmental Protection Agency, and Head Start."[7]

Despite its rapid increase in revenues, ICF distributed funds breathtakingly slowly, with only 1 percent of eligible homeowners receiving assistance seven months into the program. Critics of ICF's operations noted that it was unresponsive, and its eligibility requirements were burdened by confusing rules. Stunningly, ICF's contract with Louisiana lacked clear performance benchmarks, prompting the state to demand their development. By 2007, ICF's payment system for homeowners was found to contravene federal regulations, resulting in a $1 million fine; negotiations to establish further performance metrics collapsed, fueling public and political discontent. In New Orleans, ICF provided applicants $55,000 less than the average homeowner needed, with the shortfall rising to $75,000 in the predominantly Black Lower Ninth Ward. Moreover, the program required that applicants provide titles to their properties, which adversely affected New Orleans's poorest communities, where homes had been owned for generations without legal documentation.[8] Despite these glaring and oft-reported shortcomings, Louisiana governor Kathleen Blanco increased the size of ICF's contract to $926 million to support program improvements in March 2008. However, ICF's failures persisted, leading to significant fines totaling more than $14 million. By the time Louisiana terminated ICF's contract in 2009 and barred the company from further business in the state, ICF was "generally reviled by Louisianans."[9]

ICF's failed administration of the Road Home program occurred within a broader context of lightly regulated free-market conditions that were designed to speed the recovery process. Soon after the storm, the Bush admin-

7. Associated Press, "Consulting Company Targeted"; Flaherty et al., *Floodlines,* 59–60; Hammer, "ICF's Oversight of Road Home Program Comes to an End."

8. Flaherty et al., *Floodlines,* 59–60.

9. Associated Press, "Consulting Company Targeted"; Flaherty, *Floodlines,* 59–60; Hammer, "ICF's Oversight of Road Home Program Comes to an End"; "Blanco Administration Quietly Gave Raise to Road Home Operator"; "State Signs New Road Home Contract with HGI Catastrophe Services."

istration temporarily suspended Occupational Safety and Health Administration regulations, affirmative action requirements, and open competition for reconstruction contracts. It also paused requirements for contractors receiving federal funds to pay prevailing wages, to document wages paid to workers, and to verify worker eligibility documents. Meanwhile, the state government removed collective bargaining requirements from public infrastructure contracts, and city governments stopped enforcing regulations to prevent contractor fraud.[10] Regarding home rebuilding, the Bush administration required Governor Blanco to shift the design of the Road Home program in March 2007 from a phased reconstruction payment system, in which contractors would have been paid as they completed stages of the work, to providing contractors lump-sum checks up front.[11]

This free-market, neoliberal-oriented context created an environment that nearly obliterated workers' rights while pushing cash-strapped survivors to use volunteer labor to rebuild their homes. In *Renew New Orleans,* Aaron Schneider documents how immigrant and, ultimately, native construction workers experienced rampant abuse and exploitation, including exposure to toxic chemicals, dangerous working conditions, inadequate training, and wage theft.[12] Meanwhile, contractor fraud, in which contractors took large down payments and absconded with the money, ravaged the often meager payouts that survivors received from insurance and Road Home claims.[13] According to Southeast Louisiana Legal Services director Brian Lenard, "Most people receiving funds were required to repair and move into the house in a certain period of time, but they couldn't when the money was lost to contractor fraud or the money was not enough for repairs. So, the government then tried to get the money back."[14]

Unable to afford licensed construction companies, forced to work with a virtually hostile bureaucracy, and facing seemingly arbitrary deadlines to complete the reconstruction of their homes, New Orleans's most vulnerable homeowners called on the charitable sector, and more than a million

10. Schneider, *Renew New Orleans,* 5–6, 100–101.

11. Hammer, "Examining Post-Katrina Road Home Program"; Southeast Louisiana Legal Services, "Katrina Stories"; Welch, interview.

12. Schneider, *Renew Orleans,* 97, 104, 107.

13. Schneider, *Renew Orleans,* 101.

14. Hammer, "Examining Post-Katrina Road Home Program"; Southeast Louisiana Legal Services, "Katrina Stories"; Welch, interview.

volunteers answered their plea. Local media reported that many New Orleanians credited the nonprofit sector with providing critical aid to the city. As *New Orleans Times-Picayune* reporter Scott Threlkeld wrote, these organizations "have made a significant difference in the lives of those they've helped and the larger life of the community. That won't be forgotten."[15] Yet, to a certain extent, it already has.

Although the scholarship about Katrina is extensive, the experiences of those involved in New Orleans's long-term recovery through charitable organizations have been mainly ignored. Early works on Katrina did not consider the volunteer responders at all. Instead, they revolved around notions of New Orleans's exceptionalism, survivor narratives, and government incompetence—areas somewhat predetermined by press coverage of the catastrophe.[16] Three works in 2006 embodied this focus: Spike Lee's documentary *When the Levees Broke* and books by Douglas Brinkley, *The Great Deluge,* and Michael Eric Dyson, *Come Hell or High Water.* In the exceptionalist mode, Lee portrayed New Orleans as a particularly "Black" city with a syncretic cultural heritage, with much of the documentary implying that the federal government neglected New Orleans because of its historic racial difference. Brinkley and Dyson both contributed to *When the Levees Broke,* and their works expanded on themes in the film, with Brinkley providing a detailed rendering of each day of the catastrophe and Dyson arguing that the Bush administration's version of limited government offered "poor protection to the most vulnerable."[17]

Oral histories documenting survivors' experiences soon appeared. Although these works have provided invaluable testimonies, they are analytically limited. For example, Rebecca Antoine's collections, *Voices Rising* and *Voices Rising II,* presented poignant testimonies in various genres, including interviews, short stories, and poetry. Still, Antoine acted more as a documentarian than an analyst of the materials. In *Overcoming Katrina,* D'Ann Penner and Keith C. Ferdinand showcased a diverse spectrum

15. Threlkeld, "A Job Well Done."

16. Cedric Johnson best articulates the concept of New Orleans exceptionalism in his article, "Working the Reserve Army."

17. Brinkley, *The Great Deluge;* Dyson, *Come Hell or High Water;* Lee, *When the Levees Broke,* film.

of members of New Orleans's Black community. Nevertheless, they organized the book somewhat arbitrarily by generation and simply asserted that New Orleans has a unique racial heritage. Swinging to the political right, Nona Martin Storr, Emilee Chamlee Wright, and Virgil Henry of the free-market–oriented Mercatus Center presented seventeen testimonies to argue simply that New Orleanians were "resilient."[18] Moreover, none of these works described the editors' methodology or addressed the deeper cultural and subjective meanings of their interviewees' testimonies, elements that oral history theorists have asserted as critical since the 1980s.[19]

Diverging from this pattern, memoirs and biographies have addressed the recovery, but their creators' proximity to the struggle has made for a lack of perspective. Rasmus Holm's documentary *Welcome to New Orleans* chronicled former Black Panther Malik Rahim's efforts that led to the formation of the Common Ground Collective. The collective was a radical, grassroots organization that achieved widespread recognition when it defied martial law by beginning recovery efforts well before the waters receded. Holm, however, did not situate Common Ground within the broader recovery movement, which included more than five hundred new organizations that sprang up in response to the storm. Nor did he address any controversies surrounding Common Ground, such as its alleged infiltration and destabilization by FBI informant Brandon Darby.[20] Unfortunately, memoirs written by ACORN founder Wade Rathke and Common Ground cofounder Scott Crow followed a similar pattern of vindicating their organizations.[21] In a different approach, Luisa Dantas's documentary *Land of Opportunity* explored the battle to determine the fate of New Orleans's public housing between early 2006 and late 2007 from the perspective of movement activists, displaced residents, and even developers and migrant laborers. Although Dantas did not articulate a methodology for analyzing

18. Antoine, *Voices Rising;* Antoine, *Voices Rising II;* Neville, "How We Survived," 28–30; Storr et al., *How We Came Back;* Penner and Ferdinand, *Overcoming Katrina;* Wooten, *We Shall Not Be Moved.*

19. Lummis, "Structure and Validity in Oral Evidence," 273; Kennedy, "Oral History," 351; Portelli, "What Makes Oral History Different," 69.

20. Adams, *Markets of Sorrow,* loc 2297.

21. Blakely, *My Storm;* Crow, *Black Flags and Windmills;* Rathke, *The Battle for the Ninth Ward;* Holm, *Welcome to New Orleans,* film.

WE CAME TO REBUILD NEW ORLEANS

her data, thus limiting the ability of scholars to assess her findings, she nevertheless painted a nuanced and complex picture of the struggle.[22]

A rich area of scholarship focused on both the catastrophe and the dynamics of the recovery as a result of America's embrace of neoliberalism, defined by Cedric Johnson as "the ideological rejection of the planner state . . . and the activist promotion of a new order of market rule."[23] Naomi Klein and Paul Street used this lens as early as 2007 but more or less in passing within broader discussions beyond New Orleans.[24] However, *In the Wake of Katrina,* a 2010 collection edited by the late Clyde Woods, placed this type of analysis squarely within a Katrina context by documenting multiple patterns of the "privatization of publicly held assets" and the "dismantling of the welfare state" in New Orleans that effectively rendered working-class African Americans particularly vulnerable to the destabilization created by the storm. In the following year, editor Cedric Johnson brought together an even more robust set of essays in *The Neoliberal Deluge,* which explored the impact of neoliberalism in a range of areas, from media coverage of the storm to nonprofit and radical movements' recovery efforts.[25]

Within this critical framework, a subset of scholars focused on the evolution of radical and grassroots organizations in approximately the first three years after the storm. In a 2008 examination of Common Ground, New Orleans's most well-known radical-turned-nonprofit organization, Rachel Luft argued that the failure of the neoliberal state to respond to the people's needs drew a tremendous influx of mostly well-intentioned volunteers from outside New Orleans. Luft and Jordan Flaherty found that these newcomers gravitated to radical organizations like Common Ground, which participated in a broad array of community-based activities, and

22. Dantas and Tannen, *Land of Opportunity,* film.
23. Johnson, "Obama's Katrina," xxi.
24. Klein, *The Shock Doctrine,* 4–6, 513–522; Street, *Racial Oppression,* 12–15.
25. For examples of analysis executed through a lens critical of neoliberal-influenced policies see Sexton, *Obscurity of Black Suffering;* Arena, *Driven From New Orleans;* Advancement Project et al., "And Injustice for All"; Brown, "Wade in the Water"; Camp, "'We Know This Place'"; Diamond, "Naturalizing Disaster"; Lovell, "Reformers, Preservationists, Patients, and Planners"; Dixon, "Whose Choice?"; Johnson, "Charming Accommodations"; Russel and Lavin, "From Tipping Point to Meta-Crisis"; Lapham, "Slum Clearance"; Rodriguez, "The Meaning of 'Disaster'"; Woods, "Les Misérables of New Orleans"; Wells et al., "Defining Democracy in the Neoliberal Age."

the People's Hurricane Relief Fund, which focused primarily on advocating for displaced residents' right of return. Unfortunately, these predominantly young and white volunteers inadvertently undermined local African American grassroots leadership and reinforced other forms of oppression, particularly against Black and white women in the movement.[26]

Similarly, sociologist Jay Arena situates the failed post-Katrina struggle to save New Orleans's Big Four housing projects as the last chapter in a decades-long battle to block neoliberal encroachment on the city. Arena traces federal and local business efforts to dismantle these housing projects to the late 1970s. Still, he notes that by seizing local control and influencing local political leaders, grassroots activists largely held this neoliberal agenda at bay through the 1990s. Katrina's devastation and the array of deregulatory policies touched on earlier opened the floodgates for local elites to push forward with nationally and globally driven privatization plans, exemplified by the Road Home program's property-owner–driven approach to reconstruction; Governor Blanco's closing of Charity Hospital, which had provided free healthcare to a largely local working-class clientele; and the state's transformation of the public schools into the nation's most extensive charter school system.[27]

The demolition of all four of the city's housing projects in December 2007 and the conversion of that land into private commercial areas also figured prominently in these privatization plans; Arena contends that radical, grassroots activists' transition to a nonprofit approach abetted this process.[28] He frequently critiques nonprofit organizations in New Orleans for drawing hundreds of thousands of volunteers into gutting and home rebuilding work, rather than funneling them into the public housing movement.[29] He goes so far as to suggest that protests confronting the bulldozers set to begin the demolition of public housing could have attracted "the thousands of volunteers involved in purely self-help work" and created "an arena for democratic self-organization and debate."[30]

26. Flaherty et al., *Floodlines,* 84, 97, 100–101; Flaherty, *No More Heroes,* 59–67; Luft, "Looking for Common Ground," 20, 23; Luft, "Racialized Disaster Patriarchy,"16.

27. Arena, *Driven from New Orleans,* loc 80, 176, 184, 193, 200, 305, pp. 29, 36, 51, 56, 122, 147–149, 221.

28. Tulane School of Architecture, "After Hurricane Katrina."

29. Tulane School of Architecture, "After Hurricane Katrina," loc 149, 161, 172, 183 and 199.

30. Arena, *Driven from New Orleans,* loc 199.

For multiple reasons, involving volunteers in these protests would have been unlikely. First, whatever coverage the protests around public housing generated, it simply did not compare to the volume of images of Hurricane Katrina destroying homes, the torrent of rescue videos of people trapped on their homes' rooftops and attics during the flooding, and the cascade of images of wiped-out neighborhoods—all of which generated the kind of sympathetic emotions that drew Americans from every state to give aid around home rebuilding. Indeed, in "Identity, Place, and Bystander Intervention: Social Categories and Helping after Natural Disasters," written before Katrina, Mark Levine and Kirstien Thompson found salient identity and a sense of an ability to make a difference to be critical motivators of volunteer support. As we discuss later, participants in this project frequently identified with victims of the storm as fellow Americans abandoned by their government. Combine this with the sense of commonality that almost any American would experience as a witness to Katrina's destruction of housing, and it is hardly surprising that millions of volunteers streamed into New Orleans ready to do the tangible labor of rebuilding homes.[31]

A more likely culprit for the lack of support for the public housing movement was the pervasive national neoliberal discourse that trumpeted a mixed-income housing model as a replacement for traditional public housing. The only evidence that the public housing protests captured national political attention was the passage of a bill by the House of Representatives to provide a one-for-one replacement of public housing in New Orleans; it later failed in the Senate.[32]

Recently, Andy Horowitz in *Katrina: A History, 1915–2015* found no evidence that the public housing movement elevated their fight into a national issue that would affect the political fortunes of legislators and policy makers in Washington, DC, in any significant way. Arguing that "the fundamental problem of where to rebuild" as a general question appears to be free market oriented only when looking at more recent decades, Horowitz questions scholars' usage of neoliberalism as an encompassing explanatory framework. On the contrary, by analyzing state politics and

31. Levine and Thompson, "Identity, Place, and Bystander Intervention," 232, 242.
32. Levine and Thompson, "Identity, Place, and Bystander Intervention"; Arena, *Driven from New Orleans,* loc 177, 182.

Louisiana's interactions with the federal government as far back as 1915, Horowitz discovers significant continuities between the Katrina era and Louisiana's distant past that predated the prominence of neoliberal, free-market ideology.[33]

Despite this claim, I agree with scholars such as Vincanne Adams and Jordan Flaherty who argue that neoliberal ideology influenced the federal and state government's adoption of a strategy to subcontract large portions of the recovery work to the private sector, notably home rebuilding in the Road Home Program, and that the early failures of the private sector to live up to their obligations to the people of New Orleans led to the city's reliance on volunteer labor. Adams writes, "The rise of nongovernmental charity and volunteer organizations was celebrated by many returning residents in part because, on the ground, this aid looked and felt like real assistance in contrast to the bureaucratic nightmare of programs like Road Home and the SBA loan program or to the impersonal nature of insurance companies. At the same time, the trend toward increasing reliance on charity to fill in the gaps left open by inadequate or inefficient federal support also poses interesting new civil society problems."[34]

Although scholars like Luft and Flaherty examine some of these problems within the context of radical organizations, this project centers testimony from recovery workers across a range of nonprofit organizations in areas such as criminal justice reform, legal aid, wetlands restoration, and home rebuilding. In contrast to earlier oral histories, I subject these interviews to a rigorous analytical methodology. The project generated its participants through snowball sampling, a process in which interviewees nominate other interviewees: snowball sampling is a nonrandom sampling method used when sources are challenging to obtain.[35] Typically, it stops after securing a suitable number of participants, but it was not the completeness of the sample that ended interviewee recruitment for this project. We sought interviewees whose work had begun relatively early in the recovery process, but it became apparent that the number of those still active had greatly diminished by 2013.[36] Once my students and I ceased

33. Horowitz, *Katrina: A History*, loc 50–116, 2999, 3368.
34. Adams, *Market of Sorrow*, loc 2243.
35. Statistics How To, "Snowball Sampling."
36. I consider the early period of the recovery to be those years in which gutting still

collecting interviews, NVIVO qualitative data analysis software was used to execute a constant comparative analysis.[37] A form of grounded analysis, the constant comparative method produces theory that arises from data—a point of departure both from the early literature's overreliance on tropes, such as New Orleans's exceptionalism and the people's resilience, and from later scholarship's determination to fix New Orleans's circumstances within a neoliberal critical framework.

In more than a decade of working through oral history theory and practice with enthusiastic and thoughtful cohorts of graduate students, I repeatedly heard calls for greater analytical rigor in the field and an expansion of participants' voices. Those students were correct. Consequently, this book features extended excerpts from some of the project's most enlightening narratives, which were edited mainly for readability. Readers who wish to hear only the testimony of these volunteers can read these participant narratives, and those seeking to understand the featured interviews in a broader context can avail themselves of the detailed notes, which place themes from the individual narratives into patterns constitutive of the bigger picture.

Although all the featured interviews reflect broad patterns that make up the larger portrait of volunteer characteristics and the feasibility of using nonprofit volunteer labor to execute a recovery of this scale, their emphases differ. In situating each interviewee's narrative, it is helpful to imagine a scatterplot, with the vertical axis measuring insights regarding volunteer characteristics and the horizontal axis assessing nonprofit participation in the recovery process. Plotting the book's featured narratives along this

---

occurred on a large scale. There is no way to verify this marker, but most participants indicated that organizations involved in housing moved from gutting to rebuilding around 2008.

37. In constant comparative analysis, interview samples are coded. When variance arises within a code, the researcher writes a memo to reconcile the new data and determine whether a new code is necessary. As the codes stabilize, the analysis moves from comparing incidents to evaluating new incidents relative to the category's broader properties. As the "underlying uniformities in the original set of categories" arise, the number of categories can be reduced to a set of broader concepts. In the end, "the analyst has coded data, a series of memos and a theory. The discussions in the memos provide the content behind the categories, which are the major themes of the theory." Continuously "challenging categories with fresh data, examining any variations, and grouping only like phenomena" yield highly trustworthy results. Glaser, "Constant Comparative Method," 439–443; Vander Putten and Nolen, "Comparing Results," 101, 105.

graph would reveal a random distribution, with some situated very high along the characteristics axis, some found very far along the analysis of the recovery axis, and others positioned in between.

Chapters 1 and 2 feature interviews with members of the largest demographic group represented in the project: young adults who arrived in New Orleans fresh out of university. This group worked in radical organizations, nonprofit home rebuilding, and wetlands restoration, enmeshed in a network of young volunteers across a range of small and large nonprofits. These interviewees' narratives vividly illustrate common patterns across this young adult demographic: their motivations to come to New Orleans, their entry into short-term volunteering, and their eventual transition to full-time recovery work. Moreover, these interviews reveal the challenges of funneling unbridled youthful enthusiasm into the swamp that was post-Katrina New Orleans.

The participants featured in chapters 3–5 likewise possessed traits that correlate with the scholarship on volunteering. These narratives were gathered from leaders who established or helped establish three nonprofit organizations that grew in response to the storm: Bayou Rebirth (wetlands restoration), Safe Streets/Strong Communities (criminal justice reform), and Operation Nehemiah (faith-based home and church rebuilding). These participants' testimonies reveal the struggles of fledgling nonprofit organizations to meet recovery needs. They indicate that, for such nonprofits to remain relevant, they need considerable support to be sustainable and centralized coordination with comparably situated, lesser-resourced organizations.

Similar concerns around coordination arise in chapters 6 and 7, which focus on interviews with leaders in two larger, established organizations that moved almost entirely to recovery work for several years after Katrina: Southeast Louisiana Legal Services (SLLS), a nonprofit law center dedicated to serving low-income people, and Rebuilding Together New Orleans (RTNO), a historic preservation organization that became one of the city's most prominent home rebuilders. In chapter 6, Jay Welch, a top attorney with SLLS, describes the organization's herculean efforts, sometimes alone and sometimes in partnership with other nonprofits, to serve low-income victims of the storm who faced incomprehensible government requirements for assistance, rampant contractor fraud, and a bottomless sinkhole of individual civil matters: they were trapped in New Orleans's broken legal system.

In chapter 7, Daniela Rivero, executive director of RTNO from 2006 to 2011, describes her quest to bring greater efficiency to the organization as it made the transition from historic preservation to home rebuilding. Rivero details the difficulties of bringing efficiency and responsible stewardship of donated funds to nonprofit work amidst the cascading urgency of the disaster recovery period. She also provides insight into a particularly dark time when the drive to assist as many people as possible led local nonprofits to use contaminated drywall to rebuild hundreds of homes in the area. Echoing themes articulated by the leaders of other large nonprofits, such as Common Ground, Operation Helping Hands, and New Orleans Area Habitat for Humanity, both Welch and Rivero reveal how difficult it was for even large and well-resourced nonprofit organizations to scale up operations to meet recovery needs; like their smaller counterparts, they call for greater centralized coordination between nonprofits, local government, and national government agencies.

I widen the analysis in the following chapters to the entire interview set. In chapter 8, I outline the character traits of participants across the study and argue that the backgrounds of the long-term volunteers adhered closely to those attributes that scholars associate with volunteering under normal circumstances, albeit with some important exceptions. In chapter 9, I draw from testimony across the interviews to contend that reliance on hundreds of decentralized charitable organizations, most of which depended on short-term volunteer labor, was an inadequate—although well-meaning—strategy for Katrina recovery in New Orleans. In the conclusion, I argue that our participants' testimony points to the advantages of an accountable, state-led reconstruction process that is highly inclusive of residents in planning and execution. Although this is unlikely given the continued predominance of neoliberalism in U.S. politics and government, this testimony can at least provide some guidance in improving practices within individual nonprofits, enhancing coordination across nonprofits operating within a recovery space, and integrating the work of those nonprofits with government for the maximum benefit of communities affected by disaster.

These interviews, beginning with the young people who arrived shortly after college and ending with the testimony of leaders struggling mightily to deal with the storm after the storm, reflect and remind us of the enormous goodwill of the American people. Moreover, I hope that they will help answer some fundamental questions that will arise when the next great catastrophe occurs, such as how we can strategically position nonprofit sector efforts in a recovery process on the scale of Katrina and how the nonprofit sector can organize volunteer labor in a manner that is both gratifying to the volunteers and empowering to the local population.

1. Adrian Manriquez

REBUILDING HOMES IN A DISASTER AREA

I feel like I've tried a lot of idealistic, radical solutions in New Orleans. That was something I've definitely gone through—coming down here with a vision of a changed society that would have been tempered by elders and comrades and colleagues in Denver where I was living. But they were not down here, and I was actually encouraged to try more and crazy different ideas. What changed me is that I got to try a lot of things that totally failed, and I've had the privilege of stopping to reorganize and reassess my ways of thinking about changing the world.

—Adrian Manriquez, Operation Helping Hands and the Common Ground Collective

In 2009 when my graduate students and I began conducting oral histories with long-term volunteers in New Orleans's recovery, I knew I wanted to start with Adrian Manriquez, whose patient management of both his client and crew of volunteers during my spring break immersion trip the year before so impressed me. His interview, conducted by students in Loyola University Chicago's public history program, relayed many of the common themes found across all our participants and within the scholarship. Like many of his counterparts, Adrian was in a place of transition—from college to the so-called real world—when he decided to volunteer. Also like his colleagues, his background had many of the characteristics that scholars correlate with volunteering, such as past volunteer experience and feeling an affinity with New Orleanians as fellow Americans. Lastly, Manriquez embodied the tendency of young adults specifically to gravitate toward high-risk volunteering.

Surprising his interviewers, Manriquez spent most of his time discussing another relief organization, the Common Ground Collective, with which he had volunteered before coming to Operation Helping Hands. This proved fortunate, because interviewees consistently pointed to Common Ground as a focal point of the recovery, particularly as a gateway for new volunteers. Manriquez painted a troubling picture of the collective, however, characterizing it as an unsustainable organization full of overworked, unprepared young adults with a toxic hypermasculine culture. In addition to his negative experiences at Common Ground, Manriquez's testimony reveals the severe financial, emotional, and physical stresses of the work in the first few years after the storm, as well as the inefficiencies of attempting to execute a large-scale disaster recovery using decentralized volunteer labor. Nevertheless, like many of his young adult counterparts, Manriquez remained enthusiastic, with plans to stay in New Orleans and live out his commitment to making the city a better place.

⚜ ⚜ ⚜

NOVEMBER 9, 2009

What was going on in your life before the hurricane hit?

I'd been in Ireland since February of '05 studying abroad in my junior year of college. I was actually abroad up until the day of the hurricane. I remember watching it on CNN while I was in the Chicago airport.

What did you think when you saw the coverage initially?

I actually didn't pay attention to it for a few days. I know that sounds terrible, but I came into town the Monday Katrina hit and was getting my schooling in order. So, I didn't watch it for several days until a friend of mine told me what was going on. I was really shocked—I guess that's the word—at the idea that an American city could be flooding like that and that there wouldn't be relief coming for several days.[1] I mean my reaction

1. Manriquez's experience of paying minimal attention to the storm while being intensely shocked by the poor handling of the rescue and relief efforts (a sense of disbelief that this scenario was happening in America) is very common to the participants in this study who were not in New Orleans at the time of the storm. This theme helps explain why these folks—mostly white, middle-class, young, and not from the South—decided to assist people who were very different from themselves. Indeed, Lacie Michel writes that natural disasters destabilize "pre-disaster differences in social and economic status," leading people

was kinda like, "It can't all be underwater," or "The water's going to be out in a little while." But with the vast majority of the city being literally underwater for several weeks, it was too fantastic to conceive that it could actually be happening.

Before Katrina, had you participated in any type of community volunteer work?

I'd been an activist. I volunteered at food banks, and I'd done Habitat a couple of times in my community. I was mostly a political activist working on international and some local neighborhood issues, not so much material volunteering but more like legislative and political work.

What was the motivating factor for you to head down to New Orleans?

This is a funny one. The literal motivating reason for me to go down to New Orleans originally was a fight with my conservative girlfriend over whether the situation in New Orleans was quite as bad as the "liberal" media made it. I'd done mostly political work, and I didn't really do a lot of hands-on volunteering; she challenged me to go down there and show up. So, we both did and after having seen what was going on in New Orleans, that led me to come back down here, stay, and volunteer.

You won the challenge, I take it?

Of sorts, yeah. (*Laughter.*)

You started with Common Ground?[2]

---

to act "sympathetically and sentimentally on the basis of human needs." Disaster areas thus become sites of convergent behaviors where the broader community rushes to help despite pre-disaster differences in identity. Michel, "Personal Responsibility," 634, 635.

2. In 2006 former Black Panther and native New Orleanian Malik Rahim, New Orleans's native Sharon Johnson, and anarchists Scott Crow and Brandon Darby founded the Common Ground Collective: activists from around the country had responded to Rahim's call for help in the wake of the government's seeming abandonment of storm survivors and the violence heaped on Black victims of the storm by white vigilante groups in the Algiers neighborhood of New Orleans. Operating on a model of "solidarity not charity," Common Ground envisioned itself as partnering with the community to build out resources. By 2007,

I volunteered with Common Ground Relief for six months before I came to Operation Helping Hands.[3] Common Ground Relief still exists but in a more limited capacity. It works in the Ninth Ward and across New Orleans. I had originally come there in March of '06 as a spring break trip. Then I came down in December of '06 to volunteer, planning to be there for two years. Unfortunately, the organization went through enough changes, administratively and politically, that it was really not tenable for me to be there after May of '07.

Can you describe to us the decision-making process in choosing Operation Helping Hands?

My decision-making process quite honestly had much to do with the fact that they paid any amount of money over zero. Common Ground didn't pay any money. So, after six months, I decided that I really needed a real job. (*Laughter.*) I moved to Operation Helping Hands because a friend of mine who worked with the Jesuits told me that they might be hiring and I

Common Ground's use of this model enabled them to gut hundreds of homes and serve more than 15,000 people through their health clinic, legal aid clinic, and Latino Outreach Project. In addition, Common Ground established seven distribution centers, which, according to Crow, "provided more than 120 tons of food and 100,000 gallons of water." During its early years Common Ground—with its daring stance against gun-toting vigilantes and its willingness to violate the evacuation order to help those in need—became the largest and most well-known grassroots response organization in New Orleans: it drew thousands of largely young, white volunteers. Consequently, the organization is central to many of the participants in this interview project, and its triumphs as well as its tragedies in using radical activism in the pursuit of disaster recovery are prominent in the analysis found in chapters 8 and 9. Manriquez's testimony, along with that of Caitlin Reilly and Colleen Morgan, highlights many of these issues. Hilderbrand et al., "Common Ground Relief," 85; Flaherty, "Corporate Reconstruction," 114; Benham, "Birth of the Clinic," 74.

3. When Manriquez arrived at Common Ground, it was known as the Common Ground Collective. This is an important distinction. Common Ground cofounder Scott Crow regards Common Ground as comprising two organizations: the Common Ground Collective (2005–2008), which he characterized as having "revolutionary potential," and Common Ground Relief (2008 to the present), which he has called a traditional nonprofit that benefits the community. His timeline corresponds with the testimony from Common Ground executive director Thom Pepper, who claimed that he was brought into leadership in 2008 to create a more professional and financially accountable organization after it had achieved nonprofit status. Cunningham, "Q&A with Scott Crow."; Pepper, interview.

might as well submit an application.[4] Almost immediately, I got a job, and I've been working there ever since.

So, prior to the trip down to New Orleans, what did you expect to see?

You know we'd heard all the stories about how New Orleans looked, that there were houses in the middle of the road, that there were still dead bodies inside of houses. I had a connection with Loyola University [New Orleans] through Bill Quigley who's a human rights lawyer. He gave us a fairly detailed description and did a lot of myth-busting in his emails. Also, Common Ground Relief told volunteers that there wouldn't be running water, and any running water you find is gonna be poisonous. So, you're gonna have to use filtered or boiled water. There is no electricity. You're gonna need to bring a flashlight. You should expect to sleep on a bare floor covered by a tarp. You should expect to have cold showers and be waiting in the shower line for an hour. You should expect to have to change your tires several times. You're gonna get nails. You should expect to see houses with everyone's belongings in some kind of way. Even though I expected to see a destroyed city in many ways, I still expected a much better response.

When you got down there, did the reality differ from these expectations?

(*Pause.*) I wouldn't say it differed. I read articles about Sudan and Afghanistan. It's one thing to read articles about things going on in the world. That's terrible. But to actually go in and see rows of houses empty and piles of trash everywhere, that was something else. It was appalling. And the most jarring thing to see was the lack of governmental agencies around. There was a lot of organizations. The Red Cross was running around blaring its food truck horn, giving out free food, and there was the occasional siren of

---

4. Sociologist Rachel Luft noted a "pervasive culture of masculinity" across movement groups in New Orleans post-Katrina, but particularly in Common Ground. As discussed in the notes of chapters 2 and 9, this characteristic had significant negative effects not only on women participants but also on the entire movement, including a "minimization of emotion and basic human needs." as can be seen in Manriquez's testimony. Luft, "Disaster Patriarchy," 18.

police and firefighters, but there didn't seem to be any kind of government response. At first, I was thinking, "It can't be that bad." A lot of people at work that I'm talking to at the time—they're pretty hyperbolic—assured me that it can't be that bad. But it was that bad.

Can you tell us about the kind of work
you were doing when you started volunteering?

When I first started volunteering at Common Ground, I was put on the gutting crew. In a few weeks I became a crew leader and was leading volunteers to gut houses. I did that for about six weeks, and then a staffing change at Common Ground put me in charge of running all gutting crews. I did that for the next several months.

Was there any kind of training, or did you learn on the job?

There was some, but it was mostly optional. Common Ground sent us a lot of information on what you should do before you got there. You should take first aid training. You should have your hepatitis A and B shots and your tetanus shots. You should take these safety precautions and be aware of biological hazards, staph infections, mold, and things of that nature. There wasn't really that much training, though. Honestly, when I went on a gutting crew, my training was in the field. Someone my age, maybe slightly older, who had been gutting for several weeks before me was like, "This is how you turn off gas. This is how you turn off electricity. And this is how you can judge structural work."

Can you describe a typical day of work?

At Common Ground the wake-up call was at 6 o'clock. Breakfast from 6:30 to 7:30. At 7:30, I had a morning brief. and it went until 8:00 or 8:30. You got your crew from the morning briefing. You got your tools from the tool room, your protective equipment you know—masks, suits, goggles, and gloves. You went out to your job site. You're supposed to be at your job site by about 8:30 or 9:00. Between 12:00 and 1:30 was lunch delivery. We normally worked in the Ninth Ward, but the lunch was cooked at a centralized location and was delivered to us most of the time by truck or van. You came back whenever you wanted to, but it was expected around 4 o'clock or so.

Had dinner at 6:30 until 7:30. The evening meeting went from 7:30 until 8:00, and then there was nighttime programming put on by the antiracist and working groups that went from 8:00 'til 9:30 or so.

Did you find that you were able to balance that?

God no! Not at all! (*Laughter.*) Are you kidding me? Absolutely not. Nobody did, at Common Ground especially. Common Ground was 100 percent volunteer. Everybody was like a self-proclaimed radical "down for the cause" type of person.[5] I think that the literal expectation at Common Ground was that you would work a forty-hour shift of gutting, and then you would work three housekeeping jobs. At the time that I was there, Common Ground was operating out of an abandoned school that was donated to us by a priest who actually wasn't even supposed to have let us in, but he violated the diocese rules and let us in because he thought we were doing good work. The plumbing didn't work. Nothing had been fixed. Electricity was put together by amateur electricians. And people who were really just volunteering were expected to work three shifts, anything from housekeeping, cooking breakfast, cooking lunch, cooking dinner, delivering lunch, cleaning up the bathroom, to security detail. Essentially everyone was expected to work around fifty to sixty hours a week. You were supposed to work forty hours plus this time, and then you had one day off a week. It wasn't strictly regulated though. I think the vast majority would just work continuously until they ran into trouble, and then they would go out drinking a lot as a way of escaping or drugs. (*Laughter.*) And when I became staff, we lived in the same place where we worked—the Ninth Ward—and we were talking about working 100 to 120 hours a week. We were basically on call at any given time.

*Okay and can you tell me a little bit more about
the background of the other volunteers like,
as far as age range or men versus women?*

5. Manriquez's description may be influenced by Common Ground's lengthy debates in the early years that stemmed from participants' differing notions of decision making within a collective: the mostly young, white middle-class volunteers had a different sense of what constituted decision making than the local African American residents whom they purported to serve. Hilderbrand et al., "Common Ground Relief," 95; Harkinson, "How a Radical Leftist Became the FBI's BFF"; Glass et al., "Turncoat"; Eustis, interview.

Majority masculine, mostly men or masculine women. And I think that's important that there's a very strong element of masculinity in the volunteer base.[6]

Age range?

They're all like my age. People are between eighteen and twenty-five for the most part. There was really nobody above thirty who volunteered at the time. We've had two outliers that are carpenters that are in their fifties. Other than that, everyone in AmeriCorps programs that we run at Operation Helping Hands is just out of college and high school, probably not knowing what they're doing with their life.[7]

Since Operation Helping Hands is part of Catholic Charities, have you noticed any spirituality or belief systems among the other volunteers?

No, but boy we try! (*Laughter.*) There's some Christians and Catholics, of course, that come into Catholic Charities. For the most part, people are kind of agnostic about it. Every year there's just a few of them like maybe 25 percent that are actually devout. The staff in the operation itself tries to remind ourselves that the spirituality is what brought us there, but I don't think that most volunteers really care that much. (*Laughter.*)

6. Given his political/philosophical bent, I do not believe that Manriquez attributes the volunteers' effectiveness to the fact that most were male. More likely, his observation is a key component of his critique of the Common Ground culture: it explains its "down for the cause" bravado and its seeming unawareness of the need for balance. Sociologist Rachel Luft explored this point in depth through participant observation in the organization, noting that many long-term volunteers believed that Common Ground in its early years had a "pervasive culture of masculinity that was supported by the hard, physical labor of house gutting projects." This culture undermined the movement's goal of equitable participation. Luft and Common Ground's volunteers noted that the organization's largely male leadership consistently disregarded concerns for women's health and safety in New Orleans, arguing that race and class took precedence over concerns related to gender. Even more alarming, women volunteers, including a participant in this study, reported incidents of sexual assault perpetrated by white men within Common Ground, who were not held accountable. Over time, these tensions led veteran women leaders in Common Ground to form organizations more attuned to the circumstances of women after the storm. Luft, "Looking for Common Ground," 16; Berra et al., "To Render Ourselves Visible," 34.

7. Many participants, observers, and scholars commented that most of the short-term volunteers drawn to New Orleans after the storm were, in the words of Common Ground

Let's talk a little bit about the people that you worked for, the
local residents. How do you feel you were received by them?

It's across the board. Some residents liked us, some didn't, some didn't
care, some thought we were just some crazy novelty and a bunch of random hippies. The experience with residents was very different between
Common Ground and Catholic Charities. The Catholic Charities' residents
for the most part are really particular old ladies. Catholic Charities funds
agencies that serve elderly and disabled people. So, we're specifically looking for that demographic. They don't have a lot of options; so, when they
come to us, they're usually very grateful. Sometimes they're annoyed at
us for being volunteers, but residents have generally been very positive.
They're very excited about us. They're very glad that we're helping, and
they usually can't get it done any other way because they are a specifically
disadvantaged population.

Common Ground had a radical analysis, though, that assumed organizations like Catholic Charities would pick up the hardship cases, while
Common Ground would look for people who were able to give back in like
a material sense, a solidarity model. Working with residents was a whole
different experience because you were an out-of-towner with a lot of privilege trying to organize residents whose houses and community had been
destroyed. And that was much more difficult than my work at Catholic
Charities, which basically gives away the farm to people who need it.

And how did you feel received by the city?

In general, I guess very positive. The city to no end showers the volunteers
with praise. I think that the general outlook is like, "We're so glad the volunteers are here because they're actually helping us." Because most of the
recovery in New Orleans has been happening through determined homeowners and volunteers working together.[8]

---

organizers Sue Hilderbrand, Scott Crow, and Lisa Fithian, "young, white, and middle class."
In addition, this study found that most of these young adults were seeking an opportunity
to do meaningful service before entering the traditional workforce. See Hilderbrand et al.,
"Common Ground Relief," 81 and 93; Luft, "Disaster Patriarchy," 16; Luft, "Looking for Common Ground," 5.

8. Local media backs Manriquez's perception. *New Orleans Times-Picayune* reporter
Jarvis DeBerry, for example, pointed to the important role of nonprofits: "Many of those

But when you get into the different political circles, there are a lot of critiques of volunteers and the dangers of seeing volunteers as an alternate solution to what is essentially a federal and systemic problem.

Let's talk a little bit about the other agencies.
Would you say that federal, state, or volunteer
organizations complemented what you did with
Operation Helping Hands and Common Ground?

Sometimes, but a lot of agencies overlap in a very negative way—negative because it doesn't focus resources the most effective way possible. A positive example of this I guess is Common Ground and Catholic Charities. They have disparate missions and work quite well in separate spheres where they don't necessarily overlap. Habitat for Humanity is another good example. Their mission across the country and even in post-Katrina New Orleans is [building] new low-income housing stock. Their mission is complementary because it creates new, good housing that is designed for low-income folks. Now Catholic Charities, Presbyterian Disaster Assistance, Mennonite Disaster Services, the Southern Baptist Fellowship, and new groups like lowernine.org, Hands on New Orleans, and others compete in a very negative way: we compete for grants, we compete for resources, we compete for homeowners, and we compete for numbers.[9]

---

people with limited resources relied on charities to help them rebuild their homes: Operation Helping Hands, Habitat for Humanity, the Louisiana Methodist Conference, Lutheran Disaster Response, the Episcopal Diocese of Louisiana, the St. Bernard Project, Rebuilding Together New Orleans." Likewise, *New Orleans Times-Picayune* reporter Scott Threlkeld wrote, "In more than six years, Operation Helping Hands accomplished a critically important task, enabling people like Ms. Thomas to finally return to homes that are whole. Operation Helping Hands and other groups that have taken on that work—Habitat for Humanity, the St. Bernard Project, Rebuilding Together New Orleans and others—have made a significant difference in the lives of those they've helped and in the life of the larger community. That won't be forgotten." DeBerry, "Hope Takes a Hit"; Threlkeld, "A Job Well Done."

9. Participants in this study repeatedly expressed intense disdain for the competition for numbers: quantifiable data used to assess a nonprofit organization's performance. In particular, they indicated that this competition undermined their core missions to engage with their clients as people, rather than data points. More broadly this theme appears in the work of scholarship and activists. For instance, Berra, Liebenthal and Incite! argue that foundations are biased toward organizations that can produce quantifiable data and against organizations involved in more long-term strategic work. Moreover, in *Markets of Sorrow,*

*It sounds like there's more competition between
a lot of the organizations than coordination?*

Yeah. There is a level of coordination for sure, but there have been uncomfortable instances where we show up at a house that we have grant funding for and another organization shows up at the house and says, "That's the house that we have grant funding for." Those things are not common, but Catholic Charities, Presbyterian Disaster Assistance, the Mennonites, and other groups all cover all of Orleans Parish. So, we're all sending vehicles and resources and volunteers on any given day across each other to different neighborhoods.

What we have now is this model where everyone goes everywhere and tries to help anyone, and there's not a lot of coordination between the agencies. There's not a lot of focus. It would be easier on everybody to organize the volunteer groups around certain neighborhoods, like Rebuilding Together or the St. Bernard Project does, where they have certain specific areas. Instead, we send volunteers across and next to each other and spend much time driving around, which is a huge issue.[10] It takes so much time to drive people back and forth across the city.

Vincanne Adams reminds readers that as members of the private sector, foundations can reflect the same neoliberal and corporatist values that facilitated the negative circumstances of the victims of Katrina in the first place, leading nonprofits to transform themselves into the image of private business to secure more funds. Berra et al., "To Render Ourselves Visible," 39–40; Adams, *Markets of Sorrow,* loc 2772.

10. A program within the Preservation Resource Center, Rebuilding Together New Orleans (RTNO) was founded in 1988 to improve "the quality of life of low-income homeowners, particularly those who are elderly, disabled veterans or single head of households." Before the storm, RTNO was already a major force in New Orleans, having worked on nine hundred homes across the city. According to their website, when the storm hit, "RTNO modified its mission to aid those displaced by the storm. Instead of only smaller projects, RTNO began to focus on the total renovation and rebuilding of storm-damaged homes. By reinvesting in and restoring the existing housing stock of the city, RTNO was able to bring homeowners back into their homes, as well as providing a model for restoring and preserving New Orleans's historic neighborhoods. RTNO's home rehabilitation program targets the urban poor, who are the population most affected by Hurricane Katrina." In 2006, Zack Rosenburg and Liz McCartney, after volunteering in St. Bernard Parish, founded the Saint Bernard Project to rebuild homes in the parish with, according to the *Times-Picayune,* "an emphasis on affordable housing for veterans and seniors." Rebuilding Together New Orleans, "Neighborhood Revitalization in Orleans Parish"; Saint Bernard Project USA, "About Us"; LaRose, "St. Bernard Project."

Now at a higher level with supplies and massive donations, there has been some coordination in the agencies. Like I'm a painter. I've got a lot of painting resources donated—more than I need. Some of those go to a centralized warehouse that any volunteer organization can draw from. But as far as working together and construction, it has not been coordinated very well at all.

Is there something that Operation Helping Hands can do to make the coordination a little bit easier?

Well, we've done some. We had a volunteer for the Mennonites who came to Operation Helping Hands as a staff person, and he's done a really good job of bringing the Mennonites into our operation in the way that they look for funding. They don't really have very good funding sources, but they definitely have good volunteers that are skilled. We have a lot of funding, and they work with us on our projects. We fund their projects, and then we get the numbers from it. That's a pretty good partnership and actually allows us both to meet our grant goals.

There could be more like that. Catholic Charities could declare that we're working with one neighborhood, and every other neighborhood would get mad about it and it would be difficult. So, it's kind of an all-or-nothing thing. Honestly, I think it takes a higher level. You need to have the city or the federal government or the state saying, "This neighborhood is Catholic Charities. This neighborhood is Presbyterian. This neighborhood is the Episcopalians." That way, everyone is focused, but instead they say, "Everyone go everywhere and do whatever you want." You end up with this this chaotic waste.

Did you have interaction individually with these groups?

Yeah, I've worked with the Presbyterians in Mississippi, and I've worked with the Mennonites. Rebuilding Together is populated by a lot of my friends. Volunteers cross-pollinate at social events cuz we're all very poor and we're all looking for the cheapest thing we can do. So, we end up being in the same places. And we're also young people who have come down here with idealistic visions about the future. So, whether we're volunteers or lowly paid staff members, we kind of end up in the same places. I know a lot of folks from Rebuilding Together, and I like their model a little bit because they actually pick neighborhoods, but they're also granted in a different way, through historic preservation. Pre-Katrina they existed all across the country. They usually go into neighborhoods that are historic and bring volunteers to make historic houses beautiful again and keep their character.

How has your experience volunteering led you to think
about relief efforts and how they should be coordinated
between the national government, state government,
local government, and volunteer organizations?

They need to coordinate it better. That's for sure. I know that as far as volunteer organizations go, they need to have more direction. The state, federal, or local government has to step in at some point and say this is where we want people to be judging by the needs that we see. Having volunteer organizations simply show up and write grants based on the needs that they're able to pull out of some statistics is really ineffective and creates other competition.

As far as general recovery dollars though, there just needs to be better coordination among the federal and the state level about where dollars go, how dollars get there, and timetables for them getting there, as well as penalties for lack of service. Catholic Charities, for example, was never designed to rebuild houses, and our rebuilding effort came very late in the game because we didn't expect to have to rebuild. Operation Helping Hands operated for years under the assumption that state money that was given by the federal government would give homeowners enough to rebuild through the Road Home program. But the organization that was in charge of putting it together was a year and a half away on its promises and still walked away with a billion-dollar contract. There were some penalties, but they weren't nearly steep enough to have created any kind of efficiency.[11]

11. Road Home, the program to dispense federal monies to homeowners in the aftermath of Katrina, was run by the corporation ICF International from 2006 to 2009. Louisiana granted ICF an $800 million contract to distribute $7.9 billion to approximately 124,000 homeowners. The Road Home contract was a windfall for ICF, writes *New Orleans Times-Picayune* reporter David Hammer, "At the end of 2005, it held $227 million in contracts. It immediately quadrupled that by inking the Road Home deal, then went public a few months later. In the past year alone, it won more than $500 million in contracts involving such agencies as the National Institutes of Health, the Environmental Protection Agency and Head

Also, some of the houses we work on get into some very ridiculous amounts of paperwork. One grant allows us to put in floors, but not plumbing. So, they have to submit again for another grant that would be for mechanical work and then submit again for other grants that would give interior belongings. It seems like there's a million grant processes. There must be some way of doing a common application or tracking someone's case file across agencies. We have so many homeowners that are filling out their personal profile with their Social Security and employment information, and it's going on like the seventh and eighth time they've done it for different agencies, government entities, and recording systems among the nonprofit sector. It's ridiculous. Another thing that causes a lot of inefficiency is that there isn't a standardized way of taking information.

It sounds like disorganization at every level.

Right. Centralizing a lot of social services would be a good idea because so many of them, in my experience down here, have been put across piecemeal and have their different restrictions that make sense in a non-disaster-related area, but they don't make sense now. Like there's no money for lead-safe work practices, but you know that you're gonna deal with lead anyways. There are enough grants for lead mediation; well, those grants are designed for houses that are in urban areas and currently have bad lead paint. So, you're gonna have to do a risk assessment on the house, but here there's no way to do a risk assessment on a house that has no walls. (*Laughter.*)

There hasn't been a way, at least so far, to centralize all these different

---

Start." Meanwhile, seven months into the program, ICF had only distributed funds to one percent of those eligible for the grants. In 2007, ICF's system of paying homeowners was found in violation of federal regulations; yet, despite this poor performance, Louisiana governor Kathleen Blanco signed another $156 million contract with ICF before leaving office that year. The state had no assessments or benchmarks for progress in the initial contract and finally negotiated a few by the end of 2007. Nevertheless, over the next several years, ICF missed most of those performance measures, gained a reputation for treating applicants like criminals, and was fined more than $14 million by the state of Louisiana. By the time Louisiana refused to renew its contract with ICF in 2009, writes Hammer, the company was "generally reviled by Louisianans" and "banned from new business with the state." Flaherty et al., *Floodlines;* Hammer, "ICF's Oversight of Road Home Program Comes to an End"; "Blanco Administration Quietly Gave Raise to Road Home Operator"; "State Signs New Road Home Contract with HGI Catastrophe Services."

federal programs and say, "Look this is a disaster area, so these all now fall under a single funding stream with a common application." Private sector money also has to fall under federal regulation, because it's a disaster area, and in a disaster area the feds say the money is spent this way. They could at least say, "Agencies can't overlap in certain neighborhoods," or say, "All agencies have to follow a set of best practices no matter what they do."

We also get away with a lot of things that would never be legal except for this nonprofit loophole. Our workers are not protected by OSHA.[12] Which is terrible because a lot of young twenty-year-olds are not protected, because they're working with a nonprofit that just signs away their life through a liability waiver.

Even more importantly, you have problems by the nature of the housing code. In Louisiana if you're contracting for more than $50,000, you need a license. You need to have a license for the mechanicals. But a homeowner can hire somebody to work on their house, and the homeowner can't pull the permit even though they are not doing the work. So, because we're acting on "behalf of the homeowners," we're doing work unpermitted, un-licensed, uninsured, unbonded. It's a joke when you have a dozen organizations whose purpose is rebuilding, and they're all working on behalf of homeowners—unlicensed, uninsured, and unbonded.

I'm gonna switch gears a little bit.
What were some of your favorite moments as a volunteer?

Oh man. (*Laughter.*) Being young and cavalier as I am, some of my favorite moments are doing really ridiculous things like hanging from rafters and narrowly escaping death by natural gas explosions several times. Those are fun stories for your kids to know: "When I was your age, I was damn near killing myself in a gutted house!" But there's just so many fun stories. I think one of my favorite moments actually was being introduced to a craw-fish boil by this dude in Mississippi, who really had no resources available to him at all. The house that we were rebuilding was just a terrible house, but to him it was the world, and the fact that we put a new roof on it made him so excited he gave us this crawfish boil. This is an experience that's often replicated, but this was my first time, which is why it's so memora-

12. Occupational Safety and Health Administration.

ble to me. He came out with two fifty-five-gallon plastic barrels just full of crawfish and a big ol' metal fifty-five-gallon boil drum, that was made into a trashcan and a big octagonal poker table with a hole in the middle of it. He put this table over the trashcan and proceeded to show us how exactly you're supposed to eat crawfish, you know: pull the tail off, suck it in the head, and throw the debris in the middle of this table, which is actually a trashcan. It was just kind of hilarious.

I mean the kind of hospitality these folks are doing is amazing. Here we are coming down, we've got a fair amount of resources, we're college-educated kids, we're young, and we're gonna go wherever we want to in our lives for the most part. But some guy who never really had anything and probably won't really have much more than a poor laborer's life in the South gets his house back and spends all the money he has to give us this crawfish boil. It's great to feel that kind of gratitude. I feel like you would hear that from a lot of volunteers. We've all done service projects, but down here we're able to make some kind of connection.[13]

I mean I know these guys I'm working with were like racist, Confederate, right-wing Republicans that I would probably never get along with in any kind of way, but I was there for my civic duty, and he was just really happy that someone had come down. We completely disagreed on a lot of things. Like one of these guys was talking about how the North was the aggressor in the Civil War, and I was like, "Wow, I am so not on that wavelength." But at the same time, we'd be civic citizens working together and have that kind of camaraderie, which is nice. It's a feeling that quickly evaporated in New Orleans. Katrina has gone from memory, and there's more political fights, but it was nice at the time.

13. Manriquez is right. Some version of surprise at seeing expressions of gratitude and "southern hospitality" was discussed as a phenomenon in post-Katrina New Orleans by Diana Cheyenne Harvey and is a common theme across interviewees who are not southern. These stories are analytically confounding when trying to understand the essence of the relationships between out-of-town, long-term volunteers and the clients they served. On the one hand, the volunteers can come across as patronizing—a negative characteristic scholars have found associated with young people involved in service-learning projects. Yet scholarship also describes how service across identities creates cross-cultural empathy. See Harvey, "'Gimme a Pigfoot and a Bottle of Beer'"; Astin et al., "How Service Learning Affects Students"; Pompa, "Service Learning as Crucible"; Borden, "The Impact of Service-Learning on Ethnocentrism"; Sax et al., "Long-Term Effects of Volunteerism."

*In contrast, were there any times when
it's been really tough as a volunteer?*

Yeah . . . I don't know if you've followed NPR at all but a couple months ago there was a segment about Brandon Darby who was an FBI informant. He was actually my boss at Common Ground. That was a difficult challenge. That was probably the worst time I've had here. Working in an organization full of self-proclaimed radicals who had done direct action, we broke a lot of laws to get people back in their homes. We had in our mind and hearts that we could change the world and that, despite all the challenges we might see, we could find a better way. We weren't breaking laws for some crazy reason. We were breaking laws because it made no sense to keep people out of their homes. When people wanted to be back, we tried to get them back. We were doing the best we could with very limited resources and with mostly our idealism driving us, because it certainly wasn't the food, and it certainly wasn't the housing, and it couldn't have been the salary.

And then there were people like Brandon Darby, who, for whatever reason, rearranged and disorganized and fought against our efforts. What he did in Common Ground caused a lot of dissension amongst our ranks. He caused a lot of fights. He played a lot of racial, class, and ethnic cards to divide people and actually put some of us in danger by fighting with local drug lords. He did all that because he thought that we were a bunch of useless radicals. That was really demoralizing and very difficult. It was hard to work with people like that, and there were definitely FBI informants among our crowd. There were folks that would cause trouble for no reason at all, and when we found out that a few of them literally were FBI informants it was eye-opening, like "Well that makes us feel better because he wasn't just an asshole. He was actually paid to be an asshole."[14]

14. Brandon Darby was among the first of the white radicals to assist Malik Rahim, along with fellow anarchist Scott Crow. Darby acted as Common Ground's director of operations from January to April 2007. Frustrated with the slow pace of consensus-based decision making in Common Ground, Darby returned to in Austin, where he began working with the FBI to identify radicals who allegedly posed a threat to the upcoming Republican National Convention. After Darby's provided information to the FBI that resulted in the arrest of two members of the Austin activist community, news quickly traveled to New Orleans, and members of Common Ground began to connect some of the group's worst problems to Darby's leadership. Characterized by his fellow activists as "handsome," "charismatic," "provocative," "charming," "macho," "violent," "somewhat crazy," and a "megalomaniac,"

So, I think the most demoralizing thing I've experienced down here is the feeling that just because we were idealistic and wanted to change the world, we would face opposition by dominant power structures. After putting in all that work, to find that people were still against our attempts to rebuild the city, to hit obstacles with the federal government's bureaucratic inefficiency and its FBI spying, and to have the police hassle us for looking kinda weird. . . . That is incredibly demoralizing and still is a challenge.

So, do you think that experiences like that have changed how you think about America?

Yeah. But it's awkward. New Orleans supposedly has had well over a million volunteers down here. I know that I personally saw probably about ten thousand volunteers come through my programs, and the people that come down here are interested in helping. Not to be cliché, but they're American citizens that are interested in each other. These are American citizens who are coming down here taking time to try and make the world a better place. A lot of them don't share my political beliefs and they definitely don't share my analysis, but when it comes down to it, they actually are interested in helping. So, when you talk about America, it's difficult for me to answer that question because there's America the power structure and then there's America the people.

The power structure certainly does not represent any of the people I've seen down here or at least not the vast majority. In fact, the only people that the power structure represents down here are the military, the police, and the bureaucrats. My view of them has become dimmer since I've been here. But my view of some old guy from Michigan who's a ceiling and tile

---

Darby was accused by Common Ground members of creating a toxic environment and in one case endangering lives by antagonizing the local criminal element. Although Darby claimed that he was contacted by the FBI after leaving Common Ground, FBI files indicate that they were in contact in 2006. Interviewees like Manriquez saw Darby's erratic behavior as caused by his acting on behalf of the FBI, in a manner not unlike the FBI's infiltration of Black activist groups in the civil rights era. "Brandon Darby"; McCarthy, "Common Ground Official Was a Federal Informant"; Winkler-Schmit, "Brandon Darby—FBI Informant and Common Ground Co-Founder"; Harkinson, "How a Radical Leftist Became the FBI's BFF"; Babcock, "Common Ground Co-Founder Is FBI Informant"; Austin Informant Working Group, "Statement from Texas Anarchists"; Moynihan, "Activist Unmasks Himself"; Eustis, interview; Reilly, interview; Hilderbrand et al., "Common Ground Relief."

installer and likes to come down here and teach volunteers how to install stock tile . . . my view of people like that is amazing. My view of people who come down here because they just think it's not right to have this kind of destruction happening in America the same way that I did is brighter than ever.

Branching off the previous question about being tough, were there ever any times that you were worried about your safety for other reasons, other than just biohazards or hazards of the job?

Yeah, there have been a few times at Common Ground when Brandon Darby was there. He had gotten in some fights with local drug lords—like the local guy on the corner who carries a gun and sells weed. A lot of our volunteers would buy drugs from people in the neighborhood, and generally we would say, "If you do that, you're not part of us, and we're not gonna be responsible for anything you do." But Brandon started a few fights with dealers because he thought that our volunteers should be protected because they're doing a lot of this good work. He picked a few fights that led to folks coming in and threatening our volunteers, threatening to steal shit, and threatening to take people hostage. One volunteer who was actually out buying drugs was taken hostage for a short period of time at the end of a shotgun in some old guy's FEMA trailer. That made me fear for my personal safety. I was constantly afraid of being personally attacked or injured in some kind of way for several weeks. It's a city. There's problems in a city, but that was really the only time that it was like not a job site thing but actually like, "This is a dangerous place for me and I'm staying here because I think I need to, but we all know that one of us could get shot if this fight keeps going on."

It sounds like you have had a contrast of experiences. So, what do you feel like you've learned about the people of New Orleans?

(*Laughter.*) The people of New Orleans . . . I don't know. I'm still working on that. It's just too difficult a question really to answer accurately. I've lived a lot of places in my life. Moving every three or four years, I don't find folks to be all that different at the core. I've lived most of my life in a lower-middle-class to middle-class lifestyle where we've had access to some resources and kind of followed the rules. We were "ingenuitive" about things, but we tried to stay closer to code and regulation, instead of edging our way around it. I think that's something that's different that I've seen here. Still, I have worked and lived in several places in the city, and it's difficult to say one encompassing view without referring to some sort of silly stereotype in some kind of way.

So how have you changed through this experience?

My experiences here have changed my views of working within and without the system. I mean I worked within that system for a little while, and then I decided to not work with that system when I came to New Orleans. New Orleans's massive disaster has caused a lot of people, myself included, to come down here with more idealistic visions than we would ever have attempted in our own neighborhoods. When we come down here and try them out, it leads to a lot of disillusionment and burnout. That was something I've definitely gone through—coming down here with a vision of a changed society that would have been tempered by elders and comrades and colleagues in Denver where I was living. But they were not down here, and I was actually encouraged to try more and crazy different ideas. What changed me is that I got to try a lot of things that totally failed, and I've had the privilege of stopping to reorganize and reassess my ways of thinking about changing the world.

Have you seen any positive changes as a result of Katrina?

I think it's really hard to look at the positive without looking at the negative because they're two sides of the same coin. There's probably about a hundred thousand people that were in poverty in New Orleans that are no longer here. When you remove that element, you remove a lot of the social stressors that exist in any city. If you were to remove the bottom 20 percent of Chicago, who have the most social stress, you would see immediate improvements in schools. You'd see immediate improvements in crime. You'd see immediate improvements in a lot of things. We've seen improvements in crime. Although the crime rate actually has not been that much better, it is now more isolated than it was pre-Katrina. Those are just observations. I don't know if those would bear out in statistical reality.

I should probably stop referring to this as Katrina and make a specific note that it is the levee failure that caused the disaster in New Orleans. The levee failures caused a lot of idealistic, young, college-educated, and radical folks to come down. People that have been working on innovative new ideas all across the country came here. A lot of folks that were doing work somewhere came down for a few months, went back. and then created relationships. People who are creating farms in Michigan, in all the thirty square miles of empty lots in Detroit, are coming down here to talk to us and work with us. The folks who are creating urban CSAs in Denver are coming down here to volunteer and talk with us.[15] The folks that have been working on food collectives and farmer's markets in Seattle have come down and talked to us. The folks who work on land trust in Vermont are coming down to talk to us. The people who are working in Austin who have been working on ground filter mediation and bio- and micro-mediation are coming down to talk to us. So, in this weird kind of way, every green builder in the country, in fact every builder in the country nowadays, is coming down to see what the hell is going on in New Orleans. So. there's an amazingly good amount of resources coming to hang out with us because there is such a blank page.

That is the flip side of the negative disaster of the federal levee failure. If it had only been a hurricane, you'd have problems. You'd have some money and a whole lot of roofers come out here. You would've had a couple old ladies get new furniture from the United Way or something. But because of the federal levee failure, you have this massive depopulation of a city that was once in poverty but had an incredible cultural history. Because of that disaster, you now have this kind of odd melting pot of various ideas. That is a good and bad thing. The privileged folks who are testing out new ideas in New Orleans are not accountable. At the same time, it is gonna create some new ideas that will be specifically thought of as New Orleans's things, or they will be tested out here because there's such a blank canvas.

15. Community-supported agriculture. Cone and Myhre, "Community-Supported Agriculture," 187.

There's a margin in which people can try and reevaluate and reform the way society works.[16]

What's next for you?
How much longer are you gonna be in New Orleans?

I'm actually in the process of buying a house right now. There's been some grant money for first-time homebuyers, and I took advantage of it. I'm also traveling next week to New York to work with the Fordham-Bedford Housing Corporation and the Sustainable South Bronx organization to talk about how to do community development in a sustainable and just way. I'm traveling with two of my colleagues to set up a nonprofit here for the purpose of rebuilding houses. We're looking at community development through the Mid-City Neighborhood Organization. So, what's next for me is a whole lot of projects. I'm developing a community garden. I'm working with this nonprofit on housing development. I'll be working with the Mid-City Neighborhood Organization to be an active citizen, and I'm running for the board of two different nonprofits to do fair housing and community work. I've got my hands full with New Orleans. I'm hoping I'll be in New Orleans for the next ten years, and I'm hoping that in the next ten years we'll have a city that is much more sustainable than it has been, a city that has a lot less blight, and a city that has opportunity for people. A city that creates its own kind of insular economy based on growing its own food and making its own crafts. A city that doesn't require heavy destructive industry and that is able to keep people here employed and that keeps its cultural and historical character. So, I got a lot of work to do. (*Laughter.*) I think it's still a challenging time for New Orleans, but I think it's still possible that we can make it better, but that's a much harder task and we got a lot of work to do.

16. In making this point, Manriquez mirrors scholars and activists who criticized the pattern of predominantly white, middle-class outsiders coming into New Orleans without building any relationships with long-term native activists or without any sense of accountability to the people of New Orleans as a form of racism. See: Flaherty et al., *Floodlines*, 101; Berra et al., "To Render Ourselves Visible," 39.

2. Caitlin Reilly

SURVIVAL IN RADICAL COMMUNITY

> Not everyone is really capable of trying to eliminate
> sexism and racism while trying to rebuild a city.
>
> —Caitlin Reilly, Bayou Rebirth and the Common Ground Collective

It was a hot late afternoon in New Orleans when Caitlin Reilly and I left town to see the wetlands. I had been introduced to Reilly by another volunteer. During my first conversation with Reilly, she suggested that we drive south through the wetlands to Grand Isle so I could see the scope of the erosion firsthand and better understand how the marsh had historically protected New Orleans from storm surge. I could tell she had a story, but I was leery of doing an interview during a two-hour drive with a person I barely knew. If anything went wrong, there would be no escape route from an awkward conversation. Nevertheless, I wanted to learn more about the wetlands, and having her as a guide was too good an opportunity to miss.

As it had for other white, college-educated young adult volunteers in this project, seeing the storm as a tragedy befalling fellow Americans had brushed aside differences in identity that might normally have kept Reilly from leaving her native New York City to volunteer in a place as different as New Orleans—a phenomenon that scholars have identified as convergence behavior.[1] Also like others, Reilly had a long volunteer history, and having recently graduated from college but not yet starting work or graduate school, she was very consciously in a period of transition.

Reilly differed in several important ways, however, from many of her fellow volunteers. With both of her parents having deep activist backgrounds, Reilly was what the literature calls a "legacy volunteer." Scholars have

---

1. Michel, "Personal Responsibility," 634, 635.

identified this characteristic as contributing to youth volunteering, and Reilly shared this trait with several of her peers in this study. Like many interviewees, she also had experienced burnout, and research has shown high risk coupled with burnout to be characteristics common to young adult volunteering. Noting her inexperience and the disorienting nature of life in post-Katrina New Orleans, Reilly reflected on her exhaustion and the impossibility of any kind of self-care more deeply than her counterparts in this study.

Reilly had entered the recovery scene through the Common Ground Collective, but unlike others interviewed, she remained with it as it made the transition into a nonprofit organization, Common Ground Relief. During these years, Reilly witnessed situations addressed by multiple interviewees: wasted resources, substance abuse, and the turmoil caused by FBI informant Brandon Darby. She also described Common Ground's perpetuation of a culture hostile to women volunteers that encouraged strong tensions between volunteers and the local community. Like Manriquez and others who started at Common Ground, Reilly ultimately left to find a healthier environment in which she could still contribute to the recovery. Although, clearly, Reilly's time at Common Ground was hugely impactful, it is not clear that its impact was positive.

⚜ ⚜ ⚜

AUGUST 26, 2011

I'm here with Caitlin Reilly, formerly of Bayou Rebirth
and Common Ground, and now with the LSU Ag Center
and Bayou Land Research Development and Conservation
District. Tell me where you were in your life when
Hurricane Katrina hit.

I was fresh out of Manhattan College, which is in the Bronx. I got my degree in religious studies and peace studies, and I had just moved into an intentional community in a Presbyterian church on the Upper East Side of Manhattan to do a social justice internship with a homeless outreach program. I remember distinctly my first Tuesday night after Labor Day, going to serve dinner to one hundred homeless and marginalized people in Manhattan, and the hip-hop radio station changed format to do all news about Hurricane Katrina. They were interviewing a woman who had been on her roof for days, and she talked about having to break out of the attic to get onto the roof with her grandmother, her family, and her children with a bag on onions: that was all the food that they had. They sat up there for days, and the helicopters would fly over, but no one would really do anything. At first, they were all out there. Then they decided to leave Grandma, and that didn't work. She was out there with just the American flag. A couple of the kids thought they were gonna die up there, and that's when they started shooting at the helicopter, 'cause they just thought no one could figure out that they were there. I remember feeling heartbroken and terrified and thinking to myself, "There's nothing I can do about that right now. But if something like that were to happen here, these people I'm gonna serve dinner to would be the people stranded." I kind of put that in the back of my mind and didn't think about it again for a couple of years.

So, what led you to be part of an
intentional community?

It just sort of fell into my lap. I was graduating college, not really having a plan for what I was gonna do next, and my mom got an email with a job opening for a live-in social justice intern. I'd get a stipend, and it included health insurance. It seemed like a cool opportunity. I applied. I interviewed. They hired me. And living in a community seemed a little less scary than going from living with a bunch of my friends to living alone, all by myself. (*Laughter.*)

You stayed there for a couple of years?

I was there for a year and a half. It was a life-changing experience. Nothing will make you stop feeling sorry for yourself like talking to somebody who's been sleeping in the rain for three days.

You grew up already theoretically conscious of poverty
and inequality issues, right? Did you become more aware
of those issues in a tangible way once you were with this
community?

Sure. Well, I would say actually the level of intentionality in that community wasn't very great. I had two days of training with a young woman who had been there before me with no background in social services, and then I went from being a kid where the grownups were always in charge, to being twenty-one years old and telling mostly men who were significantly older than me, "This is how it is."

How did you deal with that as a twenty-one-year-old?

I didn't. I certainly didn't cope with it in any sort of healthy way. Drugs and sex and alcohol were certainly coping mechanisms for me. That statement that I made, about not feeling sorry for yourself, went to a level of not having any space for my own emotional process.

So, you weren't taking care of yourself?

No. I ate food, washed my clothes and such, but I don't think that our society does a great job of teaching people how to take care of themselves in those kinds of stressful situations. I certainly didn't. I didn't become a crackhead and I didn't have a serious drinking problem, but I was definitely escaping rather than processing. I didn't have a particularly healthy lifestyle in college either. We drank. We smoked lots of pot.

So, I worked. I hung out with homeless people. (*Laughter.*) I gave out a lot of socks and underwear. The one really cool thing that I'm pretty proud of is that we renovated a space in our basement for homeless people who were living on the street and didn't want to be in a program. The outreach was pretty cool because it didn't have a demand for social services goals to be met. We were really a support service on the edge of the Upper East Side. So, the fancy churches on Madison Avenue would give us money to support our homeless outreach program. (*Laughter.*) The Greek Orthodox Church was more than happy to cook all the food for us in their kitchen, but they didn't want the homeless people eating at their nice tables. "We want to be involved. We just don't want them in our pretty building," you know?

What made you move to doing something different?
What did you do next?

The level of stress from my job every day, combined with the fact I did not have any real support from the church, made it an untenable situation. So, I got a job working for the International Rescue Committee. They run refugee camps for the U.S. and British government all over the world. People like Henry Kissinger and Madeleine Albright were on the board of overseers of the organization. (*Laughter.*) I just sat in front of a computer, processed FedEx vouchers, answered phones, and processed catering orders. I was chained to a desk for forty hours a week and commuting on the subway into Manhattan. I hated it, and I got fired from my job for like calling in sick and showing up late. I was really depressed and just miserable. So, I got fired. I lasted a week.

A month or two before, though, a friend volunteered with the Emergency Communities in New Orleans and was like, "Come with me. You'll love it. Just screw it. Blow it off." And I was like, "No. I have to have this job for a year for my résumé and my health benefits." Two years later he comes back, and now he's going down to volunteer with Common Ground and is like, "Come with me. Come with me." This time I decided that I should go. So, I wrote a quick essay to Emergency Communities and said, "Hey, I want to come down for three weeks and volunteer."

Did you have to think about it for very long?

At first, when he told me he was goin' to volunteer in New Orleans two years later [after Katrina], I'm like, "What do you mean?"

Were you one of those people who were like, "Isn't everything done already?"

Yeah. I totally thought, "Isn't that all taken care of? What have they been doin'? Two years?" I mean, if you live in the Northeast, a hurricane hits every once in a while, but it's like a heavy thunderstorm with a lot of wind.

A couple hundred times at least I've told people that everything from the airport where you flew in [to New Orleans] to Bayou La Batre, Alabama, was underwater. I still cannot fathom it. I've seen pictures of it, but I cannot close my eyes and really imagine what the hell happened. When you look in somebody's eyes, and they tell you they swam with their children to the house down the street to get to a second story, and couldn't sleep because they thought that the water was still coming for them . . . How is that possible?

So, what happened in your mind when
he asked you to consider going?

The first time, I was locked in like I didn't have a choice. But then I got fired. Getting fired was the best thing that ever happened to me. It was the kick in the ass I needed to change up my whole life. When I decided to go, I figured, "I'll just go to New Orleans; I'll volunteer. I'll be doing something productive with my time while I search for a job back at home." I sent out a half-dozen résumés, and I never heard back from any of them. While that was happening, Emergency Communities was still serving meals to people, so it facilitated interacting with the community in a pretty direct way.

Tell me about the work that you did
with Emergency Communities.

Cooking food, serving food, washing a lot of dishes. I was there for a couple of weeks. Those people were really crazy. That was an era where there were a lot of burned-out, pissed-off people in the volunteer scene. These kids had lived through Buras, which was the original Emergency Communities camp in Plaquemines Parish. There was sort of this romanticized version of a time when everyone, volunteers and residents, lived in this big hippie community. Everyone was intense and going out and gutting houses. The community evolved. Immediately [after Katrina hit], there was no food, water, or medical supplies available to anybody. So, they needed to organize as a community to bring in supplies, distribute them, feed people, and start gutting out houses.

But two years after Katrina, they had set up this place in the Lower Ninth Ward, and they're engaging with a totally different situation—they're not the whole community anymore. The place that you're in is a 'hood, and these people who are living here are not necessarily living in good situations, and people like me come in. They're foreigners, they're white, they're not from New Orleans even, never mind the South or anywhere near here, and they have come in to give them what has already been donated to them. So, yeah, they don't like you. It was a very hostile situation.[2] It was rel-

2. Reilly's awareness of tensions between volunteers along racial and native/non-native lines corresponds with very well-developed analyses of New Orleans post-Katrina.

atively short-lived 'cause they couldn't sustain it. They were miserable, angry, and had this weird relationship with the populace. And just awful stuff was going on. I mean smoking crack and stripping of copper wire.

I have very rarely heard about negativity being expressed toward volunteers—although I have met several native New Orleanians, usually outside New Orleans, who made a lot of negative comments. I'm still tryin' to place that. I don't know what it means, but it doesn't occur frequently enough that I can really analyze it.

Well, there was hostility toward the volunteer organization. Things were stolen. But what I was actually referencing was that there was also hostility from the volunteer organization toward the local residents: "They are crackheads. They steal from us. Don't lend them anything. It'll never come back. Don't trust them. They stay outside; we stay inside." Like the guys who sat and drank beer every night on the corner. I was the first person from Emergency Communities to come and keep them company.

So, would it be safe to say that the organization you were with, and maybe others, was in a space of extreme disillusionment, like when people go into things with false expectations?

Yeah, there was a lot of that, but it was also this moment where these kids had been working full tilt, ten hours a day, seven days a week, and the organization wanted you to do that. When I got down there, I was like, "Your website says you work forty hours a week for five days a week, and you begrudge me going to church and taking all of Sunday off? This is insane." So, that was obviously an untenable situation. They were shutting down, and I was wanting to be in the Lower Ninth Ward meeting people and seeing the stories my parents told me about the Bronx when they were growing up playing out in front of me in a whole new place.

So, how did you decide to go to Common Ground?

See Crow, *Black Flags and Windmills,* 14, 90, 94; Flaherty, "Corporate Reconstruction and Grassroots Resistance,"115; Luft, "Looking for Common Ground," 5, 6, 10, 13, 14.

I got kicked out of Emergency Communities. I didn't show up for work one Sunday, and they had this rule that if you miss three shifts, you had to leave. Well, you had three shifts of work a day. So, if you missed a day, they kicked you out. I was twenty-three years old! (*Laughter.*) I had come all the way to that place to stay there and work there for three weeks, and they had no problem with just telling me, "You have to leave now. Take all your stuff and leave into the night."

Was that because there were so many volunteers to go around?

It was because there were so many volunteers to go around, but they were jaded for good reason at that point.[3] There were a lot of asshole people that came through volunteerism, in all different shapes and colors and sizes. They were long-term volunteers, hardcore and down for the cause. I was there for three weeks. I was the new kid. What the hell did I know? I was just gonna go back to my upper-middle-class lifestyle and never look back, you know?

Were you resented because of that?

Sure. I speak up. I say things. I ask a lot of questions. I'm not deferential for no good reason. So, yeah, that's obnoxious. (*Laughter.*) But at that time there was this heavy long-term volunteer attitude, "We've been here since '06. We're rough and tough. We've been through it." And part of the reason they were so jaded is because it was crazy to think, "We're gonna gut and rebuild the city."

In the early days when they started, there were thousands of volunteers. They were sending out multiple crews of ten or twenty people to go gut out houses. Common Ground gutted as many houses as Catholic Charities. There were crazy numbers of young people coming through and seeing something horrifying. It's really motivating. You see this place and it hits you. You just can't get that sense of urgency from people presently.

So how did you go to Common Ground?
Did you seek them out?

3. Common Ground hosted and deployed more than 23,000 volunteers in its first three years alone. Crow, *Black Flags and Windmills*, 4.

Well, my friend was there, and it was down the road. So, I just I went there and said, "Hi. I'm here now." And they said, "Oh, there's a bed over there." They were doing nothing. That place was infested with crackheads and alcoholics. It was crazy.

In terms of the volunteers?

Yeah. The block was just a mess. The House of Excellence—the H.O. House—was kind of doing some stuff. I think they were originally in a building that was like the School of Excellence, so they renamed it the House of Excellence. For a while Common Ground had their legal clinic, their tech stuff, and their wellness person based out of there, so it was the fancy place in Mid-City city as opposed to like this dumpy, Lower Ninth Ward block.

So, it had a healthier feel?

Much more. That was where all the young, bright-eyed volunteers were hangin' out, but I ended up on the block in the Lower Ninth Ward. I wanted to be in the Lower Ninth Ward.

*So, tell me about your observations of
the people that were there?*

It took a little while to realize quite how bad it was 'cause it was a weird place for a person who was going through a huge transition in their life. Everything was weird. Like the Lower Ninth Ward was bizarre. I didn't have a car, so I didn't really leave. I just lived in this little weird, microcosm of crazy for a long time. (*Laughter.*) I remember just feeling like there're so many resources here that are not being utilized appropriately, and these volunteers are living off of the thing and not doing what they're supposed to be doing. People just sat on their ass and did nothing. They took the money that was donated and bought booze with it. That place digested so many resources over the years. (*Sigh.*) It's hard for me to be completely objective. . . . Can anyone really objectively recall their history?

At the moment that I got there it was really bad. The quintessential memory is that at some point Malik would come and hold court.[4] He was

4. Descriptions of Malik Rahim typically point to or highlight his charisma. For examples, see Crow, *Black Flags and Windmills;* Holm, *Welcome to New Orleans,* film; Flaherty et al., *Floodlines.*

the last founder standing. (*Laughter.*) He would say things like, "This is an organization founded on bullshit." And he would go on to talk about how he asked for help, and all these people showed up at his doorstep saying, "We have to form an organization. We have to do all these things." Then it mushroomed into health clinics, indie media outlets, gardening, tech centers, wetlands restoration, and lots and lots and lots of house gutting. Then they just left. They went home, and everybody was still in Malik's backyard, but he couldn't go anywhere. He's from New Orleans, and he was already at home. He had been enough of a front person in all this that everyone associated it with him. He had these grandiose ideas of running for Congress and he wasn't gonna completely walk away from it, but he had no capacity whatsoever to actually lead an organization. This was not his skillset. He talked, and I used to joke, "We follow Malik." (*Laughter.*) He's a charismatic person.

Good on charisma but not follow-through?

Not at all, and it takes a little while to figure that out. You're in this crazy situation. You know nothing about what's going on, and here's somebody who sounds good. Malik took me to the Mississippi River once and told me he could stand there and hear the people in the Lower Ninth Ward screaming for help. That gives you some insight into somebody who doesn't have any malicious intentions and still has that fire for all those things from the sixties to be real. He would stand up and hold court. Then people scurry around acting like what he was saying means things. They had just come back from Washington, DC, too, and they were talking about the Jena Six and how they were going to support the families.[5] All this was just like the complete opposite of the attitude I'd left that the "residents are crackheads and they steal from us." But people on the block were crackheads too, and half of them were goin' out and pullin' copper wire out of houses.

5. In December 2006 six African American teenagers from Jena High School in Jena, Louisiana, were charged with attempted second-degree murder for the beating of a fellow white student. The episode occurred against a backdrop of several events, including the hanging of nooses around the campus, that had heightened racial tensions in the area. The students' cases drew national attention and protests; many people felt that the state treated the six too harshly in charging them as adults and that the incident resulted from increased racial strain. See Flaherty et al., *Floodlines*, 227–251.

How were you able to function in a real job capacity
while all this was going on around you?

I think I did pretty damn well actually. I don't think Common Ground would still be around today if it wasn't for my gumption. I set up the new volunteer program. I said, "Hey, we can't facilitate people building houses en masse, but we can farm them out to other organizations that need volunteers, rotate them around and support the programs that we are actually able to handle internally."

Why weren't you all able to do it?
Lack of resources for that particular job?

It's really easy to gut a house. It is not easy to rebuild a house. Have you ever tried to get a bunch of college students to drywall something? It's a terrible idea. These young people show up with this sense of entitlement: "I have an idea. Someone should listen to it. I want to drywall. I should be able to do that." But why should someone entrust you with hundreds of dollars of materials and tools when you have absolutely no skills? So, what do you do with a bunch of volunteers? 'Cause what people need is sheetrock hung, and volunteers certainly are not gonna wire a house.

Then we also had so much delusional, weird, political weeding out of folks over time 'cause Thom Pepper, who's the director now, was basically tryin' to take over operations and move Malik into a more removed position.

Did he feel like operations needed to be made sort of
standardized and legitimate, for lack of a better word?

Standardized? No. Legitimate? Yes. (*Laughter.*) It would hard to be less legitimate than Common Ground was when I got there. It was just a mess, and they had to figure out what to do next. We had shut down the gutting program because we just pretty much ran out of places to gut.

When you decided to leave,
what led you to make that decision?

I stayed at Common Ground for a year and a half, from October 2007 'til April of 2009 with a couple of breaks. I took a two-month internship in

New York after a year, and then Thom convinced me to come back. Thom kind of wrestled control of the organization from Malik after he became the operations director. Malik just totally gave it to Thom, but the direction that Thom wanted to take the organization was very different from the direction I thought the organization should go.

I wanted not to be against things anymore. I wanted to be for something. I didn't want to be against the war. I wanted to be for this city. That's why being in the Lower Ninth Ward and working at Common Ground were important to me. I wanted to be for rebuilding. Being at Common Ground for me was being for things.

That's a good point. When you are for something,
there's also a way that you have a kind of lived
pro-activity where you're building and making.

Exactly. It was kind of youthful naïveté, but I think we all were wrapped up in this romantic concept of "Just and sustainable! Just and sustainable!" There were chants and bonfires. There was community, and I didn't need to save it anymore. Also, Thom and I just saw things differently. Nobody ever got to see the books. Nobody ever really knew where the money was. After a while, you're like, "Wait a minute. I don't know where the money comes from or where it's going. I don't understand what your vision is here or these partnerships you forge with contracting companies." These are questions that make you feel uncomfortable.

And he always had shit to say about people who used to be volunteers. So, he did to me what he's done to a lot of people. Sour grapes, you know? It's like he tried to blackball me. He denied it, but I saw him treating me the same way he treated other people he tried to push out of the organization, and I knew it was happening, but everyone had been telling me I was paranoid. Then I sit down to talk to Colleen.[6] He told her and other people all kinds of horrible things about me. It's scary when you realize that you're not paranoid, and someone is actually attacking you. I didn't know where I was gonna land, what was gonna happen, how vicious he was gonna get, and who was gonna believe what he was saying.

6. Colleen Morgan was the founder and executive director of Bayou Rebirth. She also participated as an interviewee in this project.

When Colleen told me what the hell was goin' on, I resigned. I was leaving the next day to visit my family for Easter. Thom had given the guy who was driving me to the airport an envelope with $200 in cash and a backdated letter asking that I step down as volunteer coordinator and move into different housing when I returned. When I went back, I went into the volunteer housing that he wanted me to live in. It was like a frat house. It was a bunch of nineteen- to twenty-two-year-olds, a lot of 'em boys, who didn't do their laundry.

That couldn't have been comfortable at all.

No. I was constantly saying, "You guys get it together. Clean your rooms. Do your laundry. Live like human beings." I did all kinds of stuff. I kicked people out at times. For a long time after I was sexually assaulted, I did the orientation. I would do a really intensive verbal consent training with people when they came in talking about verbal consent and sexuality.

You were assaulted at that place?

Yeah. I woke up in the middle of the night to some dude tryin' to pull my shorts off. To this day I'm not certain whether I was drugged or just more drunk than I thought I was. I really didn't freak out until the next day. I woke up and walked down the street to the house where all the food was prepared and I just realized like, "Oh, fuck. I'm really upset about what just happened. How does that happen?" I told the volunteer coordinator, and he says, "That's it! That guy's out of here. This type of shit keeps happenin'." I just didn't know about it.

Keeps happening? You had no awareness that this kind of thing had been going on?

Oh, the history of sexual assault at Common Ground was real bad.[7] I didn't know that before I got there. But I would say that I made an example of that

7. Rachel Luft's findings in "Looking for Common Ground" support Reilly's perception of sexual violence in Common Ground. Luft notes that in 2006, white women volunteers in Common Ground reported a string of sexual assaults, the vast majority of which were attacks on white women volunteers by nonlocal white male volunteers. Nevertheless, internal dialogue focused on the alleged dangers of the local Black community—a response mirroring Reilly's perception that the volunteer groups projected criminality onto the local populace. Moreover, Common Ground's leadership also struggled to address sexism within the context

young man without really realizing it. They asked me, "Do you want to call the police?" But I was not interested in sending anyone to jail. If he was losing his house and his stability, that's fine. But they came back to me and were like, "Well, he refuses to leave so we're gonna call the police to have him removed from the property. Are you sure you don't want to talk to the police?" At that point I thought, "Well, this guy is like real crazy. If you're not taking the opportunity to walk away when someone tells you, 'Leave or we'll call the police,' then you probably should go to jail." So, I talked to a military police sergeant. I walked him down to the house and picked up the condom wrapper off my floor. I was like, "This doesn't belong here." He prepared a report, and then the NOPD showed up and took another report.

So how long did you put up with this situation in this house? That was the tail end of your time at Common Ground, right?

It was. So, when I initially moved into the gutted house that I was living in, it was just absurd. That place was just disgusting. We called it the post-apocalyptic wonderland, but things ebbed and flowed a lot because of the different volunteers that were there. It got better. It got worse.

So, what happened for you afterward? You went home?

I went home. I kept in touch with people. I volunteered on the *Clearwater,* doing a couple of weeks of environmental work on a sailboat. Then I went back down to New Orleans and started living for a while with a Jesuit volunteer and her two kids who had an extra bedroom in her basement. Then I had a friend who was goin' out of town and wanted somebody to house-sit

---

of the apparent racism that led to the flooding's most identifiable outcomes. Consequently, although the trend of sexual violence was known and discussed among the leadership, Common Ground had not yet devised a coherent prevention and response strategy by the time Reilly joined the organization. Reminiscent of Adrian Manriquez's testimony regarding his perception of masculinity in Common Ground, Luft argues that a "pervasive culture of masculinity" related to the grueling recovery work in the midst of a crisis enabled "sexual attacks" without accountability. As one of her interviewees noted, "It was so blatant that there was no policy for dealing with [sexual assault]. . . . It was like we had created a situation for it, where really awful things were plausible in this environment, and there was no way of dealing with it, no space for it." Luft, "Looking for Common Ground," 5, 13–17; Berra et al., "To Render Ourselves Visible," 34.

so I lived in her house for a couple of months. I got a job in a coffee shop. I would work in the coffee shop during the week and at Bayou Rebirth on the weekend, and somehow find time to coordinate volunteers for Contemplatives in Action. Then I applied to America's Wetland Conservation Corps, and they offered me a position. So, in January of 2010, I started working for the America's Wetland Conservation Corps, which was a partnership between LSU Ag Center and the America's Wetland Foundation.

And that's when I met you actually. At Bayou Rebirth,
even though you were part-time, the staff was small
enough that you were still an important part of the staff.
Is that correct?

Yeah. When it started, I was still doing stuff with Common Ground and Bayou Rebirth. I took care of all Common Ground's wetland grasses for a while, but I never really did any of that stuff for Bayou Rebirth 'cause they were partnering with Common Ground to manage that. Then all of that came to a crashing end. At Bayou Rebirth I became one of the main coordinators in the program, and I led a lot of projects for a while. I would coordinate planting trips with whoever was in the crew. We planted a lot of grass.

Your time at Common Ground always was chaotic,
as you described it to me. I'm assuming that Bayou Rebirth
has not as been as chaotic as Common Ground.

Well, you'd be amazed ... but I didn't live there, so that's a huge, important difference. I had another job to balance out the money when I needed to finally live somewhere that I had to pay rent. So, it was certainly different. It was sort of a transition back into the normal world.

Let me ask you a quick question. After what you
experienced, what do you think about this concept of
young volunteers living together and working together?

Well, where do you get the education to form a radical community? How does a nineteen-year-old know how to do that? They don't. They have some ideas they think they might want to try, but you wind up manifesting the same ugly shit because it's so deeply ensconced in you, and when you don't have layers and layers and layers reinforcing social structures and norms, you see it real fast.

It sounds to me like if you're gonna have large communities of young people being involved in any sort of radical organizing work, it might be good to have a firm, grounded, older hand there.

The problem is who is defining "grounded, older hand." Sometimes the older hand may be the FBI agent who's actually there to completely disrupt things and reinforce the idea that you should exist in this kind of power hierarchy situation for attractive white men. We had all of that at Common Ground. We had Malik, and we had Thom Pepper.[8]

And then there's Brandon Darby, who outted himself as an FBI informant. At the very least he was an informant after he was at Common Ground, but a lot of us think there's more to the story than that. He came forward to rat people out very publicly around the Republican National Convention during the 2008 election cycle, which was at the exact same time that they started talking about all the crimes that went on in the wake of Hurricane Katrina. And suddenly we weren't talking about white vigilantes on West Bank in New Orleans. We weren't talking about the real issues that were finally being brought to light. We were all talking about fucking Brandon Darby.

At a key moment where the focus should have been to provide support and bring to light what happened here, all anyone wanted to talk to us about

8. Thom Pepper was the executive director of Common Ground from 2006 until 2019. A real estate developer from Florida who stayed in New Orleans for several months to help gut homes in 2005, Pepper started working with Common Ground in 2006 and is credited with using his business background to move the organization away from the instability associated with its anarchist origins toward a more sustainable model. Journalist John Pope wrote of Pepper: "Under his leadership, the organization worked with about 65,000 volunteers in gutting about 3,000 structures in the Lower 9th Ward; establishing centers in seven parishes for lending tools and distributing food, water and clothing; and creating medical and legal clinics, computer centers, bioremediation centers and shelters for women and families." Pepper died of cancer in New Orleans on December 23, 2019. Pope, "Common Ground Leader Thom Pepper."

was Brandon Darby. People like to ask, "What was Common Ground up to that the FBI would be spying on us?" In my perspective, it was more that people with power wanted to disrupt the potential organizing capacity of other people.

I don't know if I would make as generalized a statement, but I certainly know that the FBI has a history infiltrating organizations that in hindsight, weren't doing anything wrong. Have you heard of COINTELPRO? [9]

Oh, yeah. We used to joke about COINTELPRO.

So, I mean, we have a history of that in this country.

Oh, yeah. There was rampant sexual assault from my understanding when Brandon Darby was the director of Common Ground.

And you feel that he perhaps allowed that?

It's pretty clear from what I know, but not only Darby. I take issue with the notion that the person in charge is the ultimate responsible person. That's bullshit. If you don't want somebody around, you run them out on a rail. You don't need the guy in charge to give you permission.

Our culture is so ugly. We have so much engrained racism and sexism and classism, and we don't even talk to each other about it or try to understand how it makes all of us feel. We talk about superficial bullshit. But you can't just rush into an emergency situation, thinking you're going to forge this radical entity. You have to heal yourself before you can heal others.

Having been in these different organizations, how well do you see them communicating and working with each?

In a lot of ways they don't, but it's kind of hard to judge. Habitat for Humanity was great, but they used all Chinese drywall, and now they're rearranging all their people and re-drywalling every house they built. [10] There are

9. In 1956, the FBI founded COINTELPRO to infiltrate and sow dissent within allegedly radical political organizations. Newton, "War against the Panthers," 43–51.

10. As discussed in greater detail in chapters 8 and 9, large quantities of drywall were shipped to the Gulf states in response to the need for rebuilding after Katrina. New Or-

some partnerships. Common Ground and Bayou Rebirth for a long time worked together, and at times that partnership worked better or worse based on lots of different factors. But Common Ground and Lowernine .org—never the two shall talk. Even though we're both in the Lower Ninth Ward, they do their thing, and we do our thing. Lowernine.org grew out of the remnants of Emergency Communities. They have a narrow mission and seemed for a while to be doin' pretty well.

Out of thirty interviews so far no one has ever said that there was effective interorganizational work. Do you think there should be? If there was some sort of way in which organizations would talk to each other, how do you think they should be doing it?

This came up again with the oil spills: how people respond to a disaster.[11] Unless you have existing relationships and people you trust, trying to forge those things in a disaster situation isn't going to work. People close ranks. After Katrina, people just rushed into the void. They kept showing up because they wanted to do something. But they were in disaster mode. They're freaking out. If you don't have a network and structure in place to make rational decisions before the disaster strikes, you get crazy talk, and nobody counteracts it.

---

leans Area Habitat for Humanity (NOAHH) received a substantial donation from Interior/ Exterior Building Supply (INEX). The donation exceeded their needs, and they let other rebuilding agencies take as much as they needed for their projects. By 2008, reports of defective drywall, which caused noxious odors and disabled homes' HVAC systems, began to arise across the states affected by Katrina. At the outset, NOAHH denied knowledge of any problems with the drywall, while the nonprofits that had received and used it in their clients' homes feared the worst. Nevertheless, hundreds of homes rebuilt after the storm had to be stripped to their frames and be rebuilt a second time at a heavy financial and emotional cost. Reckdahl, "Chinese Drywall Concerns"; Pate, interview; Nolan, "Hurricane Relief Groups Are Gutting."

11. On April 10, 2010, an explosion on the *Deepwater Horizon* in the Gulf of Mexico triggered the worst offshore oil spill in U.S. history. The spill resulted in an oil slick covering 57,500 square miles of the Gulf and 1,100 miles of shoreline contamination in Louisiana, Mississippi, Alabama, and Florida. It also led to the unemployment of 8,000–12,000 people in the fishing, drilling, and tourism industries. Pallardy, "Deepwater Horizon"; Friedman, "Ten Years after Deepwater Horizon"; Lee, *If God Is Willing*, film.

*So, it sounds as if your argument would be to get
people talking to each other before something happens.
Know the people who are involved in reasonably similar
activities so that when something happens,
those relationships already exist.*

Yeah, and have some kind of like sanely hashed-out plan. Katrina was an inevitability for New Orleans, but nobody had a plan. The oil spill was an inevitability for the Louisiana coast, but nobody had a plan. And since both of those things have happened, nobody has decided to make a plan.

*It seems to me that what you all might want to do is figure
out how to have a conversation that is not charged by
fixing a problem right now. You're pointing out that once
people get invested in their own methodology or
philosophy, the time for talking to other people is gone.*

Yeah, once a disaster happens, people think, "Who is this stranger? I have my whole list of urgent priorities. I don't have to make new relationships with strangers unless I have a specific thing that they can help me with. I don't want to get to know you right now. I have shit to do."

*So, after seeing all this,
how do you feel about our national character?*

I felt inspired when I got down here. I wanted to be a part of this thing where young people cared, were active, and were doing something relevant. And for a while, Common Ground was really relevant. But what it means to me has evolved. I keep moving away from human suffering. Maybe it's sort of this like cop-out retreat into privileged, white middle-class existence that I'm entitled to being my birthright, which I say in an ironic context. But people suffer and pain is not good, and this is not new. Now we have AIDS. Before that we had the plague. Now you live longer, but you might die of cancer. I feel like I've become more and more of a nihilist.

3. Colleen Morgan

BUILDING A NEW MODEL OF
WETLANDS RESTORATION

This Bayou Rebirth thing is the hardest thing I've ever done. It's a
good thing. I consider this problem, our environment washing away
because humans have screwed it up, as the most important thing for our
generation to tackle. So, if we have one life to live and each one of us has
something important in it to do, this is what I'm supposed to be doing.

—Colleen Morgan, Bayou Rebirth

Colleen Morgan differs from many of the interviewees in this project. The
majority of the project's participants, like Manriquez and Reilly, were non-
native young adults who came into entry-level positions (usually home
rebuilding) in recovery organizations and moved their way up to be man-
agerial staff. A much smaller but significant portion of the interviewees,
whom we will meet in later chapters, were middle-aged and senior leaders
who were generally from New Orleans. With a decade-long career in journalism behind her and a freshly minted Yale University master's degree in
environmental management, Morgan was in her late twenties and early
thirties for much of the recovery period in New Orleans. She possessed all
the energy of her younger counterparts but with a much more developed
worldview and an unrelenting confidence as she set out on her mission—to
establish a nonprofit that advocated for the importance of wetlands restoration for the protection of New Orleans and helped corporations understand their economic interests in wetlands restoration. This was the vision
underlying her nonprofit startup, Bayou Rebirth, and Morgan's interview
provides a complete narrative arc of a nonprofit from concept to closing.

Despite the unique aspects of her background, Morgan's interview offers insights into themes that were expressed by many volunteers. Like
the previous two interviewees, one can see "convergence behavior" pulling

Morgan to New Orleans when she describes her shock at seeing the damage wrought by the storm. As a former resident of New Orleans, however, Morgan possessed a second strong trait that scholars correlate with volunteers converging on disaster areas: personal knowledge of the victims.[1] Lastly, although Manriquez and Reilly followed the pattern in which past volunteering contributed to future volunteering, Morgan's experience showed how service learning also correlates strongly to a long-term service orientation.[2]

As the story of a nonprofit from conception through decline, Morgan's account provides a higher-level view of the challenges associated with individuals trying to contribute to disaster recovery by founding, staffing, or volunteering for new nonprofits. As seen in other interviews with those who led new organizations, the problem of finding or generating funding to do good work in a sustainable manner was chronic; paradoxically, Morgan's interview reveals the severe strains placed on a young organization trying to adhere to the exacting requirements associated with winning a large grant. In addition, Morgan's interview reveals the problems with relying on short-term volunteers, who came to New Orleans cyclically, to tackle ongoing problems. Organizations often solved such issues by sharing resources with other nonprofits, and because most of the attention in post-Katrina recovery went to home-rebuilding organizations, Bayou Rebirth often had to rely on them for support. Unfortunately, the pairing of two fledgling organizations does not mean that either will be able to fly.

⚜ ⚜ ⚜

JULY 6, 2010

So, what was going on in your life before
Hurricane Katrina?

Well, I was a journalist for ten years, and I lived in Connecticut. I'm originally from Dallas, but I went to boarding school in the northwest corner

---

1. St. John and Fuchs, "Heartland Responds to Terror," 397.

2. Service learning has been found to be strongly associated with choosing a service-oriented career. Niehaus and Inkelas, "Exploring the Role of Alternative Break," 134–148; Sax et al., "Long-Term Effects of Volunteerism," 187–202.

of Connecticut and then I went to Tulane University in New Orleans for college. After I graduated from Tulane, I went back to Connecticut. and I started my career as a reporter in an area called Litchfield County, which, even though it's this beautiful, pristine place, had a lot of development pressures from the outskirts of New York City. There were all these New York City weekenders who had these big estates, lots of money, and lots of power and influence. Our focus was those weekenders. They cared a lot about preserving the environment and preserving the watersheds and the wetlands in that area because they were getting gobbled up by development. So, I became an environmental reporter. That just became my beat.

When things got really difficult at the paper and a series of events happened, I left, went to another paper, became a features writer, and it was horrible.

And about what time period was this?

2004. I was at that paper for maybe six to eight months before I left. I was trying to figure out a new direction for my life and decided to go back to grad school. I was gonna go to law school, but someone who works at a land trust convinced me to apply to the Yale School of Forestry and Environmental Studies (FES). I thought, "There's no way, but I might as well give it a shot." It was actually a lot easier to apply there than law school. I got in, and I started at FES in August of 2005. Two weeks into my orientation at my new endeavor, Hurricane Katrina hit New Orleans, and suddenly I was trapped in Connecticut.

Why do you say "trapped"?

I couldn't come to New Orleans as a journalist, or helping out, or anything. I couldn't leave. I'd just started the hardest thing that I ever did in my life—grad school at Yale.

So, you felt an immediate desire to get down
to New Orleans?

Immediate, to the point where I couldn't watch television. I actually had to block it out to avert the emotions.

Before we get into that,
tell me what had made you think about going to law school?

Well, I always knew that if I went on to grad school, it would most likely be law school. I was interested in environmental law. When I was at the Litchfield paper, if there were three good stories going on, and one had to do with the courts, I would take that one.

And where did you hope to go to law school,
and what were you thinking about as a focus?

Wow, you're really getting into my deep secrets. Vermont Law School. It's up near Burlington, Vermont. But a bunch of things happened around that time. I had paths in front of me to choose from, and I knew I had to pick a path. My boyfriend and I were living together in Torrington, and we were having trouble. So, I moved into my own apartment. I had all these weird odd jobs. I was applying to law school, and I ended up feeling that I needed to connect with the important people in my former career. I ended up just having lunch with people. It was during those conversations that I further developed the idea that you can do whatever you want to do. You just have to make it happen. So, when I got the letter from the Yale School of Forestry, I screamed. I called my brother because my new life started right then and there.

This is almost where we started the interview: two weeks
into the program Katrina hit and you felt trapped.

I remember we hadn't moved to New Haven yet, and our house was in boxes. The orientation was at the Yale School of Forestry. It's like you go out into the woods, and then you go through urban ecology for a week. I came back from a week, and my boyfriend was trying to fill me in on what had gone on. I had just gotten back from a week in the woods, and I was two days away from starting my classes. I was just like, "I can't handle this." It was like my home was being destroyed.

I'm guessing when you were an undergrad at Tulane,
you made a strong connection to the area.

Yeah. I didn't realize how strong it was until the storm. More than anything I wanted to jet down here and be a journalist again, but I couldn't. It all just kind of welled up inside me, and I'll be honest, I really had to ignore it because I knew I couldn't do anything. I couldn't actually physically do anything.

So, you didn't really pay attention to the
press coverage to protect your own mental state?

Yeah, for my own emotional stability. A couple of weeks into school, our dean called a meeting to talk about how the school and the students could help Katrina victims in some way. He was giving a call to arms. I remember that I was standing up against a wall, and this gal, who became a good friend, started talking and broke into tears. She was like, "We have to do something. We have to. We can't live with ourselves if we don't." Well, I decided to speak, and I said, "I have no idea what we can do but whoever wants to do something, meet me on Wednesday at three o'clock. Write it down." So, I had a group that met with me, and we started down the path. Then I started reading more about what was going on down here and specifically about wetlands deterioration and how it basically exacerbated the impact of the storm.[3]

Right. It opened the door for the storm to
walk right into the middle of the living room.

That's a really good analogy. (*Laughter.*) So, I put out another call to the whole school saying, "Who wants to be involved in researching wetlands and maybe going down there?" I ended up setting up a project class with a whole bunch of professors. I figured out the curriculum for it. I got five professors involved, and those five professors juggled the work of doing lectures and meeting with students. We ended up having twelve in the class, and then ten people came down here during spring break of 2006.

I came here for the first time during Christmas break, right after the storm, and just toured the area. I met my mom here. and we went everywhere. I actually met with some local professors and was setting up the project course at the time. I was trying to connect with some local people that could help us down here. Then we ended up doing this thing during

3. For more on the wetlands' deterioration see Morrish, "After the Storm," 1008; Van Heerden and Bryan, *The Storm,* 4, 160; Adams, *Markets of Sorrow,* loc 421; Flaherty et al., *Floodlines,* 57.

spring break where we did actual wetlands research in the marshes down in Cocodrie,[4] and then we just met with a ton of people, including the Army Corps of Engineers. We went to the National Wetlands Research Center and met with the head of the Coalition to Restore Coastal Louisiana. I was in charge of everything having to do with that trip. I set up all the logistics. I planned it. I manned it. I was the primary contact when we were here, as well as the van driver. That was my first experience really coming down here and researching. We did presentations in New Haven about our various research. That was really just the beginning for me. It was like the foundation because, during the summer, in between your two years at Yale FES, you have to do an internship.

This is the summer of 2006?

The summer of 2006. I came down here, and I worked with the LSU Ag Center. My research was a contingent valuation[5] of the ports and the oil industry in terms of trying to set a value of wetlands as protection, but my main project was with LSU Ag Center. I rebuilt a greenhouse in City Park and turned it into a wetlands plant center. I ended up getting donated plants from all over Louisiana to stock that plant center. I utilized volunteers to propagate those plants, and the first place that we utilized those plants was in the lagoons in City Park. That's where I learned to be a volunteer coordinator. That's where I learned how to propagate plants, and that's how I learned how to restore the environment.

Other people have talked about their initial impressions
on arriving to the city. What were yours?

I was so busy, but we went to the Lower Ninth Ward—a place that everyone feels like they have to go. When I drove through there with my mother, there were trees on top of houses and houses pushed in the middle of the street. There were cars in trees. There were cars on top of houses. Cars on top of cars. Houses on top of houses. It was like a war zone.

I knew this was where I had to be. I couldn't let that happen again, if I

---

4. A small town in Terrebonne Parish, Louisiana.
5. In the *Encyclopedia Britannica*, Pamela C. Jones defines *contingent valuation* as "a survey-based method of determining the economic value of a nonmarket resource. It is used to estimate the value of resources and goods not typically traded in economic markets. It is

had anything to do with it. This Bayou Rebirth thing is the hardest thing I've ever done. It's a good thing. I consider this problem, our environment washing away because humans have screwed it up, as the most important thing for our generation to tackle. So, if we have one life to live and each one of us has something important in it to do, this is what I'm supposed to be doing.

You finished organizing the spring break trip in 2006. Bayou Rebirth was started in 2007. What happened between that spring break and the genesis of Bayou Rebirth?

I finished grad school and was here as an intern for the LSU Ag Center.

Tell me more about that experience.

Well, I wanted to do this particular research called a contingent evaluation, which is the economics of natural resources. It's basically where you go to people in a neighborhood or business and ask them what they consider is the value of a particular environmental resource. I was going around to companies related to the ports and the oil industries to get the value of wetlands as protection from storm surge. I got it funded through the LSU Ag Center, but the deal that I made with the LSU Ag Center was that I would work part-time as a volunteer coordinator to help with this offshoot that was gonna happen that summer. This other gal wanted to do this project, and I would help her part of the time. Well, my research was a full-time job, and the gal I was supporting was a full time job. It turned out that my research was awesome, but it was huge.

You mean the scope of the project?

The scope of the project was huge. I could have done a PhD on it. And I did this volunteer coordinating thing. She would assign me a group that was comin' in on Tuesday, and I'd go out and work with that group. Then on Friday I'd have another group. I did that ad hoc for a while and then I grabbed onto this project that our boss, Mark Schexnayder, had started

---

most commonly related to natural and environmental resources." Jones, "Contingent Valuation."

a year before. He had written a grant to turn a greenhouse in City Park into a learning center where kids could learn about and work on wetlands plants. That grant never went anywhere. I took that grant, rewrote it, and he helped me usher it through the process. Then we got the grant, and I administered it, but it was so much more than his original proposal. I took this greenhouse in City Park, which is the greenhouse that actually grows out the plants for the Botanical Garden. That greenhouse was completely destroyed by Katrina. It was flooded. I rebuilt it with volunteer groups. We were using all this found, recycled material from Shell. We also took this other part of the property, which had been basically kind of overgrown and hadn't been used and brought in wetlands plants from all over the state. I was drivin' all over the place and digging up different types of plants that I didn't really know. I was tryin' to figure it all out as I went.

You didn't have any guidance?

Oh, I had all kinds of guidance. I learned everything that I needed to know about plants that summer. Some volunteers worked with me like every day for the whole summer or for a month at a time. Mostly they were volunteers from Operation Nehemiah. I worked with so many organizations: Operation Blessing and volunteers from Common Ground Relief. These were all total bohemians. They rode in the back of my truck. They loved "getting" in the water and "getting" dirty, and most of them were vegetarians. That summer was incredible. I never thought that I would end up spending my days at a greenhouse working with power tools in what seemed like 110-degree heat, 100 percent humidity, with volunteers that had nose rings, literally waist-deep in the lagoons in City Park, planting all these different types of grasses, and spending most of our time propagating grasses that we had just hauled in from five hours away.

It all culminated on August 3rd of that summer. We promoted this huge planting at the City Park lagoon. Those lagoons are gorgeous and normally filled with fish, and there's irises everywhere. People get their pictures taken at City Park when their wedding's coming up. Well, City Park was flooded with saltwater, and all those plants on the shoreline died. And the fish that were left suffered terribly because the water was so salty. So, the whole point of the project was to set up a wetlands plant nursery to help the Botanical Garden rebuild its greenhouse. In exchange, we'd get some of the property to build up wetland plants stock and use that stock to replant the shorelines in City Park for the purpose of fishery recovery. That was the project.

Was that your idea?

No, it was my boss's idea. That's what he wanted from the project. I grabbed onto that because it was all about wetlands plants, I could travel around the state, and I could also learn a lot about working with volunteers and salt marsh grasses. I wasn't goin' out to the wetlands of coastal Louisiana, but the truth is that I needed to start in City Park. I needed to start somewhere where it was something that I could do. I learned so much about how to work with volunteers and how to keep them safe, hydrated, and cool.

We planted, and after a month and a half of working with volunteers on a daily basis or every other day, we planned this really big planting for local volunteers—anyone who wanted to come. It was on a Saturday, and we put it on the radio. I remember wakin' up at the crack of dawn and gettin' on TV and just promoting the effort everywhere and then planning this huge event. We had to have zillions of plants, all this equipment, trucks, and the whole nine yards. It was the hardest thing I had ever done.

The whole community came out. One hundred and sixty people showed up. I had a whole team, and I was in charge of the whole thing. All those volunteers that had been working with me over the course of the months became my team leaders. It was the first time that I really made something big happen in a single place, and we got so much feedback about how wonderful it was. What a great experience it was for the kids that were there!

And what was the name of the event again?

Bayou Rebirth.

Oh, so that's where the name happened?

That's where the name came from. I didn't coin that name. My boss Mark did. I was on the phone in his office with Rebirth Brass Band, and I was trying to convince them to come and play at the event. I was on the phone with them, and he sits there, and his brain starts working. They couldn't come because they were gonna be in San Francisco or something. I get off the phone and he said, "I just figured it out. It's gonna be called Bayou Rebirth." Everybody got a Bayou Rebirth t-shirt. The lagoon where we planted is called Bayou Metairie, and it's in the very front of City Park. It's gorgeous.

So, you feel that the event was a real success.

Oh, it was a huge success. Everything after that was like anticlimactic.

How so?

I didn't know this, but the whole summer was building up to that point. After that, the plant center was set up. We didn't do another planting. School started again at the end of August. So, I left two weeks later, and those two weeks were spent just buttoning up everything.

How did you feel? Were you up or down after things were over? Sometimes when you finish something big, there are these weird left-over emotions.

Sick. I got sick and it laid me up for a couple of days. I mean I had not slept or eaten for a week or something. The same thing happened when I was in drama. I was in plays when I was in high school. I'd always get sick right after the play.

So, there's an emotional connection there?

Oh, absolutely. I was on more than I'd ever been. I was communicating with team leaders. I was teaching 150 people. People in the various groups sent out my cellphone number somehow. So, my phone was just goin' off all day. (*Laughter.*) Anyway, that day was the very beginning.

Did you know it at the time?

No. I went back to school. I had a meeting with my adviser to talk about my research from the summer, which had pretty much disintegrated. I was gonna propose that I start over. Earlier that day I hung out with a friend of mine who was in a PhD program. She and I were kindred spirits. I told her all about my summer and how great it was. Then she was like, "Why don't you take what you learned this summer and make it something that can be a long-term, sustainable thing." It didn't take much for her to convince me. It was like she gave the rubber stamp on what I was feeling deep down but hadn't realized.

Was your adviser supportive of that idea?

Oh yeah. My adviser knew as soon as I walked in there that I'd been swept away by something. It was so much more real than what I had proposed, and he was excited about it. He passed me on to one of the professors that I had worked with the previous spring, and he ended up becoming my project adviser. He knew more about plants as opposed to economics. Also, that summer we did a planting at City Park with seventy local high school students. I did surveys of all those students as well. Those students that came with me from Yale were the volunteer group, but at the end of the week, they became my team leaders. They taught all the high school students how to plant. So, I was team leader the whole week except for the last day when I was the site supervisor in the lingo that I now use.

Could you go back to something? I'd be interested to know what are the things you had to learn about working with volunteers and how to take a bunch of people who aren't graduate students in environmental studies and getting them to be people who are doing environmental work?

Well, a lot of what I consider my landmark experiences with volunteers was when I was working with the greenhouse in City Park. At the greenhouse there were two different types. I already told you about the bohemians. Then there were the folks from Operation Blessing, and they were very different. Operation Blessing folks came there as a mission trip, a religious-oriented thing. Two very different types of groups. I learned a lot from both, and they learned a lot from me. I got to know them very well because we not only worked very hard in the heat, getting very dirty and all that stuff, but we also drank and partied heavily. I think I partied harder that summer than I did the whole time I was at Tulane.

With the mission trip people also?

Oh yeah. They did it kind of surreptitiously. With me they felt they could let their hair down 'cause they weren't necessarily with their group or whatever. I knew where to take 'em. So, they felt really comfortable hangin' out with me. I had certain bonds with more of them than others, and certainly with the Common Ground volunteers. We had so much fun. We just played in the mud all day and danced all night, and it was all for coastal restoration from the storm. I made sure they knew they knew how important it was. I was always saying that this was a step in a larger direction. Those plants in the greenhouse might not be the plants we put into the shorelines today, but the great-grandchildren of these plants, we will eventually put in coastal Louisiana. That was the purpose of the Wetlands Plant Center.

I started the process of developing my education program when each one of those volunteers walked up to me. I would tell 'em why I was there, why these plants were important, and the whole purpose of the project. I do PowerPoint presentations for almost every volunteer group that comes to us. I'm always tryin' to tell students that they can educate Americans about a huge problem and that they can go home and advocate.

The volunteers must feel really small relative to the vastness of the expanse they're working in. You can see the boundaries of a park, but if you're in the wetlands, you'd just see a few people.

Well, what's cool is that we can say, "You guys in front of me are twenty folks from Wisconsin, but on Thursday we're gonna have thirty folks from Seattle. Then on Saturday we're gonna have fifteen people from Quebec." So, they can see that it is a movement and not just a movement from within New Orleans. People have been coming down to New Orleans from all around the world forever, but now they have a really damn good reason to do so.

In a previous conversation you mentioned that you have volunteered with gutting and home-rebuilding organizations. Did your time as a volunteer inform how you train your own supervisors?

Oh, completely. There are actually some other organizations that do plantings around here. Any time there's a planting that's within an hour from me, if I can, I volunteer for it because I get to connect with those organizations who are doing similar work. Sometimes that's the only time we actually get to chat. The other thing is that I'm just a volunteer that day, and I can chat with the other volunteers like I can't do if I'm their supervisor. I also can experience the work and have a different perspective. It's really important to do that every now and then.

How did you go from the big event in City Park
to starting the organization?

I studied how to do a case statement, which is like a proposal, and then I studied how to work with volunteers. I did surveys. Then I did this big trip in the spring of 2007 with a whole group of Yale students where we did different projects every single day. At the end of the week, the Yale students became team leaders with a group of I think eighty high school students, and we did a grass planting in City Park. I did a presentation for the kids, and we surveyed those kids as well. Then I analyzed the surveys and wrote about it. The elements of making a spring break trip happen, all the different restoration projects, and the planting projects were the big pieces that prepared me for starting Bayou Rebirth. I already had a network of people. The only component that I wish I had was more research on how to fundraise for nonprofits.

Has that been difficult?

It's been horrible. It's been very hard.

How much of it is the difficulty of fundraising,
and how much of it do you think might be the
state of the economy the last few years?[6]

Fifty/fifty. I didn't know how to do a lot of fundraising. I did a big grant application as part of my master's project. We had to answer all these questions and do a budget. That was a big learning process. That was the only fundraising portion that I did. I submitted it. I didn't get it—all stuff that is part of the learning process. (*Laughter.*) I'd been a journalist for ten years, and I really didn't want to write anymore. That was a problem. (*Laughter.*) Not that I couldn't write. I did it all the time. But when I came down here and started the program, I really had to develop the educational programs from scratch. Also, the process of getting all the things that I needed to set up volunteers and supervising the volunteer groups when they got down here took a lot of time and effort. And I had a part-time job that was very demanding. So, I didn't have the time that I needed to write grants. I was doing grants like a day or two before they were due, and it was like really hellish.

6. These interviews occurred just after the Great Recession of 2007–2009.

I did end up getting one big grant, $32,000 from the Gulf of Mexico Foundation. In December of that year, I got an almost $10,000 check and suddenly had the wherewithal to do a lot of work. It was fantastic—and I was way in over my head. (*Laughter.*)

Really? You've been so prepared for everything else.
It sounds out of character.

Well, I didn't have any help. I was all by myself. I had volunteer groups for that whole first year from Common Ground Relief, this other volunteer organization that cared a lot about wetlands restoration projects. I had a partnership with Common Ground, and their wetlands coordinator became my right arm. Their wetlands coordinator was always that person who helped me with the education program and helped in the field—making sure that all the kids were doin' the right things, helping me move dirt, all that stuff. That didn't necessarily help me with developing the program because none of the people that took that position at Common Ground were experienced enough. I'm the one that had the knowledge and the ability to make the project happen. That person kind of learned from me, and sometimes I gave away some responsibility to that person.

What else was happening with you at that time?

I took on this part-time job at the Audubon, and the woman at Audubon really believed in my research and helped me develop it. She's the founding member of my board. I had all these people that really wanted to help me make Bayou Rebirth happen. So, I had all this confidence. I had this plan. I put every piece of me into this. I worked from the time I woke up until the time I went to sleep, every single day, for a long time. It was very stressful. I also committed to doing a four-day camp, and I had to figure out what I was gonna do in those four days.

Who were you gonna do the camp for?

It's called Operation Reach. It's a camp for low-income kids, and it goes on all summer. At the very end of the camp, they wanted to do this four-day, hands-on, outdoor, community outreach session. I literally got here on June 1 and by July 15 or something, I had to have a curriculum ready.

That was really tough, but I still use that program today. We developed it into an eight-session program that lasts a semester. Once I developed that, I started selling it to schools. I also did a lot of presentations for people that were here for conventions or volunteer groups that wanted me to speak, and I charged an honorarium for that.

I promoted my plantings and education programs by going to these volunteer organizations that were already established here in the city and told them that I'm looking for volunteer groups for just a day. There were only a certain number of organizations that were even interested in referring people to me, but slowly those referrals started to build, especially after my reputation spread. I was also working at the nature center, so if a group had the money and they really wanted to do a wetlands planting, they could do a wetlands planting. If they didn't have the money but still wanted to do an environmental project, they could go to the Nature Center, 'cause I was the volunteer coordinator. All the time I spent connecting to these volunteer organizations and promoting Bayou Rebirth, I promoted the Nature Center on Nature Center time, but my boss Amy was cool with that. She wanted me to make those partnerships and whatnot. It was all about partnering with people who believed in their heart that we needed to save the wetlands to protect the city, and teaching volunteers from all over the country about wetlands. And I was tryin' to do it just all by myself. I was a one-woman show for two years.

What do you envision as the mission of Bayou Rebirth? You said it had an environmental mission but without bashing entrepreneurship or business.

The business community is the tail that wags the dog in terms of environmental issues. The vast majority of environmental issues are caused by or somehow related to business. And the destruction of wetlands in Louisiana is directly and indirectly caused by the growth of our oil production in coastal Louisiana but also because of navigation, canals, and that kind of stuff.[7] I feel that those industries and the players in those industries should be involved in restoring the environment. We can bash them because

7. For more on the relationship between canal building and wetlands' deterioration, see Adams, *Markets of Sorrow,* loc 421; Flaherty et al., *Floodlines,* 57.

they've broken our coast, or we can sit down with them and say, "Listen, we're trying to restore the coast; we're trying to educate people about the coast. Help us do that. You have the money. We don't have the money. We know how; you obviously don't. Let's involve you in the solution." That's how we're going to become a greener country—by changing how our industries interact with the environment from inside.

And what activities does Bayou Rebirth do in that program that you've outlined? You've mentioned the plantings and the education. I'm just tryin' to understand how the different things you do fit together.

So, the mission is to educate Americans about coastal Louisiana land law through stewardship projects. So that they get a little bit of knowledge, and then they go back to Minnesota or Seattle and they have a piece of Louisiana in their heart. The other piece, that I haven't done such a great job on, is to not only encourage those volunteers to act once they get back home by educating their community, their church, or their college but also to garner a little movement by, at the very least, writing their congressman. I say Congress because Congress is the boss of the Army Corps of Engineers, and the Army Corps of Engineers is in charge of coastal restoration in Louisiana. The Louisiana Department of Natural Resources has a very large role in planning and executing a lot of projects, but the state doesn't have the kind of money that the Army Corps does. But even the Army Corps doesn't have enough money because Louisiana coastal wetlands loss has not become this huge issue that Congress is gonna appropriate half of its budget to. The only way that Louisiana coastal restoration is gonna happen on a large scale is if the entire country is pushing Congress to do it.

Last year I got Tulane students to do these state fact sheets, showing that the State of Illinois has these top five industries that use these major commodities and 75 percent of those commodities come to Illinois on the Mississippi River through the Port of New Orleans. The idea is that if you connect people to this issue and have them understand how it connects to the larger economy, then they start to see how important the larger restoration projects are for the larger economy. Volunteers can write their congressman, but if a group of volunteers convinces a car manufacturer in Kentucky that New Orleans is important to them and that car manufacturer talks to the congressman, then we're really making headway. That's how the tail wags the dog. That's why I talk about how the oil industry and the ports are connected to their specific state. I did this commodities support research all for free.

Given that you respect and understand business,
what are your feelings about the oil industry?

I feel that it is our industry. We created a demand for this industry. We demand this oil and that's why there's four thousand platforms in the Gulf of Mexico—because we want to put gas in our cars twenty-four hours a day, we want plastic bottles, we want our air conditioning and our heat whenever we flip the switch. The oil industry is just part of a market economy responding to a demand by the American people, and the demand for energy in this country is the largest, by far, of any other country in the world.[8]

In other words, industry was created to satisfy our demands—that's number one. The fact that industry is having this huge backlash about climate change is totally understandable. How is industry supposed to change its ways when there is a demand for their product, and the only way that they have to produce those products or services is through the energy sources that we have right now and there aren't other energy sources that are comparable in terms of price? Number two is that the oil industry, in Louisiana in particular, raped and pillaged the environment, but there were no laws about what to do or not to do in a marsh until the seventies. All these canals had been built by then, and back then all the oil was produced out of the marsh. That was a way to derive value from what was considered "wasteland." Now there is an infrastructure of 15,000 miles of pipeline in coastal Louisiana that moves oil mostly from the 4,000 offshore platforms and producing wells in the Gulf to 17 refineries in the coastal area. We created that infrastructure through our demands over the course of the last hundred years. We cannot put that infrastructure at risk by letting the wetlands deteriorate and not restoring them. They're becoming exposed as the wetlands deteriorate.

8. China's energy demands surpassed those of the United States about one month after this interview.

You're connecting the health of the environment to
the health of industry, as well as acknowledging the
extent to which the American consumer is implicated
in the situation that we have.

Hell, yeah. And that's why every single volunteer group that comes to me walks out realizing that the wetlands of coastal Louisiana are important to them because the pipeline moves the natural gas that heats their home or the oil that goes into their gas tank. It's our investment. Yes, they're owned by the oil industry, but I don't consider the oil industry the enemy that everybody talks about, because the oil industry is a product of our society. Yes, they play by their own rules and all that stuff. That's another issue. But the companies that care about regulations and actually try to be good stewards of the environment need to be brought in because they want to be part of the solution. I have a very good relationship with Shell in general because they know I care about this stuff, and they know that I understand. A lot of the environmental groups down here vilify those companies publicly, and I don't think that's fair at all.[9]

What makes that relationship with Shell good as opposed
to other companies that you did not mention?

Well, first of all, the guy who first told me about the pipeline is Ed Landgraf. He is with Shell Pipeline, and he's trying to convince the oil industry in this area to support wetlands restoration because it protects the pipeline. It costs the oil industry so much money to re-bury pipeline as the wetlands degrade and shrink in size that it is in their best interest, monetarily, to protect them. If a boat comes through, hits an exposed pipeline, and somebody dies, it's a liability. So, it's not only good for the environment but it's also good for their bottom line to actually protect and restore wetlands.

Another guy in materials management with Shell was taking pieces of the platforms that weren't being used anymore and trying to donate them to various organizations around the country that would need those materials. When I rebuilt that greenhouse at City Park, a big component of

9. For an example of what Morgan means by her assertion that some "vilify" the oil companies publicly without addressing people's demand for oil, see Gelbspan, "Nature Fights Back," 23.

the rebuild were oil platform cable trays, which I got from the materials management guy at Shell. That was a way of recycling materials.

So, Shell came to you?

They came to me. I have companies all over that have done some sort of volunteer thing with me and write a check for $5,000 here or there, but this is the only company that has formed a relationship.

Would it be your goal to have a similar relationship with more companies?

Absolutely. I'm really excited that the first company that I had this kind of relationship with is an oil company because of how I feel about industry. My goal was to bring industrial players into wetlands restoration because of their connection to it. I also would like to have port-related companies be involved in it and then the other companies that benefit from New Orleans being a port center, like Coca-Cola. That's the third piece.

So, you're trying to develop a coalition of industries who want to be a part because they understand the importance of the environment surrounding New Orleans, not because they're doing something nice.

Right. The key is that I want them to understand that their involvement in wetlands restoration is not only good for protecting their city and homes but it's also protecting their infrastructure. They know it innately. If we restore wetlands on the coast side of the Coca-Cola plant, we're gonna protect the Coca-Cola plant. It's the same with the oil industry for Shell. Restoring wetlands protects the pipes.

I realized a long time ago that I could go out and try to get grants from foundations and federal agencies, or I could convince industry players that they need to be involved in this. It's good for their environmental performance as an industry player to be involved in wetlands restoration, as well as good for their bottom line if it ends up protecting their infrastructure. And on top of that, I want their company employees to become volunteers, get their hands dirty, and be a part of restoration at their own stockyards.

Say I get a group of volunteers from Coca-Cola to come out and do plantings. Then they go back and talk about it, and they tell their families. Then some other company hears about it, and it just grows from there. I would rather industry players be my partners in that regard. Also, the company pays the fee as opposed to the employees or the volunteers paying the fee, which has been how I've done this all along.

It sounds like you're working really hard to get rid of this false dichotomy between business and the environment. You don't see that as a dichotomy at all.

I see that industry is intricately tied to the environment and environmental health. In the case of the oil industry and wetlands, it's the health of people in the community because the wetlands protect the city. So, all the differences between all these things are just completely broken down here.

I want it to be funded by a coalition of industry players that are invested in wetlands restoration in Louisiana through Bayou Rebirth. Whether this will actually work, I'm still trying to implement.

AUGUST 23, 2011

So, it's kind of refreshing. I can be more honest with you than I can with other people.

What do you mean?

Right now, I'm talking with interns, board members, and with potential grantors, and I have to be "glass is half-full." Students and whatnot call me up and say, "I'm thinking about starting a nonprofit and I'd love to talk to you." I say, "I'll take you out to dinner and I'll convince you not to. Because the main thing that you have to give to start a nonprofit is about five years of your life." (*Laughter.*)

Does it work better to make the budget large when you're applying for grants?

I'm not trying to make 'em larger than they need to be, but the general process that you're supposed to go through is: What would you really like to do? How much would it cost? So, it's a planning process and a budgeting process. Then you take the budget and the plan and turn it into a grant application. We've done a bunch of different types of things. But we can't do anything without money. The next step is to get more referrals from other organizations that utilize volunteers. As long as all the other organizations that use volunteers know about us, then we might get referrals. Volunteer groups pay a fee. So, the more volunteer groups we have that do projects with us, the more money we have in the bank. Sadly, that's what I have to focus on. I can direct people to do a planting or a rain garden, but I can't do any of that unless we have money moving through. At the same time, I have to keep all our plants alive, regardless of whether we have money. So, I have to recruit volunteer groups that don't pay a fee and volunteer leaders that I don't have to pay to keep our nurseries alive. There are multiple layers of nonpaying things. Right now, I'm spending an hour or two every day just maintaining our nursery sites because I'm the only one that can do it.

Did you get hit by the economy?

No, but that's what I say to people who ask, "What happened?" I've never spent a ton of time writing grants because I've had to work on making things happen. I never had a grant writer until this spring. So maybe I didn't keep enough things in the hopper. I also had a grant in 2009 that was an enormous headache and absolutely burned me out.

It was a federal grant for $30,000. It had all sorts of administrative requirements that I didn't realize in advance. I could do it again, but I don't want to. I got gun-shy about writing grants, especially since I spent so much time writing on deadline, into the middle of the night, trying to get these grants done in time. It was just always the last priority. In the first year of our existence, I probably wrote twenty-five to thirty grants, and we got two. It just wasn't a good use of my time.

In the summer of 2009, the year that we had the grant, I had several people working for me, but during the summer things just tanked in terms of how many volunteer groups we had and how many projects were available. I had to tell my staff, which is three people, that I didn't have the money to pay them anymore. I had grant funds, but I had to use them for other things. So, in August or late July I had to tell them: "You either need to go find a new job or I need you guys to work for free." They ended up working for free, and I paid them back once fall came, but that was really detrimental to them.

Then the following year was really hard for me financially. I had stopped taking a check for months before I finally asked them to. I was like workin' on fumes by that time. That was 2009 into 2010. I had actually planned to cease operations at the end of May 'cause that's when most of the school programs stopped.

In anticipation of what happened the year before?

Right. I said we're gonna stop plantings in the summertime, and I told everybody to get summer jobs with the idea that I'd focus on renewing our insurance, raising money, and working on the school programs, so that we would have lots to do in the fall.

So, you could hit the ground running?

Hit the ground running when summer was over. Then it all happened. I couldn't find insurance to cover us. This was after the oil spill. Nobody wanted to insure a wetlands planting operation. I was never able to raise enough money for the insurance, and therefore there were certain things we just couldn't do. I can't expose people if we weren't insured. So, I put together a partnership with Common Ground Relief. It took us a long time to get to the point where we could actually do projects together because we had a big learning curve. I had to train people, and we had to recruit team leaders. We didn't actually start the partnership until November of 2010.

I set up the partnership with Common Ground Relief because we already had a partnership working with the primary nursery in New Orleans East. In the spring of 2009, sort of through that grant, I had to set up a nursery where we would grow out our plants. Well, we did this nursery as a partnership with Common Ground Relief. It's in New Orleans East. We shared the nursery, but the organizations didn't really collaborate on plantings or projects. So, when Bayou Rebirth was having trouble, I went to Thom Pepper and said, "I don't know if we're gonna survive." And he said, "Let's figure out a way to make it work." We came up with all the different things that needed to happen for the plantings, the school program, the nursery, and some other little projects. We came up with this agreement where Common Ground Relief would take on the plantings, the supervision of the volunteers, and coordinating the volunteers, and we started instituting it in late 2010. He promoted the gal who was our nursery manager to be a volunteer coordinator. I knew her really well, and we worked together really well. I also knew that I had an AmeriCorps Vista volunteer who knew Bayou Rebirth really well and whose Vista term was gonna end in February of 2011. I knew I wasn't gonna get another Vista, and I wasn't gonna have enough money to hire someone forty hours a week. So, I was trying to actually take what she had been doing and give it to Common Ground Relief. I had to start doing other things to make ends meet and keep it alive in some ways. That partnership worked out really well for the spring. At the end of the spring, however, we had a drought. For fifty-plus days we had no rain. But, like I told you, we had all these projects, lots of volunteers, and lots of cash flow.

Even up until the spring cash flow was good?

Yes. Part of our partnership is that volunteer groups would pay the fee and then we'd pay all the expenses of that particular project, and then we would split the rest. Common Ground Relief got half, and Bayou Rebirth got half. The idea is that both of us reaped the benefits of the projects we did together.

And then this drought happened?

We had over the course of the winter and spring set up rain gardens and three neighborhood nurseries, which was Bayou Rebirth's. It was one of those other projects. I was trying to have nursery spaces on blighted lots around the city that would improve the look of the area. It would also give me spaces where I could grow our plants and engage the community in helping us grow out those plants, and we can put 'em in places that were wet.

The three additional impacts that neighborhood nurseries would have, hopefully, was they could decrease local flooding because rainwater during storms would go into our ponds at neighborhood nurseries. We have lots of flooding when we have a big storm, and the water just sits there. The second thing is it improves blighted properties. Then, lastly, we would work there with volunteer groups that were coming for conventions and only had a couple of hours.

Anyway, the idea of the neighborhood nurseries had many benefits. I had lots of people say it was a great idea, and when I would tell volunteer groups about it, they'd say, "How much money do you need?" I came up with a budget as to how much one of these things would cost. Volunteers would pay for it. They would come in and help build it. It was like this cool thing. So, I built three neighborhood nurseries in four months. They happened quickly. The first one started in November, and the last one was with the American Society for Microbiology in May. They actually helped build up the nursery before they got here for their conference. So that was a Bayou Rebirth-specific source of income, projects, and things for volunteers to do during that time period.

It was great. Then we had a drought, and suddenly I didn't have any money comin' in. The number of volunteers available out there from the end of May every year just plummets. So, I had very little cash flow. I had people that on my staff that suddenly didn't have enough to do. When we had a lot of volunteer groups, the staff would be paid to supervise the volunteers. But when we didn't have volunteer groups, I was asking them to water, weed, mow, and take care of these things. I need them to do it, but that's really more work, and I don't have enough money to pay them to do it. Then it became a matter of needing them go out there and recruit volunteers to do this work, because once I'd been paying people to do it, it's hard for them to do it for free.

So, in the end, it's me. I was mowing for two hours yesterday afternoon. And I think I'm doin' the same this afternoon. That's what it comes down to. The drought happened, and we just couldn't keep up with it.

Sometime in June, maybe early July, Thom had to get Common Ground's insurance renewed. When he started meeting with insurance people, they expressed a lot of concern about the neighborhood nurseries and the ponds. I think he ended up going around with an insurance guy to all the sites where Common Ground volunteers might work to get an idea of the exposure and liability.

Was it the same kind of problems that you had the year prior when you were tryin' to get insurance?

Yes. Except that when I was tryin' to get insurance, I couldn't even get people to call me back, much less give me a quote.

What are they so concerned about in particular?

I think the biggest issue the year before was that when I told insurance company people that I brought groups of volunteers with a paid supervisor to sites in the marshes and wetlands of coastal Louisiana, they just imagined oil everywhere. I finally got some fairly reasonable quotes, but I couldn't raise the money to pay for it. Once I finally got insurance, it was the recession, and I only was able to get volunteer insurance. This past spring Thom was trying to get insurance that not only covered his volunteers but also his team leaders. He went to all the sites where the volunteers might be working and the sites were overgrown, and the stuff wasn't looking good because it was right in the middle of the drought. It was that tiny timing.

I started the neighborhood-type nurseries so that the plants would be in a better environment. Well, that means more maintenance, more weeds, more mowing. God forbid, you don't mow for a week. The community won't come out and mow, certainly won't come out and help. And another thing I've found is that the community engagement piece was hard to do. Really hard to do. I've given up on the local neighborhood surrounding that particular nursery. I can get transient volunteer folks or students. I can get other volunteers from around the community, but not in that immediate neighborhood. It depends on the neighborhood, but so far, it's not been successful.

Well, Thom goes through his process with insurance agents and gets this outrageous quote. He is basically told that our neighborhood nurseries are uninsurable because the ponds fill up with water and a child could drown. That becomes a bone of contention, and then it becomes, "Everything looks like hell. All the plants are dying. You said that you would take care of the nurseries, but you don't have the resources. You've just left everything out there to die." Thank God, this was right around the time that I was getting summer interns. Amanda, my summer interns, and other people who I recruited began to help watering and weeding. We would have these weekly meetings where we would figure out how to keep up with everything, 'cause we didn't have volunteers.

There's this time from the middle of May to the middle of June that nobody comes to New Orleans because people are graduating, and this was around the time that I was finally able to recruit enough help to get back on top of it and my summer volunteers started coming in. We set up this watering schedule, and I asked Thom if he would take a day to water one of the sites. He wouldn't do it. He was givin' me all sorts of hell about how everything looked. I was trying really hard, and Amanda was helping me to recruit more volunteers to get things lookin' better. Around the same timeframe—the spillway was opened.

The spillway?

The spillway is a flood-control project—a diversion. When the Mississippi River gets at flood stage, they open the spillway and let the river run into the lake. That May it was the biggest opening ever in the spillway's history since 1932. That meant that a whole bunch of plantings that we had planned with volunteer groups were gonna be at the spillway and we had to move them. We found a new planting site, but we had to find cypress. I started looking for cypress and found a donation of nine thousand cypress trees and we decided, Thom as well, to take these trees that were bare root seedlings in bags and pot them. So, we ended up in this situation where neither of the organizations had any money and it was a drought. We didn't have volunteer groups coming through, and these trees needed to be potted and watered on a very regular basis. That's why we had the watering schedule and people going out to the nursery in New Orleans East every day. Watering nine thousand trees takes a long time. We were putting out the word to every volunteer organization to send us volunteers because we didn't want the trees to die.

Halfway through the summer, Thom had a huge water bill. He sent me a letter saying that Bayou Rebirth had not abided by its contractual obligations and that we owed him all this money. I wrote him back saying, "We've had a lot of trouble. This has been a very difficult summer, BUT I have a whole bunch of interns and volunteers who are keeping those trees and the neighborhood nurseries alive. I'm not gonna let those plants die, and I'm not gonna pull out my interns just because you think that we've not abided by our obligations. So, let's sit down." He had helped buy some equipment over the last year, but it was mostly our equipment, and it was in a shed at the nursery in New Orleans East. I told him that I was gonna do an inventory of the equipment, find all the receipts from the last year, and talk about a sort of separation agreement. I told my board about everything, and we had a plan. Then he sent a letter a couple of weeks later saying we owed him like $9,000 for dead plants and money that he had put into sponsoring the development of our education program. I told my board and they said,

"Get everything of yours out of there." So, we basically just went through a divorce. It's not been fun or pretty, but a great thing that happened was that all these interns, volunteers, helpers, and the board rallied around me. They worked overtime to help figure things out during this crisis situation.

Where are you now in terms of next steps?

We've retreated. My interns and volunteers had to finish up their work mid-August, but I have interns that are starting next week. Also, my board and I have been working on grants, and a communication intern is working on my website and the social media.

I'm working on a budget. I was able to look at that budget critically and say, "You know what? I need to put double the amount that I'm estimating here because prices could go up. And, before we do any plantings, we need a new goddamn truck because my truck isn't gonna make it anymore. I can't use my personal vehicle anymore for this stuff." The other thing that I have in this budget is a director, and it's not gonna be me. It's gonna be somebody who's paid, has expectations, a job description, and enough support to be able to do their job effectively. I never had that support.

Generally, people who are good at starting things are not good at running things. I'm in a phase in my life now that I want to go and start something else or go and work on some other project. I've made all these connections and I want to do some other things.

What do you see yourself doing next?

I'll always be on the board of directors, no matter the life span of this organization. I'm the founder. But someone told me a long time ago when I was just planning things "I know it's hard for you to think about now, but you need to start planning for your departure." I wish I had thought about that a lot earlier.

4. Robert Goodman Jr.

KATRINA AND CRIMINAL JUSTICE REFORM

It's not about you. It's not about me. It's about the people. That's what I encourage everyone. You have to take yourself out of the equation, because there's gonna be times when folks disagree with you, and you lose focus on why you even came to the table when you take it personal. It's not about you. It's about the people that you represent and fight for and our kids and our kids' kids. That's my last encouragement to anyone that's wantin' to get in this fight.

—Robert Goodman Jr., Safe Streets/Strong Communities

When I met with Robert Goodman Jr. of Safe Streets/Strong Communities, I knew little about police brutality in New Orleans after Katrina outside of what I had seen in Spike Lee's 2010 documentary, *If God Is Willing and da Creek Don't Rise*. Indeed, while images of so-called looters flooded the national media, police misdeeds remained unspoken of in the manner typical of the days before the widespread usage of bodycams and smartphones with powerful video capabilities.

Long before the storm, New Orleans already possessed a disturbing history of police brutality toward its African American citizens. A case can be made, writes Leonard Moore, that the New Orleans Police Department (NOPD) was "one of the most brutal, corrupt, and incompetent units in the United States in the postwar period" with the local African American press reporting brutality on an almost weekly basis.[1] Conflicted by their support for "law and order," middle-class African Americans in New Orleans initiated only tepid protests, and it was not until the 1960s and 1970s, with the arrival of the civil rights movement and Black Panther Party, that

1. Moore, *Black Rage in New Orleans*, 5.

grassroots protests with wide community support arose. Nevertheless, in the decade before Katrina, the NOPD still "had the highest number of citizen complaints of police brutality in the country."[2]

Heartbreakingly, the storm only worsened this social pathology. Biased reporting, a declaration of martial law by Mayor Ray Nagin, and a "shoot to kill" order by Governor Kathleen Blanco combined to create an inflated fear of crime in which New Orleans's civilians were often deprived of their constitutional rights, and a rash of supicious officer-involved shootings (OISs) terrified the Black community.[3] Among the victims was Robert Goodman's younger brother Ronald, who suffered from schizophrenia and lived with his elderly mother in Algiers, on the west bank of the Mississippi River, where neighbors called him "a quiet man who didn't cause problems."[4] After the storm, Ronald was unable to get his medication, which led his mother to call for assistance to take him to a hospital. What was supposed to be a routine visit turned into an eight-hour standoff with the NOPD. At the end of this confrontation, Ronald lay dead from three gunshot wounds to the head. Ultimately the New Orleans Office of the Independent Police Monitor characterized his death as a likely case of excessive force against a person suffering from mental illness who may not have even understood the circumstances surrounding him.[5]

2. Moore, *Black Rage in New Orleans,* 2–4; Rogers, *Righteous Lives,* loc 1622, 1899.

3. New Orleans Office of the Independent Police Monitor, "Hurricane Katrina."

4. Powell, "Algiers Man Dies in Standoff"; New Orleans Office of the Independent Police Monitor, "Hurricane Katrina."

5. The independent monitor wrote, "In May 2006, when Ronald Goodman's elderly mother called the Orleans Parish Coroner's Office to temporarily take custody of her son and get him back on his medication for schizophrenia (because of a Katrina-related disorder, Goodman had been deprived of his medication since the hurricane), she never imagined her call would result in Ronald's death at the hands of NOPD officers. Officers claim that Goodman fired a shotgun at them after an hours-long standoff. The autopsy revealed that Goodman was shot three times in the head. The coroner's report also revealed that Ronald's hands tested negative for gunshot residue. The autopsy file given to the family by the coroner's office contained photos of Goodman's dead body with hands secured in handcuffs. While the NOPD crime scene pictures show Ronald handcuffed and dead on the floor, the majority of blood and body tissue was found on the bed, which led the family to conclude that Ronald died in his bed and not on the floor." New Orleans Office of the Independent Police Monitor, "Hurricane Katrina."

When Robert Goodman, an ex-convict who taught himself to read while incarcerated and who had led protests against inhumane conditions in Louisiana's infamous Angola Prison, learned of his brother's shooting, he returned home and soon became a leader in Safe Streets/Strong Communities.[6] Jordan Flaherty writes, "Safe Streets has had a fundamental influence on the city's framing of the debate around criminal justice. Because of their work, journalists and politicians began—one by one—to confront systemic issues and examine the roots of the problems."[7] Early on, Safe Streets unearthed major concerns regarding the local prison system, including a finding that individuals jailed before Katrina went an average of 385 days without trial.[8] The organization joined other groups in protests that resulted in an overhaul of the city's indigent defense board, the appointment of an independent police monitor, and a wide-ranging consent decree to reform policing in New Orleans.[9]

Although Safe Streets' focus differed greatly from that of most of the organizations profiled in this study, Goodman's interview revealed themes consistent with his counterparts. Like many others, he had a long history of activism; it dated back to his youth with the 1970s New Orleans Black Panther Party. Goodman's motivation also falls within a small subset of individuals who saw their work as driven by God. Lastly, he described the difficulties of fundraising and sustainability for new nonprofits and grassroots organizations like Safe Streets. Goodman's recollection has an air of regret to it similar to that of Colleen Morgan, but he diverges in a critical way. Although many of our participants focused on the granting process, Goodman argued that the concept of the 501c3 tax-exempt status was inherently inappropriate for grassroots organizing because it leads organizations to depend on foundations, rather than to cultivate the independent, grassroots spirit that brought them into being in the first place.[10]

6. Flaherty, "Corporate Reconstruction and Grassroots Resistance," 111.

7. Flaherty et al., *Floodlines*, 177.

8. Flaherty, "Corporate Reconstruction and Grassroots Resistance," 112.

9. Flaherty, "Corporate Reconstruction and Grassroots Resistance,"113; Flaherty, et al., *Floodlines*, 49–51, 177; Greater New Orleans Roundtable, *10 Years after Katrina*, film.

10. Goodman was joined in this position by Robert "Kool Black" Horton. Horton was a grassroots community organizer who founded Black Men United for Change, Justice, and Equality in 1992. This organization focused on improving the circumstances of young African American men in New Orleans's St. Thomas housing project and succeeded in its mis-

⚜ ⚜ ⚜

AUGUST 20, 2013

Where were you in your life when the hurricane came?

At that moment I was livin' in Dallas, drivin' 18-wheelers back and forth from Fort Worth to Orlando, Florida. When the storm hit, we only knew it was headed our way, and I couldn't take I-10 like I normally do. On my way back to Fort Worth, I saw a lot of cars parked on the side and in parkin' areas. I couldn't understand what was goin' on until I went to refuel. They didn't have no fuels, and I understood why all the cars was parked on the side of the road. They all ran out of fuel. I wasn't really on empty and by the time I got to Fort Worth, picked up a trailer and headed back, that's when the storm burst. I couldn't get through to my family that was livin' here. My concern was about them and how they made out. I have an elderly mother. Did they get out? I got back to Fort Worth and turned in the truck, but by that time my family was in Houston with my niece.

What neighborhood did they live in?

The West Bank in Algiers Point. There wasn't no flooding there. Even though the mayor was encouragin' everyone to leave the city because the water wasn't good, there was no flood damage there—just a lot of wind damage. We heard two stories. They really wanted Black folks out of the city. They had a plan for that, but we didn't know it at the time. We realize now, that was just to get folks out because the goal was to not let folks come back, right. We understood that was their purpose.[11]

---

sion; the number of murders in the project dropped from thirty-one per year to zero within a three-year period. Of the 501c3, Horton told our interviewers: "We are not wholeheartedly in agreement with applying for 501c3. The work that folks really wanna do around this country in their heart of hearts they can't do because their work is being dictated by the 501c3 idea or concept. If I wanted to start a Black nationalist organization full of brothers who wanted to be self-empowered and believe in the idea of the red, black, and green, that kinda language wouldn't be digested well." Horton, interview.

11. Goodman's perception that the city leaders were in league with business interests and purposely used the evacuation of African Americans as a pretext for gentrification is consistent with many Black activists involved in the community after Katrina. See, for example, Salam, "Below the Water Line," xvi; Berra et al., "To Render Ourselves Visible," 39.

You felt that already, or did that come about
as people tried to return?

Well, we found out through the years with the housing projects that they tore down. A lot of these projects were still strong. They needed some fixin', but even though the water came up in some of 'em, they was still livable. But they wouldn't even let folks come back to get their personal belongings. They fenced everything off, and that let us know that they didn't want folks to come back. In fact, FEMA was payin' folks to stay away. The only folks that really received benefits was homeowners. The people that was in rentals didn't get anything. It seemed like the gentrification was takin' over communities. People was pushed out, or they took over their homes. They want a lot of this property, especially down in the Ninth Ward. So, a lot of folks are still misplaced—didn't come back home to this day.

When you were driving, did you learn about the
storm over the radio, or did you watch TV coverage?

By the time I got to Houston I saw a lot of TV coverage. Plus, I met a lot of folks who was actually in the water. I ran into a guy who was able to get his kids up on the roof, and when he went to grab for his wife, her last words were, "Don't worry about me. Save my children." She went back under. A lot of sad stories was talked about by people in Houston that was actually in the flood.

What was going on with you when you heard that?
Did you feel like you were getting the right story?
What was your gut reaction when you saw and
heard the media coverage?

Well, I don't believe everything the media say. I've always been trained that they're usually tellin' us only what they want us to know. I just didn't believe that the levees burst. I believe they blew up the levees. I think it was a man-made disaster. They always use Hurricane Katrina, but a lot of folks said, "The hurricane came and gone. I was outside washin' my car, and the next thing I knew, I went inside, and the water was just risin' and risin'." Plus folks in the Ninth Ward heard the explosion. A lot of that got swept under the carpet. I think that when Ray Nagin was encouragin' people to leave the city, he knew, politically, that somethin' was gonna happen.[12] We go through this a lot, and most of the time, a lot of folks don't leave. But I can tell from the way he was sayin' it. He was really begging folks to leave before the storm got here. I think they had plans for New Orleans, and Katrina just gave them the opportunity to implement those plans. Since that time, everything has been gentrified.

What was your perception of Nagin?

When Hurricane Gustav came, we did an evacuation, and a lot of people spent money to get out of town. Unlike Katrina, they wasn't given anything. People used their rent money and bill money to leave, and they was stuck out. We went to the mayor's office to tell him, and he sent some representatives sayin', "The mayor's on the phone talkin' to other mayors from different cities who had water and floods in different parts of Louisiana." We just listened to them for a minute when somebody called the director at that time, Norris Henderson. He said, "We're at City Hall but the mayor couldn't see us 'cause he's on the phone." And they said, "Oh no, he ain't. We at this restaurant right now lookin' at him." That let us know that all his talk about the Chocolate City was just really about him, and we saw that as time went on.[13] As you see, he's goin' to court and stuff right now.[14] The Black politicians in the city have never really looked out for the best interests for Black people here, though they had the power to do that.

12. Goodman is not alone in this belief. Spike Lee and Douglas Brinkley documented the suspicion held by many African American New Orleanians that the Industrial Canal breach was deliberately caused, with many claiming to have heard an explosion and others arguing that a barge was deliberately run into the levee wall. There was precedent for the intentional destruction of a levee. In the Great Mississippi Flood of 1927, the city government dynamited the Caernarvon levee in a largely African American neighborhood to minimize flooding in the French Quarter. During Katrina, St. Bernard Parish president Junior Rodriguez told Lieutenant Governor Mitch Landrieu that he had a plan to blow a hole in the levees if the death toll caused by flooding kept rising in his parish. Lee, *When the Levees Broke,* film; Brinkley, *The Great Deluge,* loc 338, 961, 974, 6466, 11387; Miles and Austin, "The Color(s) of Crisis," loc 874–934.

13. In October 2005 Mayor Ray Nagin referred to New Orleans as a "Chocolate City" as part of a pledge to bring back as much of the African American population as possible. Trujillo-Pagan, "From the Gateway to the Americas' to the 'Chocolate City,'" loc 2114.

14. On May 27, 2014, U.S. District Judge Helen G. Berrigan ordered Mayor Nagin to pay $84,264 in restitution and sentenced him to ten years in jail for "conspiracy, bribery, honest

Who is Norris?

Norris Henderson, who was the ex-director of Safe Streets/Strong Communities, is the director of Voice of the Ex-Offenders [VOTE]. We're closer now than when we was workin' here together. I just left him a few minutes ago.

Okay. So, what happened for you and your family next?

We came back 'cause I had a mentally ill brother who never left New Orleans. My older sister stayed with him through the storm. It wasn't livable, and we went back to try to get him, but he didn't want to leave. My family had came back, but it was five or six months after Katrina when he was shot.

Yeah. It would have been a few months after if your family was back.

Right. The mental facilities had broken down. He was a schizophrenic, and there was nowhere for a lot of mental patients to get treatment or get their medicine. That was the circumstances for my little brother. Even though he didn't mean nobody harm and he wasn't violent, Mama felt like she needed to get him in a hospital. Usually the police come 'cause sometimes if you're off your medicine for a while, people don't want to go. But we've been goin' through this for many years, and we usually just say, "Carl, why don't we just go to the hospital and get some medicine?" He usually cooperates. That particular day it didn't go that way.

The police showed up and they couldn't see him 'cause it was a shotgun house—one of those historical houses at Algiers Point. The police officer heard gunfire from the back of the house. He had my family evacuate from the porch to around the corner. I had Yvette Thierry, who's the executive director now [of Safe Streets] and is my ex-wife, go see about my family, and she was there the whole time keepin' me informed of what's goin' on. They barricaded everything. This went on from six that evening to around twelve or one o'clock. That's when we heard all the gunfire, around one

---

services wire fraud, money laundering and tax violations" that occurred before and after Hurricane Katrina. U.S. Attorney's Office, "Former New Orleans Mayor C. Ray Nagin Sentenced"; Murphy and Perlstein, "Ex-New Orleans Mayor Ray Nagin Sentenced to 10 Years."

o'clock that mornin'. They had a police officer stationed by my family the whole time, and maybe an hour or so later we heard someone say over his radio, "He up here weepin' for his mama now."

There was a lot of confusion, and we couldn't put the puzzle together. An hour later they come and tell us, "We gonna shoot tear gas in the house to see if we can flush him out." That didn't make sense. They were already in the house, but we're still not thinkin' that at the time. When they shot it through the windows, it gave off a lot a noise, "Boom!" I think that's when they were finishing him off, 'cause he was still alive. He was shot with an M16, and he managed to move from the table to the front door. That's where a lot of bullets was comin' through. I went back to the house and documented everything. You could see a puddle of blood where he was probably standin' before he made it back to my mother's bedroom. I could see the blood print on the phone where he was tryin' to call, but they had cut the lines. It took over two years to get the police report, and they were sayin' they found him on the floor, but I found blood soaked through the bed and there ain't no blood on the floor. It was already dried on his face and stuff, from layin' in bed all night.

But goin' back to that night, an hour later they said, "Send in the dogs." They did and then they told my family, "We got him. He's still alive." But we found a few minutes later that he didn't make it. So that's what happened. But I truly believe he was shot with that M16 and made it through the house. Then they put him in the bed and handcuffed him. We know they handcuffed him because they forgot to take it off when they took him to the car. That was in the report and the autopsy: they brought him there in handcuffs. Why would you handcuff a dead man? He was already handcuffed in that bed, and they finished him off, 'cause I found flesh and everything else in that bed.

Did they ever produce a firearm?

Yeah. My brother had owned a .22 rifle, but I think they shot it themselves. They found no residue or gunpowder on his hands. Bein' in a standoff for so many hours, I believe he was just sittin' in a chair. By the time all that went down, he probably was frightened and scared. He is schizophrenic. He didn't see his family, and he might have been in a bad state of mind when they showed up.

There was another mental patient killed at that time. Two years later, there was folks that they killed that was patients. It became a pattern. When they come in, they don't ask 'em questions. They didn't have a squad to actually deal with mental folks. They just went in, no questions, shoot to kill.[15]

What happened next for you?

After seein' him on the slab, with his face blew out to the back of his brains, I knew I had to be his voice, as well as bein' there for my family. We was able to get in touch with Darren Hill. He's a civil lawyer for the NAACP in New York, but he's back and forth down here. He recommended us to Ms. Althea, and she invited us to the Safe Streets meetin'. I think that was their very first community meetin'.[16] I was pretty much the spokesman for my family, tellin' the story of what happened. A lot of them to this day are too emotional to even talk about it. We joined the organization, and I instantly became a leader.

How did you become a leader?

I couldn't leave. I was stayin' to be supportive for my mother who was takin' it real hard. She was blamin' herself for his death 'cause he wasn't botherin' nobody, and she was tryin' to get him some help. When I went to the first meetin', we see Mary Howell, the lady lawyer. Then I look over and I see Norris Henderson. Him and I go back to reform school, as well as prison. So, I know I was in the right place. We connected. I tell a lot of folks when they see how close we are today that we never spoke through reform school and prison. We knew each other from seein' the kind of work we was doin'. We never really encountered each other 'cause Angola was so

15. At a public hearing on police misconduct held by the grassroots coalition Community United for Change, Goodman argued that his brother's death was part of a pattern of police brutality made apparent in the shooting of Ronald Madison. He argued that, unlike Madison's case, the case of his brother was easier to cover up. Hing, "New Orleans Activists Want Feds to Get Real."

16. Althea Francois was among the founders of Safe Streets/Strong Communities and a former Black Panther. Louisiana Justice Institute, "Rest in Peace Althea Francois"; Angola 3 News, "Join Us in Helping to Send Sister Althea on Her Journey Home"; Ailsworth, "Remembering Althea Francois."

big.[17] Anyway I became a leader, and we applied for a New Voice fellowship for myself to come on that staff, and I started with 'em in '06. By '07, I was a staff member.

That's a big transition, right?

Yeah, from a truck driver to doin' this. But this kind of work didn't start here. This is somethin' I've been doin'. It started in prison, and it's just somethin' I've been knowin' that God was gearin' me to do. I never thought I would be comin' back to stay in New Orleans 'cause I had made a place in Dallas. I used to see so many guys comin' back [to prison], and that almost happened to me when I first come home 'cause I was still dealin' with my drug problems.[18]

So, I left town, and things got better for me. I developed the trade of drivin' 18-wheelers. But even drivin' trucks, I always knew that that God was callin' me to do this work. Like when I was joinin' this church in Dallas. They start off with me and an assistant pastor, and it developed into three or four hundred men. I had the abilities to draw folks—the same thing I was doin' in prison.

What sort of issues were you seein' in prison?

Abuse of power, livin' conditions, and things like that. At my first demonstration, I didn't even know my ABCs, but I knew that somethin' was wrong, and I needed to do somethin' about it. I brought some brothers together, and we created a demonstration. At that time, I had moved from Angola to a smaller prison for first offenders. Angola was so ferocious and dangerous for any young man. Most young men won't risk going back, but we decided that we wasn't gonna go to work. That's where it started. That demonstration would lead to other things. I became very vocal and outspoken. My reputation for that started in prison.

So, psychologically, I was already prepared to do this work. When I

17. Well known for its horrific conditions, Angola is one of Louisiana's most notorious prisons. Flaherty et al., *Floodlines,* 141 and 241; Voice of the Experienced, "Norris Henderson."

18. After first going to jail at the age of thirteen, Goodman got hooked on heroin at age fourteen. He remained in jail and addicted to heroin until the age of thirty-two. It took another ten years and his move to Dallas to get himself clean. Flaherty et al., *Floodlines,* 75.

learned how to read and write, I spent many years tryin' to understand our history, culture, and why things happened the way it is and how we so readily fall victim to this system.

So, you were here when the organization was beginning. How did it start, and what was its initial growth and development?

Safe Streets was created from the JJPL, the Juvenile Justice Project, and another organization called FFLIC, Family and Friends of Louisiana Incarcerated Children. Safe Streets developed out of those two organizations. It was juveniles 'cause JJPL and FFLIC deal with young folks, but then a lot of other folks began to come 'cause a lot of their loved ones, adults, was bein' misplaced. Then folks like myself begin to come when the police violence was takin' place and folks was bein' killed.

They saw the need for Safe Streets because of all these reasons. People from the community didn't have anywhere else to go to have a voice. Seven of us came on board, all staff, but that still wasn't enough for the work that was goin' on and the things that had to get exposed, especially the police killings. There was twenty-one officers indicted. That never happened before in the history of this country. We just kept pushin' it and pushin' it. It took time, years. Even when it got in courts, we kept pushin' at it and kept encouragin' the families. One of the key elements for the families was just bein' able to connect to deal with that psychologically.

Someone can say, "You can tell me, man. I sympathize with what happened to your brother." But when you lost a loved one yourself, then I know you can identify with my pain. Those same families still talk and meet to this day, and I'm one of the glues that keeps them connected. So, I know bringin' those families together, if nothin' else, helped the healin' process. About a year ago, I took those same families to Savannah, Georgia, where we met a mother who lost a loved one to police misconduct, and for the first time, she was able to connect with families who'd been through or can identify with what she was going through 'cause they was there to tell their stories. So that's how we got connected with Safe Streets, and we created the independent [police] monitor.

*Was the primary emphasis going after abuses of
power during and after the storm?*

It was to reform the criminal justice system, NOPD, and Orleans Parish
Prison, which is the jailhouse. We worked with families who was bein'
impacted through the criminal justice system, the police, or the jailhouse.
As you can see in the city, now, there's two consent decrees that's goin' on.
That's not just Safe Streets alone. There's other organizations and activists
that's involved with the Orleans Parish Prison Reform Coalition, OPPRC.
Safe Streets was dealin' with this by itself at one time, but when we lost
staff members, we had to build a coalition. So, we meet like every other
Monday to push that agenda. The police part is pretty much taken care
of now.[19]

*In 2009, one of your former associates who was still
in prison brought up your name in relation to a
crime committed thirty-six years ago to try to cut a
deal for himself. That brought you back to prison.
What did it feel like for you to go back after all this
work in the community?*

It was pretty devastating. I had been out for over ten years at that time.
On the day of my release, you know, me and the guard got into it, and they
brought in a lot of goon squad. I just tell 'em, "You need to go on the computer just to see who you're dealin' with." And for some reason, they come

19. The formal legal process that led up to the consent decree began when Mayor Mitch
Landrieu invited the Department of Justice to investigate allegations of misconduct on the
part of the New Orleans Police Department in May 2010. On March 16, 2011, the Department of Justice released findings accusing the NOPD of "unconstitutional conduct" and
expressing concern about "NOPD procedures and policies." According to the City of New
Orleans NOPD Consent Decree website, "On July 24, 2012, the City, the NOPD and the DOJ
entered into a Consent Decree, which was the nation's most expansive Consent Decree. The
Consent Decree contains a broad array of separate tasks and goals detailed in more than 490
paragraphs and 110 pages; it reflects a shared commitment to effective, constitutional, and
professional law enforcement. The Court approved the Consent Decree on January 11, 2013."
Contrary to Goodman's testimony, the website does not mention a second consent decree.
Perhaps Goodman is referring to the appointment of the Consent Decree Monitor by order
of the U.S. District Court for the Eastern District of Louisiana on August 9, 2013. City of New
Orleans, "NOPD Consent Decree."

up with a different attitude when they find out who I am. I experienced that several times. One of the guards said he had been watchin' me on the monitor for six months while I was here, and he noticed how everybody, whites and Blacks, get along. He knew I played a big part in that. Every day I made sure that everybody—white, Black, whatever—spent an hour or two reading and talkin' about how we can make a difference while we're here and once released out of these jails.

So I was still organizin'. It didn't matter whether I was in or out. At that point I realized that God had a purpose for me whether it was inside or out. This is somethin' that I was gonna do. People wrote letters for me across the country, even Angela Davis. I had met her in Oakland at Critical Resistance.[20] That's the organization she helped develop that's across this country. It had a ten-year anniversary, and I met her 'cause one of the guys from New Orleans was the executive director and he introduced me. But anyway, folks from around the country wrote me letters, and even at the hearing young folks stood up for me as their mentor and all the folks stood up for me as a pillar of the community.

How did it feel to see all that?

It felt real good. I received a lot of letters. You really don't get paid for this work. For years I spent seven days a week on the ground, pushin' and pushin'. That was very rewardin' to know how folks felt about me and to see the courtroom packed with folks.

Did you expect that?

They had three or four setbacks, and I had been hearin' that the reason it took the judge so long was all those letters. A lot of people wrote beautiful letters about me. Even professors from some colleges wrote letters about me. I spoke to their students. I think that helped the judge make the decision. I think he was mostly concerned about what I had to say compared to what everybody else was sayin' about me. I told him, "I'm gonna take a page from Michael Jackson. I'm gonna start with the man in the mirror." I knew years ago when I was incarcerated that I wanted to come home and

20. Critical Resistance is a grassroots organization dedicated to ending the prison-industrial complex.

make a difference in my community, to work with other young men to help them understand the decisions that they make and the consequences that comes behind those decisions. I knew this was somethin' I wanted to do. I wanted to change my life and be an asset. I told him, "Whatever choice you make today, judge, whether you choose to release me or not, I'll continue to do the same work." And he released me. October the 23rd, 2009. And I came right back to work.[21]

What was the state of the organization at that time?

At that time, it was just one or two staff here, and they was creatin' another director. We had a lot of internal discrepancies. That happens in all organizations, and it took the focus away, to some degree, from the fight on the ground. The work pretty much stayed the same. Safe Streets is a community-based organization that's built off the community, like me comin' from the community, as staff and now director, and Yvette. She really didn't know much about this work at all, but she did a lot of good organizin' and she's now executive director. There's just so much that's goin' on, and we don't have the capacity to deal with a lot. So, what I do now is help train leaders to put out fires themselves without support, rather than me try to put it out for you. Our goal is helping other folks to advocate for themselves along with the coalitions and organizations that's been established.

Another good thing that happened in 2007 was our first U.S. Social Forum.[22] That brought a lot of grassroots organizations from across the country together in Atlanta. Safe Streets brought fifty-somethin' folks there along with other people that left New Orleans.[23] It was my suggestion to Dr. Kim, with the People's Institute for Undoing Racism, and Monique Hardin, who works with the environmental rights situations, that we shouldn't stop here, and that when we get back, we should continue working with one

21. Jordan Flaherty confirms Goodman's story in his book *Floodlines*. Flaherty et al., *Floodlines*, 176.

22. The U.S. Social Forum (USSF) of 2007 in Atlanta was the first such event. The USSF gathers activists from across the United States to discuss contemporary issues and ways to synergize their work. The forum seeks to connect local movements to form a larger national movement. Making Contact, "The Road to Detroit."

23. For more information on Safe Streets/Strong Communities' participation in the 2007 USSF in Atlanta, see Guillod, "The First US Social Forum"; USSF Book Committee, "The United States Social Forum"; Greater New Orleans Roundtable, *10 Years after Katrina*, film.

another.[24] That's when the Greater New Orleans Organized Roundtable was created.

When we did a fundraiser to create money to go to the next U.S. Social in Detroit in 2010, we raised about $10,000. We used the roundtable as a model. Many groups around the country wanted to find out how we was able to bring an organization together. I always emphasize that before we're able to do things collectively on a national level, we have to learn how to work with each other on a local level. Our accomplishments in this city have been through a collective process. When we show up at City Hall, we have orange t-shirts. Other folks wear orange to show solidarity. So, it may look like we got 400 or 500 members, and we may just have 50. Me and Norris laugh a lot of times about this. If this city really knew how many folks that was really pushin' this, they would be really angry for all the things that's happenin' now. (*Laughter.*)

Do you feel as though the city is worried about what you could do?

The city is not scared of us, but they know we have an incredible group to be reckoned with. They know everything they're tryin' to change in this city is things that we pushed them to do right—not because they saw it themselves. The mayor's still fightin' about it. He don't want to pay for the jailhouse consent decree. But at the end of the day, he gonna have to do it.

You talked about the decline in staff. What caused that?

First of all, I think they would like to see this organization fade away. Any effective group in this country, goin' back to the Muslims, the Black Panthers, was infiltrated, and I think even Safe Streets has been infiltrated 'cause of the confusion and stuff that went on.

Allegedly, Common Ground was infiltrated.

Well, they was. I know Malik. I grew up around him, his younger brother, and his older brothers. We was real close. They said he allowed in some-

24. Here Goodman refers to Kimberly Richards of Undoing Racism: The People's Institute for Survival and Beyond and Monique Hardin of the Deep South Center for Environmental Justice. People's Institute for Survival and Beyond, "Dr. Kimberly Richards"; Deep South Center for Environmental Justice, "Monique Harden ESQ."

body who was working with the agency, but you never know that. I tell folks that all the time, "Shit. It could be me." You know what I mean. (*Laughter.*) I learned from the Black Panthers how folks that we thought that was about the cause, was the infiltrators. That's how it's worked.

And, granted, the funders loved Norris Henderson. When he left, a lot of credibility left the organization. A lot of funders began to pull out, and it's been difficult. We had a dream team. I think we all now realize how valuable each person was.

I been tryin' to say this for years when we was gettin' all those resources, but nobody thought about bringin' all these minds together in one big buildin' to have at our disposal everyday. We meet at the Roundtable once a month, but if we had this at our disposal every day, it'd give us a better voice and support mechanism to help one another who may be fallin' short on resources. Plus, you leave a legacy behind. When we get too old and can't do this, we have somethin' for the young folks. They haven't actually saw that picture yet, but they're beginnin' to. A lot of organizations are feelin' that because funders is pullin' out.

And another thing, the 501c3 to me was never created to help organizations on the ground to be successful if you just think about who the funders are. They spend billions of dollars at conferences, but it would take one hundred-thousandth of that to buy a buildin' for an organization to do this work, to strengthen them or to give them money to create business to sustain themselves. You got your restricted grants or your unrestricted grants, but nevertheless, this money is only there for two years or three years. Then you're on your own.[25]

Are you saying that organizations, especially when money is flowing, need to put energy into making themselves stable and providing longevity?

Right. 'Cause funders couldn't stop that if we had decided all to work together. Even the main organization here spent a lot of money for this buildin' that they don't own. After Katrina, when a lot of places were renovated, enough organizations could have put their money together and bought our

25. Goodman shared this view with fellow interviewee Robert "Kool Black" Horton—a core trainer with the People's Institute for Survival and Beyond and the cofounder of Black Men United for Change. Flaherty et al., *Floodlines*, 22, 176; Horton, interview.

buildin', rented out space. Instead of us goin' out payin' for food we could create a cafeteria. A lot of groups that come to the city spend a lot of money on big hotels in the French Quarter that don't serve the purpose of this community. That money never trickles back here. If we had a big enough buildin' where people could gather, we could tell organizations, "If you want to invest your money in the community, then this is where you need to invest it."

What do you think is next for your organization?

Well, I got an organizing class that's about to take place around the first week in September. A lot of local cab drivers are bein' pushed out. One of 'em [a taxi company] is Black owned. They tryin' to use the same principles against them as they use in New York or Chicago where they have two airports. We only have one. A lot of them came along and built solidarity with us 'cause they want to work with us to get support. So, they gonna be part of this organizer training. We got a lot of new folks that done came on board and other organizations that has an interest.

It sounds like you're in this for the long haul.

I hear older folks say, "It's time to pass the torch," but that don't mean you fade out of the picture. The work still goes on. I think that's what happened after civil rights was passed. We dropped the ball like everything was over, but we're fightin' for the same things today.

Is there anything else that you would like people out there to know about?

No. Just get involved. My encouragement is to get involved with any local organization that's on the ground tryin' to make a difference in your community, whether it's about education, housin', the criminal justice system, prison—whatever your interests are.

The other part is please, no matter what your interest is, work collectively. We at war, and a lot of us just don't know it. As we can see across this country, our middle class is beginnin' to feel the bulk of this pressure on the economy too. It's not about you. I use myself as an example. My little brother had a case that I put on the side to help other families because we knew that these was the high-profile cases to get some light on it and to get some things done. Part of me feels guilty about it 'cause my brother's case has never been looked at, but it makes me feel good to know that some victory came to those families. It's not about you. It's not about me. It's about the people. That's what I encourage everyone. You have to take yourself out of the equation. It's about the people that you represent and fight for and our kids and our kids' kids. That's my last encouragement to anyone that's wantin' to get in this fight.

5. Fred Franke

RENEWING FAITH THROUGH
REBUILDING COMMUNITY

> I was in major mobilization mode on what God was puttin' in my heart to do. I kept hearin', "I've got to contact all these people. I've got these churches comin' down. We've got to get back in there and replant, get our church up and runnin' and bring these people down so we can go help the communities that need help. We need to bring our people back." That's recyclin' in my mind over and over. I just put my phone down and said, "God, will you talk to me? If this is what you want me to do, I got some serious problems here." I tell people often that I argued with God like Moses [did]. I said, "God, I own two businesses or at least I had two businesses. Now, I don't even know how I'm gonna bring in the next dime to support my kids and my family. I don't know where I'm gonna live. I don't know how I'm gonna do all this." And He laid a blanket of peace over me as if He told me, "You take care of what I'm askin' you to do, and I will take care of you and your family."
>
> —Fred Franke, Operation Nehemiah

Nehemiah was a high-ranking Jewish servant to the Persian emperor Artaxerxes in 445 BCE. He learned that, although Jews had returned from exile to Jerusalem nearly a hundred years earlier, the city's walls were crumbling, and the people were suffering from constant attacks. Neighboring enemies launched attacks as Nehemiah organized the rebuilding of the city walls, but he led their defense and completed the work in only fifty-two days—bringing about a renewal of spirit. Many years later, Nehemiah found that the city had slipped in its faith, so he once again helped lead them back to their beliefs—reminding readers that one's spiritual journey requires constant renewal.

In founding Operation Nehemiah, Fred Franke sought to bring about a similar renewal of faith. A deeply felt Christian ethos framed and pervaded his narrative far more than those of his counterparts. Franke's story begins with his family's harrowing escape from the city with the storm at their heels. Like a small number of other interviewees, Franke's religious belief was the primary driver to his desire to provide aid. Unlike his peers, however, Franke's civic engagement before the storm was limited, and he did not simply shift an ongoing pattern of political, civic, or community activism into efforts to rebuild the city. Instead, during his evacuation, Franke experienced a sudden, intense, and inexorable calling from God to return to New Orleans and dedicate his life to its recovery.

In many ways, Franke's story mirrors those of the founders of many other small, grassroots nonprofits that came into being at this time, but his basic operating philosophy differed. Long before the storm, Franke worried about survey data showing that the majority of Americans believed in God, yet increasing numbers wanted no part of organized religion. Drawing from his own experiences, he lamented that the church had a tendency to criticize, rather than show the power of religion to do good in the world. From this concern, he founded Operation Nehemiah to bring Christians from across the country to New Orleans to rebuild its church communities, which he believed could serve as anchors for renewal across the city and show God's love in action. But that was not the end of his mission. He then charged his volunteers to go back to their homes and find ways to improve their own communities. In so doing, he hoped to demonstrate the value of the church and revitalize the faith in a manner not unlike his organization's namesake—a lofty yet inspiring vision indeed.

In addition to exemplifying those long-term activists whose work in New Orleans was grounded in Christianity, Franke also epitomizes the strong do-it-yourself (DIY) tendency among the recovery community. The perception of federal and local government failures in the rescue effort and the failures of all levels of government in the recovery led many to espouse local control. This circumstance led to a curious array of out-of-town, mostly white anarchists, religious groups, and local, largely African American organizers joining together to champion local control of the rebuilding effort. As will be discussed in the last two chapters, the circumstances of New Orleans's recovery call into question the efficacy of myriad small and large organizations executing a response of this scale. Nevertheless, in Franke's thoughtful and authentic testimony, the rhetorical power of the argument for local control of the recovery is on full display.

⚜ ⚜ ⚜

JULY 8, 2010

What was going on in your life before the storm?

Before the storm, I owned two businesses and was very happy doin' the work that I was doin'. Was and still am married to a wonderful lady and got three young adult children. At that time, they weren't all young adults. Our youngest one was still livin' with us. She was in tenth grade. The storm hit. We were thrust out of the area, and we head out of town like we do almost in any hurricane. I remember somebody with a small Christian periodical sent a blanket email to a lot of folks that were in "hurricane land" and asked, "What's goin' on out there?" I told him, "You grab two to four days' worth of clothes, grab your important papers, get the kids, get the wedding album, and head off to friends or hotels in another state. We usually return in three to four days after the storm, unboard the house, pick up the debris layin' around, and get on with our lives. This time I don't know where I'm gonna live. I don't know what I'm gonna do to take care of my family." I didn't even know what state I might be able to reside in. It was very different from previous hurricanes. We had received many strong blows with hurricanes but nothing that ever took the levees out like this one.

I got the impression that a lot of folks
didn't take it as seriously because of
past experiences with hurricanes.[1]

I think it's something else. If you do an internet search for satellite photos of south Louisiana from 1970 'til today, you see a lot of our land is wetlands. You can see that there is land there, even though it's very wet, like marshes. If you look at current satellite photos, especially within the last fifteen years, the loss of those wetlands has been drastic. In the last decade people know for sure that when a hurricane is headed toward us, we have less protection. The wetlands slow and reduce the strength of the storm. When it gets to ya, it still will be a powerful storm, but for every mile of wetlands that we have, there is a reduction in the tidal surge from a half-foot to

1. As late as 1998 only one in three New Orleanians evacuated for Hurricane Georges. Van Heerden and Bryan, *The Storm,* 49.

a foot. Forty years ago, the Gulf used to be about one hundred miles away from New Orleans. Now from the southern areas of the city we are as close as thirty-five miles. That is major frightening.[2] So, a lot of folks head out of town. There are plenty of those who are somewhat cavalier in attitude and don't want to leave. They feel that they're indestructible, nothin's ever happened to 'em before, and they're gonna make it. But a lot of folks that don't leave are the ones that have no means to leave. The majority of folks that stayed probably fell into that second category.[3]

Let me take you back for a minute.
What kind of businesses were you involved in
before the storm?

One was parkin' lot maintenance, and the other was a playground equipment company. I owned the first one since 1978, the second one since '87, and was quite happy doin' what I was doin'. My life was goin' on a track. Then the storm hit, and I did not imagine that I'd be doin' what I'm doin' now. I do see several things that have occurred all through my history that helped prepare me for such a time as this.

Tell me about some of those things.

I can remember that my dad was always instillin' in us and in me, in particular, to excel and work hard at accomplishin' whatever you set out to do. Whether it was school or cuttin' the lawn, it was to be done with excellence. When I started working, I always wanted to do the absolute best for my employer, and usually in a short period of time I was one of the best employees. That led me from a young adult to now. I was always either an independent contractor or a salesperson of some sort, and I have owned my own businesses for about thirty-some odd years. Now, it's a little different because I am the head of the nonprofit.

2. The U.S. Geological Survey writes, "About half of the United States' wetlands have been lost over the past 200 years. The losses are greatest in Louisiana, where about one-quarter of the state's wetlands—an area the size of Delaware—have been lost since the 1930s." U.S. Geological Survey, "Louisiana's Changing Coastal Wetlands"; Van Heerden and Bryan, *The Storm*, 4.

3. Like Franke, testimony in *Voices Rising II* points to a widespread knowledge of the dangers that hurricanes could cause and an inability to evacuate. Antoine, *Voices Rising II*, loc 2477.

*Did you always conceive of yourself
as a person working for yourself?*

I learned a whole lot from others, but you learn most when you are in the proving ground of doing it yourself. From a work standpoint I believe that helped prepare me for some things I'm doin' now. I think one of the other most important things that helped me was that I come from a faith-based background. I've been a Christian since the seventies. I walk and live accordin' to that.

So, you weren't raised in the church?

I was brought to church. I don't really believe that I was raised in the church.

What do you see as being the difference between the two?

We were taken there, but there wasn't a lot of it, if you know what I mean. Today, there are so many great activities where youth interact with and derive a lot of strength from their peers. I didn't have that. That's the primary distinction. I will say that foundation that was set as a child, where I was told that there would be places of comfort when you struggled, helped drive me back during struggles in my early adult life.

*Yeah, that foundation really makes a difference. My family
took me to church as a child, but I wasn't really raised in the
church. I think that in some ways that's a benefit because if
you're raised in the church, when you go through that
rebellious phase, you might rebel too far away. I eventually
ended up being baptized as Methodist about eight years ago.
So, I was kind of glad that I wasn't as tight as a younger person.*

I agree with you on that. I have seen young adults and even old youth go through that rebellious stage. Hopefully, they still got the grounding to where God will draw them back. I've also seen incredible folks raised in the church in such a way that it just captured them. But my church days, especially some very difficult struggling church days, absolutely helped prepare me for this time period.

The first church I sought was very small. It was in the neighborhood, and it was the same denomination of the church that I was taken to as a youth. I went there, met some great people, was uplifted, and saw the need to give my life to Christ. Things were good, although God never promises us a rose garden.

So, you found another church home?

Found another church home. It was like going from the storms into a quiet garden. That church was the church I was an elder in when the storm hit. When the storm hit, all the church members were scattered all over the country.

Tell me more about your evacuation experience.

We would normally leave two to three days prior to a storm. If you wait within twenty-four or even thirty-six hours before a storm to get wherever you're going, it just takes an extremely long time. We got lots of friends everywhere, but we'd usually go to Houston. Houston's typically a six-hour drive from New Orleans, but during a hurricane evacuation it could be eighteen to thirty hours. Katrina was supposed to hit in the panhandle of Florida somewhere in the Destin, Fort Walton, Panama City Beach area. Then it kept trackin' west, and the probability of it hittin' us was in the ninetieth percentile. It was also lined up to be one of those worst-case scenario storms that could dump and flood the entire city.

You were very aware of that from the outset?

Oh, everyone knows that. When you see the hurricane comin' in at a certain angle, you know the chances are high of it pushin' the Mississippi River flow backward and of it pushin' the Gulf into the two lakes that run into Lake Pontchartrain. Lake Pontchartrain is on the north side of New Orleans, and if it fills up it could top the levees.[4] Those are the worst-case scenarios, and it was lined up perfect for that. So we made an effort to leave town on Saturday, and that was late 'cause this is gonna hit Sunday night. Instead of goin' west, my wife and I and my son and my daughter—my son's girlfriend at that time—we were gonna head east to the very place that the hurricane was originally supposed to hit. Once it passes, a hurricane very

---

4. New Orleans lies below sea level in a virtual bowl rimmed by Lake Pontchartrain to the north and the Mississippi River to the south; these bodies of water are at higher elevations. Southeast of Lake Pontchartrain is Lake Borgne, a lagoon off of the Gulf. Given this topo-

seldom backs up. Its momentum pulls it a different direction. We figured if this hurricane doesn't hit us and continues to track westward, Houston is probably not where we want to be. So, we chose to go to Destin. We made reservations at this resort that we happened to have timeshare points at. It was very simple.

Everyone's pretty much ready, except my oldest daughter who's married. She tells my wife, "Hey, we're not goin'." Her husband is a fine man. They always evacuated with us, but he also believed that it was always a waste of time. They were gonna stay there, because no hurricane's really ever hurt them. I'd gone through lots of hurricanes, but once we had less wetlands, I always thought it'd be safer to take my family out of harm's way. They refused. She would have gone, but she agreed to not rail against her husband and that they would be all right.

What was going on inside of you when you heard that?

It caused me struggles. This is my daughter and I love my kids dearly, and I love that man that protects and takes care of and provides for my oldest daughter. He's a great son-in-law. But I also thought they were makin' the wrong decision. My wife was pleading with him. I even told 'em, "You will have very few seconds, maybe a couple of minutes to make split decisions if it tops any of the levees or if any levees break. If you see the waters comin' up into your house, don't think or contemplate. You run to a two-story home. If no one's there, break into it and climb to the second story because you will not have another chance to save your life." Those were my parting words with her.

We decided to leave Sunday morning. I did sleep, but I woke up around five o'clock and this hurricane was a 165-miles-an-hour Category Five, headin' right at us. We needed to get out of town quickly. My wife was frantic again because of our daughter not leavin'. So, I called my son-in-law's dad and his mom. His dad hates to evac too, and that's maybe where he gets it from. His dad had arrived back in town the night before, and he didn't even know what was goin' on. So, I woke him up early in the morning. I said,

---

graphy, a storm surge of sufficient power can push water back up the Mississippi River and through Lake Borgne into Lake Pontchartrain, causing water to flow into the city with only a series of human-made levees and other protections to prevent flooding.

"I apologize for callin' you so early, but I need to talk to you about something. It might mean the safety or life of your son and my daughter. I don't know if you know what's goin' on, but there's a Category Five hurricane out in the Gulf, 165 miles-an-hour sustained winds, headin' right at us. And I ask you to please call your son and see if you can encourage him to leave." He said, "A Cat Five?" And I said, "Yes." He said, "A 165-miles-an-hour winds?" I said, "Yes." He said, "We're getting' out of here." I said, "Whoa-whoa! Wait a minute. Before you get out, will you call?" He called. About three hours later, we get a call from my daughter, and they preferred to go to Destin with us, rather than Huntsville, Alabama, with his dad. So, they did evac, but that was major angst and pain and struggle within my wife and, to a degree, within me.

We had four cars in tow, and we were headin' for Destin, about a five-and-a-half-hour trip. It took us ten hours to get there but that was better than twenty or thirty hours goin' to Houston.[5] When we got off the interstate it was dark, and the storm had started hittin' hard. The resort we were stayin' at was right on the water, but I chose it 'cause it was a high rise, concrete, hotel and they had a highrise parking garage, also solid concrete. We figured even if we had a large tidal surge, we would be plenty safe, and all our vehicles would be safe. That was a scary trip because there were places where the water had covered the road. But we got down to the coastal highway, and when we headed east toward the area where we needed to get to, we were experiencin' strong winds and rain literally sideways. We drove down that coastal highway basically and got there around ten o'clock. We felt safe, and that hurricane took out that bridge overnight.[6]

While you were driving, were you able at all to
think about what was going on back home?

5. It was common knowledge that large-scale evacuations drastically increase travel times, leading many to try to evacuate to safe areas as close as possible to New Orleans. Flaherty et al., *Floodlines,* 6.

6. The ability of Franke's family to caravan using multiple functioning vehicles and to afford to stay at a resort in Destin, Florida, points to how economic privilege made their evacuation feasible. Nevertheless, the harrowing journey and severe emotional distress they experienced reveal that evacuating during Katrina was an extraordinarily difficult experience for anyone who attempted it, regardless of class position. For examples, see Fussel, "Leaving New Orleans"; Woodmansee, "On the Run," loc 1314–1374.

Well, you always wonder about what's goin' on back home, but you don't want to go off into some water on the side of the road. Monday night at 1 a.m. is when I saw Brian Hunter with Fox National News receivin' a call from a lady. She was in a position of some kind of management at Tulane Medical Center, and she was pleading for help, sayin' that she had called the National Guard, the police, the fire department, everyone, and no one will come help, and he said, "What do you need?" She said, "The levees have broke, and water is floodin' into our medical center. It's already on the first floor, and if it gets to the second floor, it knocks out our generators and we're gonna have people dyin'." When he asked for further confirmation, she said, "Well, I'm standin' here in the Tulane Medical Center and on Canal Street. We can see the whitecaps."

That brought tears to my eyes. We knew if it had breached the levees, it was going to literally encapsulate that city and we did not know when we would come back. So, your heart just dropped, like the whole world dropped from out from under you. I realized that when the hurricane passed and the horrible winds stopped around four, five, or six o'clock in the evening, the city's people were breathing a sigh of relief that the levees had held. But they didn't know about the damage inside and underneath the levees, of soil bein' displaced, and helping to cause floodwalls to move a little; then the water starts comin' in. Even if it's a small amount, once it starts to break, the floodwalls are gonna come down—one, two, three to where we had a gap of over a football field long on the 17th Street Canal. The London Canal had a gap of about 100 yards as well. It was royally messed up. That's when our hearts sank. As an elder of the church, my heartfelt job in my soul, in my heart, in my mind was to find our people and to see that they were okay.

Did you get started on that right away?

Oh, right away. Emailin'. Phone callin'. Well, phone calls was virtually impossible. We had, I think, six cellphones among us. We made over one thousand phone calls on one of the first two days. We got through three times.[7]

---

7. In "Water in Sacred Places," Donald Devore finds that African American pastors in New Orleans acted similarly to Franke in attempting to reconstitute their churches after the storm. DeVore, "Water in Sacred Places," 765.

I remember you told me to always to use
text messages in this circumstance.

You're right there. That's how we started getting information back from some of the folks on where they were, how they were doin', and what their next steps were. We couldn't get through any other way, and my cellphone turned into an office of what God placed on my heart to do. I didn't know He was really placin' it on my heart that first day. The first day, I was thinkin' like, "Hey, you got to find out where these people are. You got to make sure they're alright. You gotta help them where they are, and you got to help prepare them to come back." That's what I was doin' and I was nonstop. And, at the same time Bobby Ross from the *Christian Chronicle* had taken part of what I had sent back to him, put it on the front page of the *Christian Chronicle* with my contact information. So, I was gettin' phone calls from all over the nation. People in transit said, "We got truckloads of goods comin' down, and we've got money and people to help rebuild, and we're on the way. Where can we meet ya?" (*Laughter.*) I said, "I'm in Florida with my family 'cause that's where we evacuated to, but you won't be able to get in the city 'cause we're underwater. But go to all those cities that surround the north and west of us—Lafayette, LaPlace, Baton Rouge, Houma, Hammond, Covington, and Slidell. Get in there because we're wantin' to get back and when we get back, that's where we're going to be. They're gonna need the help. They're gonna need the money. They're gonna need y'all ministering to them." Sure enough, Baton Rouge doubled in size in thirty days. The churches were exploding at the seams. The schools, the gymnasiums, everywhere you could put anybody, they were just explodin' at the seams. So, the second day, I knew that He was placin' it on my heart.

Anyway, the first day I got like three or four, maybe six emails, and I responded to 'em. The second day I got fifty some odd. The third day I got three hundred and some odd. It was snowballin' very rapidly. I was in major mobilization mode on what God was puttin' in my heart. That second day, I just put my phone down and said, "God, will you talk to me? If this is what you want me to do, I got some serious problems here." I tell people often that I argued with God like Moses. I said, "God, I own two businesses, or at least I had two businesses. Now, I don't even know how I'm gonna bring in the next dime to support my kids and my family. I don't know where

I'm gonna live. I don't know how I'm gonna do all this, and you want me to do this?" Then he laid a blanket of peace over me as if he told me, "You take care of what I'm askin' you to do, and I will take care of you and your family." And God opened His barracks and His storehouses and sent His people and His funds.

Maybe I was put into leadership of this small church for such a time as this, because He had prepared me beforehand to be who I was now. To be able to take all these things that are bein' onslaught at one time and not have a problem siftin' through it and marchin' forward. That's who He made me to be. I'm not blowin' my own horn in that area. I would fail miserably if he put me in a room of four- and five-year-olds and said, "Take care of 'em."

How did that conversation with your family go when you were telling them what you felt was your calling?

They sort of saw it happening. But there was a disconnect there. I'm on the phone with these incoming groups. I'm on the phone with some of our best friends and fellow church members. I'm tryin' to get them help wherever they're at, tryin' to give them some kind of guidance, some kind of encouragement and hope for the next day. But I would hear an echo every so often in the room: "Hey, we were impacted too. We are also them." I took a little time to deal with that.

On Wednesday morning we're headin' out of Destin to my son-in-law's family in Huntsville, because we can't get back into New Orleans. Where we lived, just west of New Orleans, there was martial law. You couldn't get in. When I was in Destin, I found that one of my fellow elders was in north Alabama, and so was our preacher. They were both within about an hour-and-a-half drive of Huntsville. So, I asked if we could meet in Huntsville for me to share what I believed that God gave on our heart on how we can move forward. We met at some kind of little Mexican restaurant, and my fellow elder says, "Yeah, let's go with it." He could have said anything, and it wouldn't have mattered. I would have still gone with it because that's what God had given me to do, but the preacher also thought it was very wise. We prayed about it and went our separate ways.

That had to make you feel pretty good.

It was good just to be face to face with somebody more than anything else. We were a close-knit church. You really knew everyone there, even new-comers. We were a likable, friendly, welcoming, hospitable church, and place of grace. We had people that had been beat up from churches all over the city, but we only had something like $12,000 in the bank, and that disappeared overnight. We had a million dollars' worth of damage on that buildin' and no flood insurance. We were still underwater in September. Even into October there were still parts of the city underwater. But October 4th, the first team came from a Texas church. They gutted out the church pews and put 'em outside out on the street for the FEMA crews who, by that time, were pickin' up debris.

We'd sent out an email to all our members that, if they could, to meet us at the small, little La Platte church to worship, and then afterward we were gonna have a family meetin' and let them know in what directions the elders were gonna go. At that meeting, we told 'em to look at the website. We had set up a website where they could see the before-damage pictures and pictures after we gutted the inside of that buildin'. Hearing from us three elders helped them see that we were not giving up. We were going to restore God's church in that community, and we were gonna do every-thing possible to bring anyone back that wanted to come back. That was the message that we gave. Now we had no money, but I would be paid as a minister to accomplish this task. In fact, they said that they also believed that it had been put on my heart by God.

That's a lot of responsibility.

Well yeah, it is. But I will tell you this: if you hear a call of God and you go that direction, there's gonna be people lookin' at you real strange some-times sayin', "What? You're gonna give up your job to do that? Are you crazy?"

Let me take you back to Huntsville. Your family said,
"Pay some attention to us. We're going through this also."
How did you all move forward as a group on that issue?

I felt it was very important to do it first and foremost with my wife, because no matter what happens with the kids, my wife and I are one. I explained to her more fully at that time, and that made her scared initially. She was still having great difficulty, and I said, "Open my laptop." I wanted her to read some of the emails from the last three days. She's readin' the emails from some of our best friends, and she starts to cry all over the place. Then I said, "Now read all these emails from these people from all over the nation that you don't even know yet." She started cryin' again and said, "I can't believe these people are wantin' to come down here to help people they do not even know." And almost every one of these folks at that point are Christians. So, she was deeply moved and touched. I had to work on her on that drive northward to Huntsville, before we could even attempt to work on our children, because she needed to be strong and resolute even though she may not know where our future was gonna go.

So, we get up to Huntsville and we share a little bit more with the kids, but we're there for a short night. I'm gone because I'm havin' a meeting with the elders, and the very next day we're goin' to north Mississippi to pick up my wife's parents. They took major hits, power outages, and they were frightened to death. We drove over there because her brother and sister-in-law needed to get back and they could no longer take care of mom and dad. So, we took her mom and dad and the rest of the caravan from north Mississippi to Little Rock, Arkansas, where some good friends of ours stayed. We were all in their house, and we looked at our houses by satellite. Our house was spared. It was on a lot with trees all around us, and the trees all around us came down, but not one of 'em hit the house.

That is very fortunate.

That's what we thought, until two years later when we got the check from the insurance company. We had $186,000 of damage, and we got only $23,000 from the flood insurance. If a tree had come down on the house, we'd have got full money. That's something that we did not realize. We had paid insurance for thirty-some odd years. Before flood insurance was even required by anyone down here, I always had it. That was something that we did not know that we were going to go through. We did not know that we were going to be livin' in a FEMA trailer and all those things to come. Eight days later, I sent my son-in-law and my daughter down to look for houses for rent or even to buy. We agreed that if we could not rebuild our houses now, we would buy or lease a house as far away as one hundred miles. Just find a house and let's get this thing done. I had a lot of contacts bein' in the parkin' lot business, and I was reachin' out to every construction company, home builder, and real estate person I knew. It was bidding wars.

A house went up for sale for $200,000—it would sell for $300,000. There were so many bids that were comin' in on it. Rentals were the same way. So, when they left, I called some friends of mine that had parents livin' in Houma. It's about a forty-five-minute to an hour drive away from New Orleans, before the storm. After the storm, it became about a two-hour drive. But I wanted to know if there was anything down there that they could find. I said, "Go find the penny and the nickel newspapers at the grocery stores. See if there's any listings for houses for rent." We found a house for rent by a deacon from a Baptist church, and he had raised his kids there. I got on the phone with my daughter right away and said, "Whatever it takes. If it takes $1,600, whatever it is, rent that house."

She was negotiatin', and he says, "I don't want any more money. I just want to know that you can pay, that I got the right people in here, and that you will take care of this house because all three of my children from birth on were raised in this house." Here's a fellow Christian, an elder of the church so that helped. So, we signed a six-month lease and I drove down the very next day. My son, his girlfriend, and my youngest daughter came with me. So, my wife's left up there with some very good friends of ours and her parents. That tore her up, but she needed to stay while we set up the household. This was a house that needed appliances, that needed furniture, that needed and needed and needed. She came down two to three weeks later, and we had a household set up. I drove to the church building every day, and we busted the swollen doors open on the church building.

You could get into the city with no problems?

No. It was near impossible at that time. I was settin' up some things to make it easy for me. One of the companies I derived most of my income from was a medium-sized asphalt and concrete company that built parkin' lots. We did their striping, bumper signs, and whatever they wanted on top of their parkin' lots. They also did streets, water lines, sewage, and all that underground stuff. Jefferson Parish and Orleans Parish were askin' them to take a look at all the broken water pipes, sewage, and street damage, and I got one of their passes. It let me go anywhere, even into the Lower Ninth Ward where they had to bulldoze all those homes later on. You couldn't even drive through the streets before they came in with a huge military vehicle that resembled a gigantic snowplow. They used that to clear those streets so you could get through. That was then all blocked off by troops, but we could get in with that pass.

What did you see?

Oh, man. That was rough. I'm lookin' at a city that I loved that was virtually destroyed. Eighty-eight percent of our homes and 98 percent of our land mass was underwater—all the businesses, all the restaurants, everything. It was a dead city. Even in December, there was only five thousand people in the city, for a place that was a vibrant city of a half-million plus. At any rate, my thoughts are still on what God wants me to do. The first point I drove to was that church building. We saw water stains outside that were about eight or nine foot tall. But we got to get in. There were these giant wooden doors that were swollen shut. We broke the doors open, and the flood damage was incredible. You go in and you smell the stench. You see black/green/yellow and other colors of mold all around you. My lungs hurt for two weeks after walkin' into that place.

I immediately saw what we needed to do. I went next door to our preacher's house that the church also owned at that time. Underneath it was totaled. But we had a usable space upstairs, and I said, "This is gonna be our office. This is where we will work out of." So, I set up an office there. We had no phone lines. We had no cable. We had no internet. We had no nothing. We needed phones and internet. So, I got a Verizon dial-up card for my laptop, and I had my mobile phone. Sporadic, very sporadic, but it kept getting' better and better and better. The first, second, and third months I had 12, 14, and then 16,000 minutes on my phone. (*Laughter.*)

What did you focus on first? It sounds like you were really trying to get the structure of the church back together.

That is part of it, but more important than getting' the church back was seein' who of our members were there and how we could help them. If they were in New Orleans, they were without electricity, they were without natural gas, and they were without any kind of safe running water. So, we had to somehow help them. My other concern was if we're gonna get people to go out into the community, I had to have a place for 'em to sleep. God opened a door there with a FEMA camp across the river. They were only lettin' first responders in, but lo and behold, this lady, when she heard the story that I told her, she wanted me to answer "yes" to at least one question. Every question that she asked was a "no" or "not exactly." (*Laughter.*) She was tryin' to find some kind of way to get us in that camp. She took all the information and said, "I got to put this before higher ups and see." Two days later she called and said, "You can bring your volunteers to our camp." That was important because their camp had a full-scale kitchen, latrines, these gigantic tents that had wood floors, and air-conditioned tents with cots already in them. So, when we brought the volunteers in, they could work in the community and go back to a safe and secure place.

These are the people who had gotten in contact with you back in Destin and Huntsville?

Some of them were. The big numbers started to come when these people asked how they could help, and I said, "Get with the leaders of your church. Maybe get two or three other churches together and get an advance team down here. Come down here, and I'll show you what needs to be done." When they did come, I would take them to the like-named churches that they were from. I would go inside those buildings, and I would show them the mass disaster. Then I would take them outside that building and say, "This is the neighborhood this church needs to respond to. We need to re-build this church. We need to go out in that neighborhood and touch people's lives so that they will see God through us."

Having them go to the same-named church gave them a kind of stronger connection?

Oh huge! This might have been their church while they visited down here. I know it was for some of 'em. We would take 'em there. Then they would go back home and say, "We got to get help down there." Then they would come with a team—10 people, 20 people, 80 people, 50 people—and bring checks—$4,000, $16,000, $20,000, $80,000—and say, "Use this to help in the rebuilding." Most of 'em believed that whatever manner we put it to use was okay. Some put restrictions: "Half of it to your church building, half of it to a predominantly Black church building. We want this to go into the home of an elderly couple." Whatever it was, we honored it.

At the outset then,
was everything happening through your church?

Not really. I was a member of the church and the ministry was at the church, but it was not a ministry of the church. Slight distinction. It was a ministry that God gave to me but not necessarily to the church. Everyone at the church was thrilled when they heard it, but hardly any could participate because those that were back needed help, needed their house rebuilt, or they were helpin' their mom and dad's house be rebuilt. So, it wasn't a ministry of theirs.

It was a ministry that God put on to my heart. But I was an elder there. I was one of the shepherds. We were movin' and active. People would come in, bring the troops, and we would send 'em out. Every day, wherever we slept 'em, we always brought 'em into the church. And from there, we sent them out from the church so that the people that were around would see activity around that church and they'd know that there was some life in that neighborhood. It wasn't about us. It was still about givin' God the glory.

What I'm hearing is that you acted like a logistics person
for other Christians who wanted to send help and you
anchored them to local churches as a way to help inspire
the community by seeing their church come back.

That's a real good analysis, but we'd probably have to draw back in just one area because so many of the other churches in town, at that time, and even for almost two years afterward, were nonexistent. Where we were able to find 70 percent of our people in the first week, there were churches that did not know where 90–95 percent of their people were two years after the storm.

Was that because you all were so close-knit?

That's partly because we were close-knit. Partly because our church was diverse in every realm that you could think of—40 percent Black, 18 percent Hispanic, 3 percent Asian, and the rest white. We were very diverse in cultural backgrounds and very diverse in education. We had folks that had multiple PhDs. We had some folks that didn't even go to grammar school. We had different kinds of people, and not one of them was overlooked. The whites with the Blacks. The Blacks with the Hispanics. The Hispanics with the Asians. It was all intermixed. It was a body of very radically different people from different backgrounds that came together and found a cool church. Many leaders are leaders for whatever reason, but they're not necessarily the leaders that God called when a calamity occurs. At other churches we saw paralyzed church leaders—no clue, no desire. They were just paralyzed.

They got overwhelmed by the storm?

They didn't know what to do. I visited several church leaders. We sought to find out where many of the church leaders were—and they were in Atlanta or in Houston, this and that. Where I really saw it happen was when the Clinton/Bush Katrina Foundation was established, and they came to New Orleans. They sent invitations to churches across Louisiana and even into Texas. They met in New Orleans, and there were thousands that were there. Me and another gentleman went to that Clinton/Bush Katrina thing, and as we heard these other leaders go up to the microphone, we were just flabbergasted.

Why?

One church leader said, "Twenty million dollars! That ain't nothin'. I had a congregation of 8,000 people. We need $20 million just to go back in our church." I'm hearin' this kind of stuff and I'm jottin' notes down. I show my fellow minister the notes and suggest that we ought to go up there together, and he nodded in agreement. So, here's a Black minister and here's a white minister/elder/shepherd. Just as we're gettin' ready to go up, they shut the microphone down, but I was gonna tell those folks, "Don't depend upon the federal government. Don't depend upon the state or local governments. Depend upon God first, and then seek every contact you know within the denominational groups that you have, go get the help and bring it in. That's what we're gonna need."

No one else was expressing that mindset?

At that mic that day, not one person. Not one person. And it was a shame.

I read the Pew Research surveys all the time, and the research that I like to read about most is the status of church in America. I tell the churches' two statistics. Number one: for the last two-and-a-half decades, a 90-some-odd percent of the people in this country believe in God. Number two: 60-some-odd percent of the people believe in Jesus. At times I ask which Jesus? The teacher, Lord and Savior, good man, good prophet? Well, for me, my Lord and Savior. But still, that is a very high percentage. But the third one confounds me as a church leader and a Christian, even before Katrina. Sixty-some-odd percent did not want nothin' to do with organized churches and religion or Christians in general. There's something messed up with that figure. But whether it's messed up or we accept it, that is our reputation. It was before and it's been so after the storm, except in New Orleans. In New Orleans after the storm, you could go into every neighborhood, do surveys, and ask them what they think, and 90 percent want everything to do with the churches.[8]

***Because they're seeing what the churches
are doing in the community?***

'Cause they have seen it. They saw churches comin' down here, and people of different colored skins comin' down to help people with people of other colored skins, and never asking anything except "Tell me about your story." They saw churches doing everything to help move that person further along in their health or encourage them to live another day. They are so thankful for the churches. Even atheists have told me if it wasn't for the churches, nothing would be goin' on in this town. That speaks volumes to the churches that I give orientations to where I say, "Folks, when you go back home, you've got to do what Jesus said in the story of the good Samaritan, 'Now, go do likewise.'"

⚜ ⚜ ⚜

JULY 16, 2010

So, what exactly does Operation Nehemiah do today?

Well, one of the biggest things that we do is still push very hard at getting churches, school groups, and business or corporate groups down here to

8. In *Markets of Sorrow,* loc 2190, 2254, Vincanne Adams notes New Orleanians with similar perceptions.

continue to go out in the community to help not only rebuild the walls of people's lives but help rebuild the community in general.

It sounds like that developed from how you started at the outset.

Very much so. It was very similar to the very beginnin', but we adjust and adapt dependin' on what the specific needs are of the community around you. When we first started, it was very important for us to gut out churches so they could get back up and then bring in volunteers to the community— but we had to be very open to the idea that a church may not desire to do that and may want to return the way it used to be, which a lot of churches wanted to do. They felt if things was returnin' to normal, it would be okay.

What do you do for business groups and non-church groups?

Well, business groups and schools are a little bit different, but I approach them in a very similar way that we do churches. I may not use language that a church person may know, but I'm still sayin' the same stuff. Let's say I've got ten groups in town, maybe three hundred total people. I go to their websites to find their mission or vision statements. If it's a church, I'm lookin' for their ministry. If it's not a church, I'm lookin' for their service or humanitarian work. Ministry and service are basically the same. And I found the similarities of the desire to help folks in the community, whatever that help might be, very interesting.

The big difference that I find between churches and non-church groups, whether it be corporate or school groups, is the word "mission" itself. The churches and others understand that they're comin' down to help folks and rebuild, but the church folks do it as a mission, like God had vested them to serve Him and to serve others. The scripture says love your neighbor. They push that and, they want to wear themselves out. Non-church groups will come down here and work their tails off, but the mission team will work until they can't work no more. When they're drivin' home, everyone is exhausted and knows that they really put in 100 percent plus.

Do you believe that your background as an entrepreneur helps you talk to business groups?

Yeah, but I don't speak real corporate-ese. I speak natural language that a corporate executive or a janitor can understand. I tell a lot of stories. Truthful stories of the events that have occurred down here have made a major impact.

What has it been like for you to learn how to
organize the volunteers?

I mentioned that I believe He prepared me for such a time as this. I really do. Because it really isn't difficult for me to organize an army. I sift through things, troubles, and problems, and I'm a solutions guy. I don't want to know why it can't be done. I want to know how to overcome it. As far as keepin' 'em motivated, I know that I've got to touch a person's heart. So, I tell 'em stories of not only how we've made impacts on people's lives but how they will make impacts that very week. When I do that, they're ready. Sometimes I get more energized by the group dependin' on what group it is. I'll hear the crowd start to get really motivated and get a lot of feedback as I'm getting' 'em charged up. There is an occasional group that their mindset isn't to sit through orientation for a half-hour/forty-five minutes on what they're gonna be doin' throughout the week, and makin' an impact in their own communities. But that is one of the primary reasons I still do what I do: to change people's focus to where they're not just thinking about it back home. They're doin' it back home.

So, people call you and talk to you about things
they need in their community?

Absolutely. If I had twenty, or even ten, folks on staff that were skilled construction types, I might organize it the other way. For example, on July 25, I will have about three hundred volunteers in town. If I broke those groups down into groups of ten to fifteen, I've got a monstrous amount of projects every day that they could be on. If I had twenty to thirty crew leaders per ten to fifteen people, that model would work very effectively. But I don't have twenty people. I have difficulty with the financial challenges of bein' a nonprofit and tryin' to raise any kind of funds to keep the staff that I have.

So, you're not limited by having too few crew leaders to
handle the volunteers?

No. I have another office staff member that helps coordinate all incoming volunteers. I have one on-site project manager. I have one intern and I have one other staff member that has construction experience. He's also a full-time minister. He not only helps organize a lot of things in the office; he does quite a few things out in the field. When you count that, it's me, one project manager, one other staff member, and an intern. And the intern will be leavin' at the end of August. So, there will only be three of us. To coordinate fifty to one hundred people is fairly easy. When we get into the two hundred or three hundred [range], it's a major challenge. But I let the project manager know that his job is not to organize a crew at a project all day long. His job is to make sure that the crews are doing it at the projects, plural, all day long.

Many other organizations rely on AmeriCorps volunteers. How do you find your staff?

I'd love to have some AmeriCorps staff, especially the VISTA personnel or the AmeriCorps folks that come through the state because they're longer term. They serve about eleven to twelve months long. But all in all, we work with what we have. I'll tell ya an actual example. Two high school groups came in last year. On one of the groups, there was no one at all that had any construction experience. They knew what tools were, but they had never handled tools. The other groups that came the second week were the exact same kind of group, but they had one high-grade professional carpenter. The first week, we had a project goin' from the ground up. We had the piers on the foundation, and we were gonna build and frame up a house with the high school kids and the adults that came with them, but none of these people had any experience. So the first week, I put a contractor out there. They went over safety issues, and the contractor showed them what was to be done while workin' alongside them that whole week. They were able to put all the floor joists in place, deck it out, and they started puttin' up the walls. The second week had within the group a highly skilled person that could read the architectural plans, and he was able to guide that group on. That group finished walling it up, decking the roof with the plywood, and decking the outer perimeter walls—all in two weeks' time. We utilized what we have, and we know that we can get a whole lot out of folks if they're just willing to give of themselves.

WE CAME TO REBUILD NEW ORLEANS

Sometimes they think they're way better than they really are, or they underestimate who they are and score themselves lower. But when we figure out what kind of crew we've got, we get them on the project and we're movin' those people further along—givin 'em hope and help to get them through the next day and the week. We also try to develop a rapport with homeowners or the folks we're working with, so that they see the personal aspect of it too.

Some groups focus on the elderly or certain neighborhoods.
Do you have any special qualifications for whom you can help?

Nope. The floodwaters hit every socioeconomic person that you can imagine. The guy that lived in the $400,000 home around the corner from the guy that lives in the $80,000 home—both of 'em got needs. Both of 'em have been brutally crushed with something that they never thought would happen. They also realized, especially those folks that have funds, that they may be able to better move through society when things are goin' okay, but when the proverbial stuff hits the fan, all bets are off on money being your solution. It isn't.[9]

That said, we do rank certain folks higher. If somebody calls us this week with a person that is handicapped and needs a ramp put in, we're gonna score that at a high priority. We'll move them up, because it is such an important need to have a degree of freedom to get out of their house. We will score the elderly, handicapped, and/or those that have lost a loved one higher. When you got somebody comin' through the door, you're colorblind and you don't look at what kind of vehicle they drove up in; then you hear their story. It doesn't matter if I'm talkin' to a rich man, a poor man, or an educated man, if he's tellin' me the story that he lost his only daughter and only granddaughter in the floods, that man needs help. He may need me more than anything that day just to listen to him, and say, "Hey, help's comin'. We're gonna help you when we can." I ask 'em if they have a church

9. Despite Franke's sense of the storm hitting everyone equally, most damage occurred in neighborhoods at lower elevations; these areas, except for the Lakeview neighborhood, were majority African American. Nevertheless, Franke's point has merit because the breakdown of private insurance and government support as a safety net made no exception for color. Flaherty et al., *Floodlines,* 54; Adams, *Markets of Sorrow,* loc 984–1153, and 11677–1701; Campanella, "An Ethnic Geography of New Orleans," 715.

home anywhere. I don't normally ask 'em if they're a Christian or anything of that nature. I just want to know if they have a church home. 'Cause if they have a church home, there's some help there that he needs to be seeking. If they don't have a church home, and I know of a real good church that will outreach to him, I recommend that he consider speakin' to the pastor at that local church. Not because he is or isn't a Christian, but because he needs help.[10]

You would like to be in a position where you have more staff if that was possible. That made me wonder what the toughest thing for you has been.

I'd love to have more staff. I don't know what's gonna happen with folks I have currently or with the folks that God will supply in the future. But that is really important. I don't mind workin'. I've worked all my life, and I work hard. But it would be a lot more of a comfort zone to not have bags under

10. Franke's colorblind and class-blind positioning of Operation Nehemiah is thought provoking and should be contextualized within an analysis of whom the flooding affected. Richard Campanella explores this best in an "Ethnic Geography of New Orleans," 711–715, and his analysis merits quoting at length:

A spatial analysis helps clarify the relationships among race, class, and susceptibility to hurricane damage and death. Throughout the metropolitan area, 40 percent of the total population of 988,182 resided in areas under water on September 8, 2005. Blacks outnumbered whites in that flooded area by over a 2-to-1 ratio, 257,375 to 121,262, even though whites outnumbered Blacks metropolis-wide, 500,672 to 429,902. People of Asian and Hispanic ancestry numbered 9,240 and 11,830 among the flooded population and 25,552 and 49,342 among the total population, respectively. Thus while one in every four whites' homes, one in four Hispanics' homes, and one in three Asians' homes flooded throughout the tri-parish metropolis of Orleans, Jefferson and St. Bernard (24, 24, and 36 percent respectively), close to two of every three African Americans' homes (60 percent) were inundated. In sum, Whites made up 51 percent of the pre-Katrina metropolitan population and 31 percent of its victims; Blacks made up 44 and 65 percent; Asians made up 2.6 and 2.3 percent; Hispanics made up 5 and 3 percent . . . There are similar statistics from those killed by the storm: African American victims outnumbered white victims by more than double, they comprised 66 percent of the storm deaths in New Orleans and whites made up 31 percent, fairly proportionate to pre-storm relative populations . . . Focusing on absolute figures lends support to the case for disproportionate suffering of certain groups, whereas reporting relative figures makes the victimization seem more ecumenical . . . There is no question, however, that those who were stranded in the inundated city and suffered excruciatingly long delays in rescue were overwhelmingly African American and poor—in both absolute and relative terms.

your eyes all the time because you're workin' sixteen to twenty hours a day during the busy months.

Most of the funds that came early on came directly in the form of large donations. Churches would bring the money because they knew they needed to do that to reestablish churches from ground zero, and it really was ground zero minus wherever we were at that point. I think there was more than a million dollars' worth of damage to our building, and because that area of the city has never been flooded, there was no flood insurance. With only about 100 to 150 members of that church, that's a lot of money to make up, and we were in an area of the city that wasn't a wealthy area. But these folks that came down first brought in the bucks—four thousand, twenty, eighty—and said, "Put it to use in whatever manner that you really need to put it to," and we did.

Earlier you mentioned working sixteen- and twenty-hour days. How do you deal with the stresses coming down on you and your staff?

That's really a great question 'cause it is stressful. Sometimes lack of sleep is stressful. Dealin' with hundreds of people is stressful. We really want this to be a phenomenal mission trip for people, so we work really hard at what we do: to bring the volunteers down here, to house and feed 'em, to secure and coordinate all the projects, and to immerse them deeply into our culture with our music, our food, our Cajun-ness, and our southern-ness. How do we handle it? One way is knowin' that there's rest comin'. The busy times are March, June, July, and August. Our summer months are just bolstered with huge numbers, while our fall and winter months are lightweight. We can do a whole lot more restin' and playin' during these less busy times.

The other thing I gotta tell ya, is it's energizing to see these groups come down and continue to come down and continue to serve others. Most of my staff gets energized off of all these volunteers. I don't mean it's like runnin' off of adrenaline, but when you go to sleep, no matter how tired you are, once you wake up it is an exciting thing to be seein' the volunteers from churches and schools make an impact and know that we are a part of that. It is also energizing to hear from these churches on what is goin' on back home in their own neighborhoods as a result of them takin' that mission of ours back home with them.

Does the reception that you get from the homeowners feed into that uplifting experience?

It absolutely does. When a homeowner comes out, even if they're workin' full-time and they just come out for a moment, we tell the groups, "Remember that the project you're working on is the person or people. Not the house. Not the park. Not the school or the library. The people." So, when you have opportunities for interaction, we ask them to slow down and really listen to what's going on. It makes a huge difference in the volunteers' lives when they interact with those folks. Many have told me, "I don't know how I could even hold up under the same circumstances that they're goin' through." Or "How can she say, 'God's gonna provide' when she's sittin' on a porch, the house is gutted out, and there's nothing going on there?" They see the rubber hittin' the road at that point. And our clients get energized too. We've had many people say, "I want to tell you what an incredible group of fine high schoolers and adults you sent us today. They were amazing." Or "I was contemplating suicide and if you hadn't sent those people to my door that day, I'd probably be dead." Time and time again, we've gotten lots of those calls.

When people look at the change going on in their house or see twenty or thirty people that don't even know 'em devotin' a whole weekend to their house, there's hope there. There's help there. When you hoped that the government would help ya, they don't, but then you see church groups from all over the country continuin' to come down, that speaks well not only for New Orleans long term but it also speaks well of the churches.

What do you mean by saying it speaks well for New Orleans over the long term?

I've got folks comin from Christian colleges thinkin' they're comin' down into Babylon, and they want to change Babylon into a new Jerusalem, to use terms of the scripture. Most folks are thinkin' Bourbon Street and Mardi Gras. And when they think about Mardi Gras, they think about women barin' their breasts or something like that 'cause that's what they show on TV. That's not typical. Yeah, people come to play, get a little bit too inebriated, and do things that they probably wished they hadn't done later. But New Orleans is much deeper than Mardi Gras and way deeper than Bourbon Street. I've been here since 1970. This city has one of the deepest spiritual roots of any place I've ever lived. It's in the city. It's in the culture. It's in the people. Folks comin' down here have no clue about the depth of spiritual maturity down here.

Do you believe that coordination between groups doing this work can make the work less difficult? It seems to me that a lot of members from organizations know each other, but I don't get the impression that there's a lot of coordination between organizations.

Well, you're more on than you're off. Early on we just dug in. If people needed help, you just helped. They were desperate. So, that's where my actions were. I heard about an organization called Greater New Orleans Disaster Relief Program, G.N.O.D.R.P.[11] I went to several of the meetings. They were talkin' about, "How can we coordinate this better?" It was a great concept, but I got tired of the meetings. I knew they were going to be very beneficial, but I had too many people that needed help. I let one of my staff members go to keep an ear open, interject what she felt the direction of our organization was, and how we might help. But that needed to be done beforehand. That's sort of like the theorist guys. They talk in theory about how a city ought to be built, but they sometimes overlook the people that are livin' in that city.

I see a lot of good that could be done in collective, and I believe collectives should do everything they can to work together because it can be very efficient. But we saw that some organizations got their funding only by what they said they were doin'. I'm not gonna mention an organization, but they asked for all our numbers, so we gave 'em all our numbers. We found out that they were usin' everyone's numbers that were in attendance and writin' grants' sayin', "This is what we're doin'." They weren't doin' anything. They were pullin' and pooling all these guys together for the better collective to go down the road together, but it seems strange that they were

11. Pronounced "no-drip."

turning around and gettin' funds. I don't mind 'em gettin' funds. I mind 'em usin' our numbers.[12] Now we share our volunteers with dozens of organizations. Somebody's got a landscape project, we got the volunteers—we're sendin' em. Somebody's got a rebuild project, but they need volunteers— we're loanin' our volunteers out to 'em. If anybody needs volunteers and we can loan 'em out, we loan 'em out all the time, and I mean thousands of 'em. They might not be loaned out for the whole week, but we do loan 'em out because it's important to do so.

These groups that you have connections with,
did you meet them through informal networking?

I have found the most productive work to be done informally. I ran into somebody here. They met one of our people there. They heard about us, and they called us, or vice versa. At more formal meeting networks, you didn't know who was really there. Whoever is runnin' the thing may know, but you may not really know 'em, even though they're there every time you're there. You got to go beyond the meeting and say, "Man, who are you with?" Maybe you build the relationship there. When I stepped out of the picture of the coordination part with other groups, it was early on when there was too many meetings and nothing gettin' done.

Yeah, it's kind of hard to do after the
problem's already there.

Exactly. In the meantime, "Hey, we're gonna be here some kind of way and we'll make a presence, but I got to get out there and help people." When we were bein' asked to do things the way a certain organization felt that we ought to do it, I couldn't agree with that one either. If the system does not take away from our vision or mission, I have no problem in that. But when another organization comes in and tells you, "It would be a lot better if you did this." Well, it might be a lot better for them, but it might not be a lot better for you or the people that you help.

12. In making this point, Franke joins many other interviewees in this project who argued that the nonprofit granting process, particularly foundations' desire for quantitative data to assess performance, can pervert the missions of nonprofits and foster unhealthy competition that makes their work less efficient within a disaster recovery context. For examples of this argument, see Berra et al., "To Render Ourselves Visible," 39–40; Adams, *Markets of Sorrow,* loc 2785–2807.

Did the Office of Faith-Based Initiatives assist
you all at all? Did you have any contact with them?

No. We never got any help from them at all.

So where do groups like yours fit with
efforts by government?

That's a great question. Some portions of government work well; some
don't. Early on there was no government in New Orleans. They had elected
officials, but they couldn't even pull permits for construction the first two
years.[13] City Hall didn't have the inspectors. So, you had people tryin' to do
things with no infrastructure. That happens with something as messed
up as Katrina. FEMA did one thing that seemed pretty good off the bat by
bringing in a liaison between the faith-based groups, FEMA, and the federal government. They told us that we could get all kinds of federal grants.
I asked 'em to send somebody out here to tell us what and who to write to,
but nobody ever came; so many of the faith-based groups didn't fully know
where to even start.

I was invited to speak at a convention of cities on how to respond to major disasters. I'm comin' from a certain point of view, but I'm also realizin'
that many folks there might be faith-based. For many folks, church was
from three or four generations ago. They've not even thought about church,
and they certainly don't think that church is the solution. They think government is the solution. Knowin' that, I said, "It doesn't matter whether
you go to a mosque or a synagogue or a church. Before the storm hits your
area, whatever that storm is, get out there and find out what groups are makin' an impact in your city. Manufacture a database of people that can help
when something like this happens. You're gonna need it, and you're gonna
be doin' it anyway. You might as well find out how they're gonna do it and
better coordinate for the future, rather than wait for the calamity to happen
and then haphazardly try to find out who's in town and what they're doin'."

It sounds like you're a believer in making a phone tree for
organizations that have the logistics and infrastructure to

13. Pulling a permit is the process of getting a municipal inspector to review building
plans to ensure that they meet city safety codes. Major construction in New Orleans and
most other cities cannot occur legally without having all the proper permits in order.

be on the ground right away, rather than waiting for
government resources to come in.

The unfortunate thing is the government prevents many of those people from comin' in.

How's that?

Every year you could sign up for a permit to allow you to get back into the city [after a disaster]. Whether you're a businessman, relief organization, church, or first responder group. They've got 'em rated one, two, and three. We should have been a one. We were back in the city doin' work immediately. They wouldn't even allow us back in the city until the number threes were allowed. But because of [owning] a past business, I was able to get a number one. Even at this point, with all the work that all these faith-based groups from across the country have done, they still don't get it. These guys should have been allowed in right away with the police and fire department.

Government does good to maintain a degree of stability and to control populations of people. We got a lot of Army and National Guard troops down here, and they did that pretty well. Beyond that, most of the money that's come down here from a federal standpoint has been for infrastructure: rebuildin' our levees, rebuildin' our roads, helpin' rebuild many of our streets, our underground plumbing, and the sewage. But while they're doin' that, there's people hurtin'. That's why it was important for us to reestablish churches. 'Cause they're on the ground, they can do things quickly and easily. The government is too big, and each step of the way, all the people can say no, but very few people can say yes. But in these kinds of situations, everything needs to be a yes. You saw the ineffectiveness of the federal [response] until Mr. Honoré got down here. I can't remember if he's a general, but he just cut through the junk: "People over there need water! Where's the water truck? Send it over there." "But we haven't got approval from above." "I'm the approval from above. Get it over there." They needed help right then. People needed to be rescued out of the trees, off the rooftops.

And did I tell you what FEMA did regardin' the boats? The Coast Guard saved 38,000-some-odd people. That is unbelievable. They got manuals tellin' 'em how many people can fit on that helicopter or how many people can fit in that boat, but when you're pluckin' people off rooftops, you also know the capacity that boat can handle. They loaded these boats and these helicopters and saved thousands. Two weeks later FEMA says, "Send all your boats from all over Louisiana so we can go in there and save more people." What do they do? When they got down to the water point. FEMA asked for the papers on all the boats. They asked for their insurance. They asked for the floatation devices. And boats were bein' turned away. Idiots. It's a boat or the top of that roof. The flotation device is the boat. That's just bureaucracy at its worst.

In New Orleans, we try to work with the city real well, but the city doesn't work real well with you. They almost seem incapable of it. No matter who you spoke to, nobody could ever give us an answer. (*Laughter.*) Even after two years, nobody would even be willin' to help get you an answer, with the exception of one or two council people.

True leaders are not the leaders that are in leadership. True leaders are people, whether they're in leadership or not, that rise to leadership when a calamity happens. Our former governor was frozen just like so many church leaders were just frozen. They were immobilized. They didn't know what to do or where to turn because they always depend on government. We saw ineffective leadership across the board. FEMA and the feds? No. The state? No way. Local government? Most people say it was a total joke. A lot of our elected leaders are not really leaders. They've just been elected.

What do you feel like you've learned about the
people of New Orleans?

For any group of people that endures something like we've endured, you are way stronger than you were. You're just way stronger. They have stretched everyone down here to their limit and then stretched us more. (*Laughter.*) So, the growth in knowin' that we've been through this means that we can get through a lot of other things too.

So many people have come down to New Orleans as
volunteers and decided to stay. What impact do you think
these newcomers are gonna have on the city?

I believe it's been an extremely powerful impact. We have lots of folks that have come here, and I mean thousands of 'em. A lot of youth and a lot of new thinking that is not our thinking. That can change a whole culture for the good or for the worse. I believe very little of it will be for the worse. I believe most all of it is for the better, whether they're faith-based or not, because you got new energy, new life, new thinking. You got people that wanted to be a part of restoring, and rebuilding and renewing this incredible city. They're not necessarily entrenched in some kind of thinking that you cannot get past. I like the new energy. I like injectin' new blood in politics and injectin' new thinking in communities, because they are now part of the community.[14]

Are you seeing the effects in politics already?

Yeah. All those folks that were in power during the storm have been replaced because the populace believed that it was an ineffective government. So many people tried to bring race into this. Pre-Katrina, we had about a 68 percent Black population. I don't think that's the percentage anymore, because many of them have not been able to come back. But the city's population, which almost always would be able to elect Black leadership, doesn't solely look at the color of a person's skin. They want results and that speaks volumes. When I hear somebody like Al Sharpton or Jesse Jackson comin' down tryin to divide us, most of the city is not interested in division at all. Ninety-some-odd percent of the people that we've helped are different-colored skin than ourselves. And the majority of volunteers, whether it was directly through Operation Nehemiah or other organizations, have been white and middle class. They're helpin' Blacks, Hispanics, Asians, and whites, and everyone in the city sees it. I believe we have way better racial harmony than we did before the storm.[15]

Some of our leaders, who stay in power or get their income by main-

14. Franke's position diverges from that of some activists of color in post-Katrina New Orleans who argued that incoming "faith-based groups, relief-based groups, and radical left organizations" were uncritical about the impact of white volunteers on preexisting African American organizing and that their remaining presence is a form of "back-door gentrification." Berra et al., "To Render Ourselves Visible," 41; Flaherty et al., *Floodlines*, 84.

15. Franke's perception of greater harmony after the storm does not seem to take into account the very large protests and political activism in New Orleans in the years immediately following Katrina around the destruction of public housing and the reversals of criminal justice reform, both of which tended to be framed as racial and class issues and both of which involved broad coalitions of groups (usually of color) across New Orleans. See Arena, *Driven from New Orleans;* Rathke, *Battle for the Ninth Ward;* Wooten, *We Shall Not Be Moved;* Woods, "Politics of Reproductive Violence."

taining that division among groups, don't necessarily agree. In fact, they're gonna stir up everything on the contrary. I've seen them stir that since almost the beginning. Early on they were sayin' that the Black churches and the Blacks in general were bein' ignored. Man, that's as far away from the truth as could possibly be. Everyone was bein' helped. But somebody derived their power and money-raising abilities by keepin' people divided.

Some folks have been very disappointed in the nation after watching the experience of Katrina. Whereas other people I've talked to feel very inspired, for example, by how many people have come from all over the country to help the city rebuild. How do you feel about America viewed through the experience of Katrina in New Orleans?

I'm a person that likes to give people the benefit of the doubt. So as far as the nation and how they have responded, they're where they're at right now because that's their life. They're in their normal twenty-four-hour cycle of makin' a livin', goin' to school, or takin care of their kids and families. I don't put it on them. I put more of it on us. We, meanin' New Orleans in general, could always do a better job. Our organization pushes real hard to let people know that this is not over and that we need massive help. Yes, you could come to New Orleans and have one of the best vacations, but we still got 58,000 homes that are blighted and block after block of what used to be vibrant neighborhoods. I was upset that the politicians locally were portrayin' everything okay. There's got to be a balance. You need to let people know that everything is okay in some areas, and please come to have a great vacation, but during your stay here, volunteer with one of our many organizations because this isn't over.

What is my outlook on the nation in general? I believe it could get worse for a lengthy period of time, but I'm the positive guy. I believe in American ingenuity and freedoms, but cycles of economies go up and they go down. Sometimes worldwide they go down. That's what appears to be happening right now.

I think I mentioned to you earlier that a minister twenty-some-odd years ago said, "If you find a hurting and needy people you will never lack ministry." That's where the church needs to step up. When government cannot do it, that's when we should be doin' it. Before Hurricane Ike hit, this eighty-some-year-old preacher calls me from New Iberia, Louisiana, pleading for help. I said, "What do you need?" He said, "I've heard that you might be able to help me. I've got leaks in the roof of my house. Ike is comin', and I just need somebody to help." Ike was comin' the next day. So, a friend of mine and I drove over there with a bunch of tarps. I was just gonna tarp his roof, but I ended up lookin' at it inside and out. We bought some roll roofing and patched everywhere there was any kind of problem. When I got off the roof, he asked, "Man, what all do y'all do?" I told him and you could see the emotion in his body. He was gettin' really excited. He said, "Man, that's a good ol' time religion. That's what we always used to do. When a brother or sister needed help, we just did it. We didn't think about goin' to the government for help. Now everybody wants to go to the government."

What do you feel like you have learned about yourself over these last five years now?

Wow. I believe the startin' point would be as a person who believes that he will always stand for his faith even when you believe God is sendin' you in a direction that seems impossible. To know that when God lays something before you, and you do it in simple faith without knowing the ramifications and see the results—that is a huge wow.

What else? I will say that I had a flaw before Katrina in that I was more impatient with people than I should have been. And then afterward, it was like just gone. I don't mean like God supernaturally removed it. It was just gone. I mentioned to you that there was only a couple restaurants and one bank open two months after the storm. People would get super impatient, but you could only do what you could do. A realization of the reality of it all. You just saw a city devastated, and it seemed like so little help at the same time. Areas of frustration didn't really sink into me. The directive to go do these things that God put on my heart was way more important. So, I didn't get distracted by peripheral things that may have distracted me earlier on like, "Why am I havin' to wait for two hours or even an entire day to go through this drive-through bank?" I didn't even think about it. I was just glad a bank was open.

6. James "Jay" Welch

THE LEGAL FIGHT FOR THE MOST VULNERABLE

I thought it would be very hard for some lawyers to understand how
to deal with the large number of problems there were gonna be,
but for what I do it's a legal emergency room everyday anyway.

—James "Jay" Welch, Southeast Louisiana Legal Services

A few years after Robert Goodman began his activism against police brutality in the early 1970s, James "Jay" Welch, then a young civil service
worker, decided that earning a law degree would be the best way to protect
himself from the corruption and cronyism he saw in New Orleans's city
government. By the time we interviewed Welch in 2010, he had spent more
than twenty years as a staff attorney in family and public benefits law with
Southeast Louisiana Legal Services (SLLS), a public interest law firm that
provides "free, civil legal aid to low-income people in six offices, across 22
parishes throughout southeast Louisiana."[1]

Attorney or not, Welch was just another scared New Orleanian fear-
ful for himself and the home he loved when Katrina hit. His evacuation
experience not only illustrates how privileged New Orleanians were able
to flee the storm but also how that privilege provided only meager protection from the extreme stresses and anxieties that came with the process.[2]
Only a week after arriving in Baton Rouge, Welch and other colleagues
from SLLS regrouped to address the countless legal issues their poor and
working-class clients would face as a result of the storm's destruction—not

1. Southeast Louisiana Legal Services, "Southeast Louisiana Legal Services"; "LSBA
Recognizes Legal Professionals, Law Students for Pro Bono Service," 136.
2. Welch's evacuation story, involving staying with a relative and quickly reassembling
his networks, corroborates with scholarly descriptions of the typical evacuation experience
of middle-and upper-class New Orleanians. Fussel, "Leaving New Orleans."

just of the city but also of the civil legal system. Indeed, their return could not have come fast enough.

Where Goodman's testimony reveals the vulnerabilities of New Orleans's poorest citizens to systemic racism in law enforcement and criminal justice, Welch's narrative outlines other areas of exposure that only legal support could address—such as employers using Katrina as a pretext to withhold wages earned before the storm, an inability of traumatized survivors to understand and complete FEMA forms, improper denials of FEMA benefits, and parents using the storm as an excuse to violate custody arrangements.

Beyond the law, Welch's testimony also expands the theme of cooperation or the lack thereof between organizations attempting to provide relief after the storm. Although he applauds the Common Ground Collective for partnering with SLLS to create a free, local legal aid clinic, he nevertheless recounts an absurd quarrel between the Red Cross and the Louisiana State Bar Association that may have prevented thousands of storm victims in Shreveport from receiving pro bono legal advice at a critical moment immediately after the storm.

Welch's experience of escaping the storm to a city that he felt was very different from New Orleans and jumping into the recovery only a week afterward was a somewhat circular and ongoing process in which recovery work distracted from the stresses of the storm while adding its own anxieties. Other interviewees, such as New Orleans Habitat for Humanity executive director Jim Pate and Operation Nehemiah founder and executive director Fred Franke, referred to the turmoil of attempting to mount a recovery response as private citizens who were themselves traumatized by the storm, but few did so with the same vulnerability as Jay Welch.

⚜ ⚜ ⚜

MAY 23, 2010

What was going on in your life before
the hurricane occurred?

Well, I've lived in New Orleans since '72 and I've been an attorney. I've practiced here for twenty-five years, since 1985. I'm fifty-nine years old, and before I worked Legal Services, I had a job right after I got out of law school workin' at the Orleans Indigent Defender Program. And I didn't go to law school for a long time. So, in my past, I've had a large number of jobs.

What made you decide to go to law school?

Back in the mid- to late seventies, I got a civil service job with the City of New Orleans. I was around for two mayors, and I got into some disputes with the way things were being run. I kept tellin' people, "It's not the corruption; it's the incompetence." So, I decided that it'd be best for me to go to law school. I thought if I went to law school, they wouldn't treat me the way they had at the city civil service. (*Laughter.*)

One of the things that I learned from workin' for the city was that if I wanted to be involved in the community, I would have to take into account that the city is very poorly run. It's so entrenched in this way that I don't think it will ever change. So, I decided if I went to law school, I could protect myself better. That was why I went. I didn't go to make a lot of money or anything. I really more or less landed the jobs I did by accident.

Can you give some examples of the types of things that you saw handled incompetently prior to the hurricane?

The city doesn't do anything except push paper. They farm everything out. So, you have all these nonprofit organizations that receive grants under various programs. When I was at the city, it was under a jobs program called the Comprehensive Employment Training Act, which I think is now called Partners Private. The city was gettin' $45 million a year, and a large amount of that money was going into jobs training. One of the things we discovered was that people were going to learn basic English, basic math, and there was one particular program that was for welfare mothers, and they were supposed to learn how to have jobs, like working as a computer processor.

When was this?

1977. It turned out that the cost per placement to take a welfare mother, put them in this program, and get them a job—usually to be like fryin' chicken at the Popeye's or workin' as waitresses in restaurants—was $100,000. In 1977 you could easily take somebody and put 'em in Harvard for that.

So, the Department of Labor was always criticizing the way we ran the programs, and I made numerous objections to how this was all done as cronyism.

And this is another example: I was very disturbed by what I saw as different types of incompetence. So, I went to the city Civil Service Commission and made a complaint about it. Naïve me. (*Laughter.*) They said, "Oh, you got a complaint about your department. Talk to this man." He came out and I told him, "We're havin' these problems. There's all this cronyism in the program, and we need to do somethin' about it." The department was predominantly Black, and there were, out of twenty employees, four or five that were white. I was one of 'em. I didn't mind workin' in the department. I wasn't upset about that. I was upset about what was goin' on. "Well," this guy says, "we can solve your problem very easily. We'll transfer you to a nice, white department," as he called it, "that runs really well like the Streets Department."

He assumed that you were just uncomfortable in the environment.

That I was uncomfortable working with Black people! I said, "Look, I'm not concerned about who I'm working with. I don't care about their race or their sex or anything like that. That's not the problem. The problem is the cronyism. It's what the people in the department are handing out to people." He said, "That's just a Black department and that's the way it is. The Blacks get to have their programs, and that's why you should go to the Streets Department." I said, "Buddy, a report I just heard on TV and saw in the papers said that New Orleans has the worst streets of any city in the United States, so how can you say that's a good department?" He didn't have an answer for that. At that point, I thought, "Obviously, this is not going to work. I can't complain to the city Civil Service about the way they're runnin' the show." Those were the types of things goin' on. The Department of Labor was constantly threatening to defund the city of these monies, but the city needed it so desperately because over half the city employees were bein' paid out of it—all low-paying jobs.

Right. Old-fashioned patronage.

Everything here comes down to that. Anyway, that has formed the basis of this place ever since it was founded, and it's something that you either accept or move on.[3] The usual response that people have is, "Well, let's go have a beer, and maybe the problem will resolve itself." There's a lot of that here, and that sort of began the prelude of what was gonna happen in the future with Katrina. Even though I hadn't worked for the city in many years, every time I would read somethin' in the paper about a city department messin' up, I was like, I don't even have to be there to know what went down.

What years did you work for the city?

From 1977 to 1979.

You said that much of what you were seeing in terms of corruption was what was gonna go down with Katrina. But from your email, it sounded like you had more immediate concerns.

When we were all getting ready to leave on that Saturday and Sunday, I kept thinkin', "This is gonna be a major disaster but we're all gonna pull together, like people did in World War II." I remember we were on the road, and we pulled over to a rest stop at about five o'clock in the mornin' on that Sunday. There was a family there with an elderly Black lady who was havin' a great deal of trouble walking, and there was a young girl trying to help her, but she needed somebody on her other side. So, I went over and said, "Ma'am, why don't you let me take your arm, and we can help you get to the bathroom." So, we were walkin' there and I said, "You know, I think that this is something we all really need to work on—tryin' to help each other. That's the only way we're gonna get through this." Everybody's goin', "Yeah-yeah-yeah." I really thought that this was gonna be somethin' that would unite all of us in some kind of positive way, because I had seen that before. You would notice during hurricane preparations for Katrina and in

3. There is indeed a popular narrative that New Orleans has, since its founding, been flexible regarding rules and regulations. Unfortunately, these narratives distracted from assigning responsibility for the disaster to causes such as financial austerity or government "hubris." Powell, *Accidental City*, 49–50; Johnson, "Working the Reserve Army"; Blakely, *My Storm*, 18–19.

the past that the lines were orderly, and people were rather calm about the whole thing. Of course, everybody's very tense and nervous and worried, but really in the past it seemed that people were very helpful to each other and saying, "What can I do?" So that was sort of what I was, expecting. Silly me. (*Laughter.*)

Did people not react that way this time?

After it became evident that the government failed to respond to the anarchy that broke loose in the city. I was quite stunned. I was in Shreveport but starting late that Monday morning, it became evident that there was this serious flooding issue, and you began to see a major breakdown in the way the governor, and the president, and the mayor were reacting. They weren't doing anything! They were makin' speeches. And in the meantime, there's all this anarchy goin' on.[4]

Given your pessimism regarding the way in which
local and state government had been run,
you were still surprised by their lack of response?

I sort of thought that if the government wasn't gonna respond, people were gonna start organizing themselves very quickly. Then I began hearin' some of the wildest stories. One was that all the Garden District had been looted—I heard it from somebody who worked sometimes with the FBI. And I was like, "Oh, my God, is there gonna be anything left?"

I started thinking, "My gosh, if this is happening, the city government is not gonna be able to respond to this very well." I was angry at all three of our fearless leaders, and then Governor Blanco started cryin'. I was like, "I feel like cryin too, but we got an emergency here and everybody's got to get on board."

How did you feel about the governor and mayor
prior to the hurricane?

---

4. Despite his self-criticism, Welch's sense of people pulling together was not entirely off. Many witnessed acts of heroism and communal support in the storm, and the perception of anarchy was largely overblown and the result of poor communication by local, state, and federal officials. Flaherty et al., *Floodlines,* 35; Boin et al., *Managing Hurricane Katrina,* loc 479, 2948.

I had voted for Mayor Nagin his first term, and I was very optimistic about him. Then about the middle of the term, I began hearing from people, Black and white, that he was doing a very poor job. It wasn't anything in particular that I saw, but I had begun to think in the next election, I'm probably not going to vote for him. I did vote for Governor Blanco. I really didn't know much about her. I think it had somethin' to do with social things. You had all these men runnin' for governor sayin' they wouldn't give an abortion to their wives if their lives were in danger, and I thought that was ridiculous. (*Laughter.*) She was the least radical of the group. So, I voted for her, but I thought during the storm that she just seemed to be in a state of shock and wasn't doing anything.[5]

While you were still in Shreveport, did you decide you
wanted to come back and put yourself in public service
again to help the city, or did you go back to the city first?

They told us we couldn't come back. That Wednesday the mayor said that 20,000 people had died and that we would not be able to come back to the city for six months.

What neighborhood are you in?

I live in the Marigny Triangle, maybe four blocks from the French Quarter on the downtown side. It's an old house. I renovated it back in the early nineties. I knew my house was okay at that point, because CNN was on my block. They took a picture of a building that is a half a block from me that collapsed during the storm, and they started comin' down the street in the van. The only buildings they showed were on the other side of the street, and they were pretty much okay, except for that one that had collapsed. So, I figured my house is still standing because CNN's not showing it. And my street was the last street not to flood in the storm.

That had to be a relief.

5. In *Managing Katrina,* Arjen Boin, Christer Brown, and James A. Richardson argue that Governor Blanco, Police Chief Eddie Compass, Mayor Ray Nagin, President George W. Bush, and FEMA Director Michael Brown contributed to a narrative of government dysfunction and anarchy that facilitated rampant rumors of looting and destruction that far exceeded events on the ground. Boin et al., *Managing Hurricane Katrina,* loc 3025, 3045, 3178–3393.

Yes. Also, I don't know if I put that in the letter, but I had a homeless person livin' in my house.

No, you didn't. What was that about?

Oh! Okay! I'd known this guy for about twenty years, named Tommy Sanders. He played a hammered dulcimer on Jackson Square. Over the years, I've seen him become more and more schizophrenic, and he ultimately became homeless. He believes that he was abducted on three different occasions by space aliens, and he doesn't want to talk about anything except space aliens, which people get tired of after about five minutes. (*Laughter.*)

So, he has a few socialization skill problems. Anyway, I was sick one time for a while. He helped me out and I had given him money—$5 here and there—to run errands for me. When we were gettin' ready to leave for my mother's in Shreveport and Tommy was helpin' out, I gave him about $80 dollars, and said, "Tommy, take this money. You've got to get out of town now." Tommy said he wasn't leavin'. He said it was all caused by space aliens, and he wasn't worried about that. He said that Bush was controlled by space aliens. So, I said, "Tommy, you can't be outside when this thing happens. You're gonna die. I mean, this thing looks really bad." Anyway, I gave him an extra set of keys to the house and told him, "We're leavin' about four or five o'clock in the mornin' on Sunday, and you can stay in the house." We gave him the keys and my mother's telephone number, and I said, "Just try and call us if you survive this." And I was real nervous about it. It wasn't havin' him in there. I was a little scared, you know, he'd start a fire or somethin' 'cause he's kind of spaced out. But what I was really freaked out about was I didn't want to come back to see the house in ruins and find his body. So that was why I was reluctant, but it was gonna be even worse if he was out on the street.

Anyway, he did call. Right at thirty minutes after the CNN shot, he called and said he was at a pay phone at Barracks and Royal Street in the Quarter. He told me that you didn't have to put any money in it and there was a line of people. And he said, you couldn't stay on the phone very long. You had to keep moving because there was so many insects that were biting people. We have these things, saltwater gnats, and if you get bitten by them, it's worse than a mosquito bite. You really had to keep movin' because the city just very quickly became filled with insects and all kinds of stuff. After Tommy said the house was okay, he said there was one problem, and I asked, "What's that?" And he said, "I smell gas in the house." I thought, "Oh my gosh. We forgot to cut off the gas." So, I said, "Can you go and find out where it's comin' from and shut it down?" He said he'd do what he could, and of course I told him, "You better be real careful."

He found it. It was behind the stove, and the gas line had snapped. He turned it off. Had he not been there it would have blown up, and the houses are so close together that it probably would have blown them up too. Havin' him there was a miracle.

Let me ask you a question about Tommy. Do you feel like he was more lucid than normal during the hurricane? He's a person who in a lot of ways had been having difficulty surviving, but when the hurricane came, he was exhibiting extraordinary survival skills.

He loved it. He'd give me the telephone number of the pay phone, and I'd say somethin' like, "I'll call you on Tuesday at six o'clock." He said, "Oh, I love your house." He felt there was a spirit there that was really neat. For somebody like him, since he lives on the edge anyway, this sort of thing was just made for him. Some French reporters actually put him on a documentary in France. So yes, his survival skills for living in that type of a situation were much better than mine would be. I noticed that he had never been so together. He stopped talkin' about the space aliens, at least for a while.

I'm not even really sure what to think about that. I guess it just goes to show that our assumptions about people and their abilities are very specific and contextual. At any rate, what were you doing in the meantime?

When Nagin said we couldn't come back for six months, I kind of freaked out and was like, "Oh my God. How are we gonna stay away for six months? People won't come back." And I thought, "Well, if I've got to stay up here in Shreveport," which I did not want to do, "I'm gonna have to do somethin'. I'm not gonna sit here and watch TV for six months." So, I called the Northwest Louisiana Legal Services—their office is in downtown Shreveport. I talked to Alma Jones, who's the director, and she said that she had six extra offices in their facility, and they had some dead computers that they thought they could revive. And so, she says, "Why don't you just spend the rest of the week gettin' yourself together and then show up on the Tuesday after Labor Day."

We basically re-created our office up there. That was where the most people were collected together. That Tuesday, a week and a couple days after the storm, we came to the legal services office there and changed our telephone numbers with the bar association on their computer to show that we were now at the Shreveport office.

Were you associated with the agency prior to Shreveport?

I knew that they existed, but I didn't know much about them specifically. I had never worked there, but there's a legal services office for every county or parish in the United States.

So, you found them so that you could have something to do?

Yes! I thought it would be very hard for some lawyers to understand how to deal with the large number of problems there were gonna be, but for what I do it's a legal emergency room everyday anyway. I did the same thing I do now, but I had a lot more of it.

Believe it or not, within hours of my changing my telephone number on the computer, I started getting calls. I think my first call was from an attorney in Massachusetts. Somebody had shown up from New Orleans there and was havin' some kind of a problem, and they needed advice on what Louisiana law was. It was a family law problem. I don't do that anymore. But because I used to do a fair amount of family law and domestic violence and all that, I knew what to tell the lady. People just started callin' in: "I've lost my job. I need to apply for unemployment. How do I do that? What am I gonna do about . . . ?" Helpin' people fill out FEMA forms, talkin' to people about problems they would have about payin' their mortgage, a lot of custody, child support issues, and then people wantin' divorces almost immediately. (*Laughter.*)

Really?

A lot of people were not reacting well, you know, to living somewhere else.

And what happened with the FEMA forms?
Was there a website that you could go to? I was
struck by people asking you how to fill out the forms.
It would seem to me that you wouldn't know much
more than they would.

Because I'm a lawyer, I can make an educated guess about it. I'm so used to doin' legal emergency room that I know a little bit about almost everything, but I'm gonna tell ya this. The first day I went to a disaster relief center in Shreveport and they had the FEMA forms out there, I looked at 'em, and they began swimming in front of my eyes, and I thought, "I'm too spaced out to even read this."

It was a big problem. I'd read it. Then I'd read it to the client, and we'd try and figure it out. I told 'em, "Look, I'm a lawyer and I'm havin' trouble with this." It was not easy, and a lot of issues came up very quickly about that $2,000 that people wanted to get.[6]

They gave all the evacuees $2,000 per household because we all had expenses. You had to give 'em an address to send the money to, and you had to fill out some forms. I was able to do it online, and I got my $2,000, within a week or somethin' like that. It was to help people, sort of an unconditional thing from the government. There were lots of problems with that. But I will say this, on the whole, I do believe that was very helpful to a lot of people. It just saved them as far as havin' to stay in hotels and bein' places where they didn't know anybody.

What I began seeing almost immediately of course, was people having questions and then people who should not have been denied were denied assistance. But you couldn't call FEMA because the lines were busy, and you had to move on to the next person. So, I would tell people, "You're gonna have to call them 'cause I got all these people behind you." I would try and steer them in the right direction.

Did FEMA do any outreach for practicing attorneys or
civil workers to help you all be able to explain this stuff?

6. To learn more, see CNN, "FEMA to Give Katrina Victims Debit Cards"; Associated Press, "$2,000 Debit Cards for Katrina Victims"; Associated Press, "FEMA to Give Families $2,000 on Debit Cards"; FEMA, "More than $2.3 Billion in Expedited FEMA Aid"; FEMA, "Nearly $690 Million in Assistance"; Government Accountability Office, "Testimony before the Senate Committee on Homeland Security."

No. Not that I'm aware of.

Can you tell me a little bit about what was going on in the
minds of you all, emotionally, working in Shreveport?

I felt a little weird because I hadn't lost my job. We never lost a paycheck, and I hit the ground running for the most part. Within a week we got ourselves together. But Mark Moreau, who was the director, got twelve feet of water [in his home]. It was up to the second floor. He lost all his furniture, and he lost his house. I think it was very difficult sometimes for him to concentrate.

All of us were quite shocked, and everybody was actin' as though they had been in a war or somethin' and their house had blown up. Actually, I'm sort of the freakiest person of the lot 'cause I'll scream and yell.... Well no, I take that back. Laura [then a staff attorney] screams and yells and curses more than me. (*Laughter.*)

So, some people were upset and yellin' about it. That tended to be me, and then other people just sort of went, "Let's just do this task. Let's do the next task. And just try and stay focused." But it was hard. Your mind was all over the place.

One of the things I get from the interviews I've done with
people that evacuated is that there's no place like
New Orleans and that the anxiety of being away from
home was as distressing as what was going on at home.

Yes. One of the Shreveport papers and, I think, the Jackson, Mississippi, papers had articles about the New Orleans people. They talked about how loud we are and how much we liked to laugh. They even said, "It's just a different culture in New Orleans." It's true. I really realized how much New Orleans has meant to me.[7]

How long before you all got back into New Orleans?

7. As of 2000, 54 percent of residents in New Orleans's Ninth Ward had been in their homes for longer than ten years—greatly exceeding the national average. Moreover, the majority of those displaced from the city were New Orleanians who, before Katrina, had never evacuated for a hurricane. Boin et al., *Managing Hurricane Katrina,* loc 296; James, "Political Literacy and Voice," 161; Flaherty, "Corporate Reconstruction and Grassroots Resistance," 9, 103; Flaherty et al., *Floodlines,* 9; Griffin and Joanne Dubinsky, "An Unfragmented Movement."

Well, people did different things depending on what was needed. Here was my special issue: I had to get back after I had been in Shreveport for six weeks. The reason was because on October 17, 2005, the bankruptcy laws were about to change. The new bankruptcy laws were unfavorable to the debtor, and nationwide, people were rapidly filing bankruptcies [in advance of the new law]. We had maybe 100 people show up, and we were gettin' geared up for this. On the day that I left our office, August 26, I knew that we were gonna have to get these things done, because we had all these people wantin' to file bankruptcy before the law changed.[8]

When the storm happened, we tried to get the law postponed for our area because the debtors were scattered everywhere, and we didn't know how to get in touch with 'em. A few people had called me, but all this bankruptcy stuff has to be done by computer, and you have to have the setup to be able to use it. You have to have the software. You have to have a computer. You have to have an email address, and of course, you have to have an office. The debtors are gone, but people are startin' to call in and say, "I want to get my bankruptcy done before this October 17th deadline." I kept tellin' the directors, "If we're gonna do that thing by October 17th, we better gear up." They tried to set up the system in Shreveport, but the computers weren't sophisticated enough to do it, and the other attorneys in the unit were gone.

So anyway, I had to come back. Several months before the storm I moved to the consumer law unit here at the main office, on the fourteenth floor of a skyscraper in downtown New Orleans. The building got two feet of water and lost electricity. We couldn't come back there for a real long time, but we had to get these bankruptcies worked on. On Friday October 9th, I got a call from one of our directors, and he said the computer was ready to go. You also had to have a credit card for the filing fee, so the client can repay us for the cost. He said everything was set. So, I came back with Linton Carney, my boyfriend. We've been together for thirty-one years. We grew up in Shreveport, and we met each other in high school in the sixties. He was the director of AIDS Law of Louisiana. He acted heroically to keep that agency open.

8. For more information on the new bankruptcy laws and Southeast Louisiana Legal Services' response to them, see Southeast Louisiana Legal Services, "Katrina Stories"; Sahadi, "The New Bankruptcy Law and You."

So, what sort of resolution was there with
trying to file those bankruptcies for those folks?

I got there that Monday. The office was fit for five to nine people, and they had twenty to twenty-five people smushed into this small building. You'd have to go into somebody else's office to use the phone and all of this. The computer stuff was in no way ready. It had none of my clients' [information], and it was an absolute nightmare. I guess I got a little upset. I started screamin' and yellin' about it. I was getting kind of angry because they kept tellin' me it was ready, but it wasn't. It was really the computer guy's problem. Finally, he calls me. The thing's got to be done by Monday, October 17. On the Thursday before he calls me and says, "Everything's gonna be great. I will be in Monday morning to fix your computer." I kind of lost it then and said, "Don't you dare come in on Monday morning! It'll be too late by then. The law will have changed. I need this now! I've been sayin' this for four days. Nobody's listenin' to me. And you better get your ass here fast!" I didn't say it that nicely. So, he was shamed into coming the next day and finally setting me up. Now I got to come in on Friday, Saturday, and Sunday to work on these things to get it done in time. You just had to get it done before that midnight. It was an absolute nightmare, but it was very typical, though, of what a lot of people went through.

So, the government was unresponsive to
your requests for an extension?

Yes, they said that the law was the law, it was going to affect everybody, and you just had to adjust. They did modify it a little bit. They waived the credit counseling requirement for like three years because we couldn't find any consumer credit counseling agencies around for us.

I want to digress for one second.
How safe did you and Linton feel when
you got back to the city?

He's fearless. Nothin' scares him. He's got nerves of steel. He doesn't really worry a lot about crime like I do. I'm always the one sayin', "Lock the door. Do this. Don't let the criminals get in." But there were so few people back that the city was almost empty. We would go out late at night, and there would just be nobody. It was really very strange. It was deserted in many ways.

Well, I have some big questions for you now.
Where do you feel like Southeast Louisiana Legal
fits into the larger relief efforts that were going on?

We were goin' to the disaster relief centers, and everybody was doing whatever they could. I think that we were more like second responders. I did feel like we were movin' a little too slowly at first. I wanted to go on and get started. Laura and Rowena [another staff attorney] and I worked up a quickie intake form: name, address, telephone number, Social Security number, date of birth, how much money you make, and what's your problem. We also made flyers, and we posted them in public places. We were fitting into the larger picture in that respect, and we were getting people who had to have things. Like the SBA application process is very cumbersome. It's like a twenty-page document that you have to have notarized. We would have to explain things like that to people. We were sort of the legal emergency room.

Did you see any type of coordination?
Were there instances where the federal, state, or local
government communicated to you about issues that
needed to be resolved from a legal perspective?
Or was there any coordination between you all and
other organizations? I know, for example,
a lot of people had to deal with contractor fraud.

Oh, yeah! I've done lots of that. I filed about fifty contractor fraud lawsuits. Also, you can complain to the state attorney general in Baton Rouge, and the Louisiana State Contractor Licensing Board. I actually have had the licensing board investigator sometimes be the corroborating witness in court. So, we were working with government agencies. Also, we were checkin' things against the Better Business Bureau. At first, the district attorney wasn't able to take any cases of consumer fraud. Now they have four attorneys, and I have found if you can get them to take your case, they'll threaten 'em. I can't threaten the people with goin' to jail. The district attorney, however, can. The best way is to have a civil lawsuit but also to have the district attorney threaten 'em.

Has your experience given you a sense of the
way in which relief should be coordinated?
Are you satisfied with how the coordination has been
occurring, or would you have different suggestions if
something like this happened in the future?

I was very critical. One thing I forgot to say was that our agency was working with a group called Common Ground. If it hadn't been for them, nothin' would have gotten done. They were a self-help organization that had an abandoned house that had been messed up in the storm. They started workin' on it. They brought in boards, and hammers, and nails, and they got a food court kind of thing. Every day they would have free food for people, and we had a little legal clinic on Saturdays. I would do that with Common Ground.[9] So there was some coordination.

There was one thing that I was really upset about. I tend to hit the ground runnin' in this business, and in Shreveport I became very anxious to get started. I thought that we should be workin' with the Red Cross. One day I called the Red Cross and said, "I'm with Legal Assistance, and we can come and give y'all some legal help." They said, "Come on over to the Hirsch Auditorium in Shreveport. Just show up and we'll get you started." So, I took Andy. He was invaluable 'cause he spoke Spanish, and we had a lot of Spanish-speaking people. So that just got him started. But it was really weird when we got there. I went to the Red Cross person in charge and said, "Hi, I'm James Welch. I'm with Legal Assistance, and we're here to help y'all with legal people." And he says, "You're not with the State Bar Association, are you?" And I said, "No, I'm not with the state bar." And he says, "Well, you can come then. We have a bad relationship with the state bar, and they don't want to help us at all."

That seemed kind of strange to me, and the person didn't really elaborate. Apparently, somebody had called and asked the state bar what could be done to help from a legal perspective, and they told 'em, "You'll just have

9. Common Ground started the legal assistance clinic in the fall of 2005. Hilderbrand et al., "Common Ground Relief," 86.

to deal with it." So, the volunteering of attorneys or using legal assistance became an afterthought. They had a private, personal injury attorney from Shreveport. He told me he had twenty evacuees livin' in his house, and he was payin' people $2 an hour to work for him. They had a big table, they had the FEMA forms out there, and he had a basket that was filled with his laminated cards. Well, it's an ethics violation to solicit business from people that you're doin' volunteer work for. That's against the bar association rules. Andy and I were there for about four hours, and all this time I hear from this personal injury attorney about what a bunch of jerks the state bar people are. Then another volunteer attorney from Shreveport told me that they were not helpful at all. Then Andy said he had emailed the state bar three times and they never got back to him, but he had heard that they were gonna have a meeting to see about doin' volunteer work at this place in Shreveport. So, he went to the meeting. After the meeting, he gets three emails from them saying, "No, you can't go." But by this time he's already gone!

I mean if they're gonna waste time, don't waste time on emailing him after the thing. Either he went or he didn't. I got kind of upset. I was really angry. So, when I got back to the office, I found the telephone number for the president of the state bar at that time. I was screamin' and yellin', and the people worked me up the line until I got him personally. And I told him, "The Red Cross says that they don't want to deal with y'all and that y'all aren't helpful. I'm hearin' this from volunteer agencies, and I'm hearin' from private attorneys that y'all are not doing anything to help people. How many people are gonna die before you get off your butt and you do somethin' about it?" I didn't say "butt." I was very loud, and my voice does carry. A lot of people were standin' at the door of the office. He screamed back at me, "I've been workin' my ass off about this." And I said, "Well, it's not very evident up here in Shreveport, and they've got thousands of people up here." The people that were listenin' to me at the office, all started goin', "Yeah, you tell 'em." He told me to shut up and hung up on me. Then I got a little worried. When Linton found out about it, he said, "You better straighten this up 'cause you might get fired." But I wasn't really worried about gettin' fired. I don't even think they had it together enough to fire people at that point.

I did have to apologize. But let me tell you somethin', and this really pisses me off. From the beginning, I kept sayin' we had to get involved and then this thing happened. A year-and-a-half after the storm we get this email that we're supposed to go to a meetin' in our library. Our main office had reopened, and they had some attorneys from the Red Cross here and they wanted to tell us somethin'. We get in there and they say, "We were thinkin' that we should have reached out to y'all after the storm and get y'all to come to the disaster relief centers immediately, because you're really, basically, sort of second or first responders."

And I'm like, "Why is it that I can see somethin' like this and I say somethin's wrong, nobody's gonna listen to me. Then y'all figure it out a year and a half later. Well, it's too late now!"

Why do you think it took them a year and a half?

I don't know. You'd hear somebody who was in charge two years later tryin' to justify themselves 'cause they were really not doin' anything or they were tryin' to take a vacation. It was all like Michael Brown kind of stuff.[10]

What could have been more effective? It sounds to me like there was a gap between the experiences at the ground level and those who were able to control the levers to move resources where they needed to be.

That's exactly what happened. There was a huge gap. You had the people like Common Ground, and I still get students all the time tryin' to help after Katrina, but whoever's runnin' the administrative aspects of this, they just don't seem to get it. I think that's exactly the problem.

Are there steps that could be taken to resolve that?

Well, one thing is getting your telephone tree worked out and having people call in as soon as possible when there's some kind of disaster. Then know ahead of time that somebody—the Red Cross, the Bar Association, or Common Ground—is gonna have a thing ready to say where you can go to do this work. They should have had all this thought out in advance. I read in the *Times- Picayune* that as early as 1998 FEMA had estimated that the worst

10. Boin and coauthors argue that FEMA, under the leadership of Michael Brown, faced severe restrictions in dealing with Katrina, but Brown did little to convey those constraints to the public. Boin et al., *Managing Hurricane Katrina,* loc 3252.

natural disaster to hit the United States would be a Category Four or Five hurricane to hit New Orleans. They knew this as early as 1998. I often said, "You've known how vulnerable we were since 1998, and nothing was done about it?" And I can tell you some stuff about that junk that happened with that barge that had crashed into the levee in the Ninth Ward. The Corps of Engineers had deliberately compromised that levee—that very spot where that barge hit. They had that done for five years, and I kept sayin' to people, "That is an accident waitin' to happen. That levee is not strong enough." I'm not an engineer but I can see that the thing's been cut in half, and sure enough, not only did they get the tsunami but they get it with a barge in on top of 'em.

Do you believe this was an engineered disaster?

People talk about a conspiracy. I don't know about all that, but I will say that was negligent homicide. I wrote letters to Michael Brown and President Bush, and I said, "Somebody, maybe you, needs to be prosecuted for negligent homicide." They all knew this could happen. Then a year later, that tape came out of Michael Brown meetin' with the president and sayin', "Well, the Superdome does not have the capacity to deal with this. If this hits, they will not be safe in the Superdome." And then there's the whole thing that happened at the Convention Center. Nagin's got a lot of blood on his hands. I can't even imagine.[11]

Let's go back for one second. It sounds like you're indicating that to deal with social and welfare issues at an emergency level we need to have a better pre-constructed network for emergency situations.

Yes.

Do you feel that there's any role for the state, local, or national government in coordinating those groups afterward? Do you feel like there should be a larger group coordinating the institutions so that they can work together?

11. Welch was not alone in his assessment of the levees. See Maggi, "Trial to Decide"; Duncan et al., "Stability of I-Walls," 681; Adams, *Markets of Sorrow*, loc 417.

Oh, absolutely. I was just thinkin' about this as you were talkin'. They need to get FEMA into agencies like us and say, "This is what we're gonna do if something bad happens." I don't think there was anything like that.

I know it was a leading question, but that's basically what everyone else has said. Most of the people I talked to are involved in home reconstruction though, and they pointed to a lot of overlap in effort in the early years. I find it very curious that although everyone seems to know that lack of coordination and communication is a problem, there still doesn't seem to be much talking to each other.

You had to do it on your own. You had to take the individual initiative, and that's how it happened. It was the American people. It wasn't the government. We had all kinds of people that didn't know anything about New Orleans. I've seen hundreds of 'em show up here just because they wanted to help. Some of 'em fall in love with New Orleans. Some of 'em don't. But it doesn't change anybody's idea that they needed to get themselves down here to do something about this because they were so embarrassed. I remember one of the things with Sandra Bullock. She had no connection to New Orleans whatsoever, and she overheard a conversation about a high school here that had lost its library in the storm, and she gave the school some x-million dollars to completely rebuild and refurbish their library. She's bought a mansion in the Garden District. She came down here. She's fallen in love with New Orleans, and the first graduating class asked her to give the commencement address.[12]

That leads me to a couple of other questions. What have your experiences made you think about the people of New Orleans? And what has this experience made you feel about the state of our nation?

I feel kind of funny. I have a lot of students, and they're younger people than me. They're very idealistic. They're very anxious to change what's wrong, and they all seem to have an incredible constitution. I really am

12. For more on Sandra Bullock's relationship with New Orleans, see Miller, "Sandra Bullock Donates Big"; Mowbray, "Actress Sandra Bullock Purchases"; Kamenitz, "Far More than 10 Blessings."

very pleased about that, but I'm afraid that the long-term prospects for New Orleans and for the United States are not very good.

Really? Tell me more about that.

Over the years, we've lost so many of our wetlands, and that is the single biggest issue. It's really not even the levees. This really started big in the 1950s and 60s when the Corps of Engineers built a ton of levees. They drained a bunch of swamps. They built a bunch of navigation canals. All of this has aided the process of coastal erosion, because saltwater gets closer and closer and closer to the city. We used to have about 120 miles between us and the Gulf, and if we lose those wetlands, then we have no protection whatsoever. They say there were 10,000 acres of wetlands that were destroyed in St. Bernard Parish because of MR-GO, the Mississippi River Gulf Outlet. That thing had caused so much saltwater erosion.

They said that had the 10,000 acres of wetlands been there at Katrina, they would have absorbed half of that water. It would have been a 50 percent loss for them instead of 100 percent, and St. Bernard got it the worst. Every building in the parish was damaged. The problem now is that we've got to rebuild these wetlands, but it's easier to take 'em away than to put 'em back. There was such an outcry about this, and they have shut down MR-GO.[13] That thing has been very controversial.

I'd like to bring you back to the question I asked before.
What are your feelings about the people of New Orleans
after seeing them go through this catastrophe?

Well, I guess the biggest thing is how much people are so attached to New Orleans. I see it in the young people too. I've supervised probably hundreds now. They come here and they fall in love with New Orleans, and it reminds me of when I was their age and did the same thing. I tell them, "You don't have to be born here to be a New Orleanian. It's something that you just are. If you're lucky, you find it before you die." So that's one of the biggest things I've seen, and it does reinforce my own feelings about it.

13. Often referred to as "Hurricane Highway" by its critics, the Mississippi River Gulf Outlet had long been known as a hurricane amplifier and criticized for its destructive effects on native ecology. Flaherty et al., *Floodlines*, loc 261; Rivlin, *Katrina: After the Flood*, loc 720.

I've done so many interviews with people who have
fallen in love with New Orleans and decided to stay.
I was struck by something I was told by Rebuilding
Together. One summer, one church organization brought
10,000 people to volunteer and then another 15,000 came
with another church organization.

That's very common. What the American people have done has been really terrific. The problem almost always has been the government, whether state, local, or federal.

Is there some sort of new effect that's being created by
all these people coming in who decide to stay because
they love the city so and want to help it so much?

In our organization, we have about three or four people that didn't know anything about New Orleans, came down here for a volunteer thing, and then said, "Wow! This is a very interesting place!" They loved it, went to finish law school wherever they were, came down here, took the Louisiana bar, and have started workin' here. And that's just in our agency.

What's interesting is that those folks exhibit a loyalty
that strikes me as similar to the loyalty of natives.
But it's new in a way also, without some of the baggage
of having been a native.

Right. Right. I think they kind of see New Orleans as this beautiful, wounded creature. It distresses them to see something that is so interesting and beautiful writhing in agony. I think that really captured their imagination, and now they're here.

What has been your most satisfying experience
in these efforts?

The biggest thing is seein' law students. This summer I have two undergraduate students from North Carolina. They have a special program up in UNC and Duke University to get a group of people here. They have about ten here. Recently I met everybody at a meeting of all the different groups, and I always tell 'em, "Look, we'll do anything. If you ever have a problem, please call us. If there's anything we can do to help." I always try to let 'em know how grateful I am personally, and they see it in how grateful our clients are. The clients have no problem if I say, "I'm gonna have a student help you." They're ready to do that. That has been the single most gratifying thing: to meet all of these really terrific people.

What is next for your organization?

We're gonna continue working. Most of my stuff is still related to the storm. Now we're doing a lot of contractor fraud. But we're also doing bankruptcies and mortgage problems. People lose their jobs. They can't pay their mortgage, and some of that is still related to Katrina. We're gonna keep on doin' that. We're now seein' how we're gonna get involved with the problems with the oil spill.[14] So we're gonna be dealin' with that too. So, our organization is probably gonna be very, very necessary to this community for a very long time.

What do you think New Orleans needs next?

I was talkin' to my barber. He's a real New Orleans native, and he's very pessimistic. He was tellin' me, "What people have to accept is that New Orleans does not want to fix itself. New Orleans is fun and nice, but very stubborn in that respect. It always will have the worst streets and the highest poverty." It's a mixed bag, I agree with him. I think that this place does not want to fix itself. It's a very un-American attitude, but it is the mentality here. Mardi Gras is very involved in that, and our kind of inability, sometimes, to get the job done. We just don't like to work. One of the students was tellin' me, "I noticed the people here will say, 'Hey, let's get together,' and they mean it." And I said, "Yeah. They won't come to work but they'll always show up for a social engagement."

---

14. On April 10, 2010, an explosion on the *Deepwater Horizon* in the Gulf of Mexico triggered the worst offshore oil spill in American history and led to the unemployment of 8,000 to 12,000 people in the fishing, drilling, and tourism industries. Pallardy, "Deepwater Horizon"; Friedman, "Ten Years after Deepwater Horizon"; Lee, *If God Is Willing,* film.

7. Daniela Rivero

THE CHALLENGES OF DISASTER
RECOVERY AT SCALE

I think that in a nonprofit environment, everybody wants to save the
world, but nobody wants to be responsible when things go wrong.

—Daniela Rivero, Rebuilding Together New Orleans

Rebuilding Together New Orleans (RTNO), along with Common Ground
Relief, Habitat for Humanity, and Operation Helping Hands, were the Big
Four home-rebuilding nonprofit organizations post-Katrina. RTNO's history in New Orleans dates to 1988 with its participation in the Preservation
Resource Center's (PRC) annual "Christmas in October" program to revitalize the Lower Garden District by rebuilding homes for elderly residents
and those with disabilities.[1]

In October 2004, the PRC rebranded "Christmas in October" as an af-
filiate of Rebuilding Together, which was a national rebuilding organization with roots in Texas in the early 1970s. After beginning in the city as
a one-month event with a budget of $450,000, Rebuilding Together New
Orleans rapidly converted its programming to focus on rebuilding homes
destroyed by Hurricanes Katrina and Rita in 2005. Leveraging a history
of relationships with corporate donors and an unprecedented citizen response, RTNO mobilized 250,000 volunteers, rebuilt one million square
feet of the city, and invested $20 million into New Orleans by 2012.[2]

---

1. The PRC played a complex role in New Orleans. Its commitment to neighborhood
revitalization in the 1980s and 1990s aligned it with the forces of gentrification that ultimately led to the destruction of the St. Thomas public housing development in 2001, despite
vociferous community protests. Yet the PRC found itself arrayed in a losing battle against its
former allies in fighting against big box retail expansion shortly thereafter. Langenhennig,
"Rebuilding Together New Orleans Becomes Independent"; Arena, *Driven from New Orleans*
34, 36, 139, and 140.

2. Langenhennig, "Rebuilding Together New Orleans Becomes Independent"; Rebuilding

Acting as its director of field operations and eventually executive director from 2006 to 2011, Daniela Rivero led RTNO through the earliest phases of rebuilding into the peak of its work. As has been the case for our featured interviewees, Rivero shares the characteristics correlated with volunteering, including her background in community development work, her level of education, and her strong sense of altruism. Yet, even as Rivero's experiences were similar to those of her peers across this project's dataset, her story is perhaps the most unusual of them all. Of Bolivian descent, Rivero came to the United States and New Orleans less than a year after the storm, and she is the only engineer in the project. In contrast to most of the interviewees whose volunteering backgrounds were in the context of church or school, Rivero's experiences included teaching chemistry in Cameroon, volunteering with Greenpeace in Mexico City, and working with a mayor and the Bolivian president in one of that country's poorest communities.

As we shall see in her narrative, Rivero became RTNO's executive director through a set of extraordinary circumstances that resulted from her passion for satisfying work paired with plain old good luck. Her account of leading RTNO from 2006 to 2011 provides the highest-level view of the volunteer-based recovery process. Alongside Rivero, the other leaders of the Big Four home-rebuilding nonprofits were Thom Pepper of Common Ground Relief, Jim Pate of New Orleans Area Habitat for Humanity, and Kevin Fitzpatrick of Operation Helping Hands—all of whom were interviewed for this project.[3] Rivero spoke of the best and worst features of using nonprofits for large-scale disaster recovery (a theme articulated by all four leaders), including problems with the nonprofit funding model, the limitations of volunteer labor, and the extraordinary dangers of nonprofits acting outside any regulation or coordination.

This last point is particularly instructive and an area where Rivero's testimony distinguishes itself from the others. In a major disaster that occurred during the rebuilding process, New Orleans Area Habitat for Humanity distributed toxic drywall to rebuilding organizations across Or-

---

Together New Orleans, "About Us"; Lee, "New Orleans after Katrina"; "Rebuilding Together New Orleans Completes 500 Homes."

3. One could argue that the Saint Bernard Project (SBP) could be counted on this list, but the SBP operated in St. Bernard, rather than Orleans, Parish.

leans Parish. The scandal broke very slowly, so that residents of recently rebuilt homes and both small and large nonprofits came to worry greatly about whether their homes had contaminated drywall. When Habitat finally confirmed that it had unknowingly distributed the drywall, the news broke like another hurricane, nearly destroying RTNO and forcing OHH out of business. Through it all, Rivero captained the RTNO ship. She recounted how the calamity affected RTNO, the other large rebuilding nonprofits, and the relationships that had been so carefully forged between those top leaders who had been engaged in the work.

⚜ ⚜ ⚜

AUGUST 23, 2011

Where were you in your life when Hurricane Katrina
was happening?

I was in Bolivia. I'm originally from Bolivia, and I remember seeing everything in the news. I'm an engineer, and I was working for an oil company doing safety and risk management. It was pretty striking. The most surprising thing was realizing that this was happening in the United States.

What was it like for you to see the lack of safety and the
apparent lack of risk management that occurred here?

Well, nobody really understood that the levee failure was a man-made disaster. The media was just portraying it as this terrible hurricane hit New Orleans and produced all this destruction. But I remember thinking, "Well, why are they not getting the people out? How many helicopters does the U.S. Army have?" That was definitely something that, even today, I can't understand. Why were people left for almost a week without any help in the middle of the summer?

In the United States, there was a lot of focus on how these
were poor people of color, and there was blame against the
administration. How did it look in the Bolivian media?

I think it was mostly focused on the disaster. The shock was that this is happening in the United States. At least the silver lining is it's happening in arguably the most powerful country in the world, so everybody will be taken care of. I remember looking at the Superdome footage and realizing that you couldn't really see a white person there.

That struck you?

Absolutely. Because you don't really imagine the United States, when you're living outside it, as the multicultural environment that we have here. You don't really imagine that you're gonna have a whole Superdome filled with African Americans, and you don't see a single white person. I wasn't as aware of the history of New Orleans with everything from the 1700s, but it was definitely shocking.

Did you talk to anybody about it? Was this something your friends were talking about?

My husband is an American, and we were together at the time. I took in so much of the coverage because he was in complete shock and couldn't leave the TV. I think the international media asked why nobody was coming to help this situation even more than what was portrayed inside. Also at the time, my mother-in-law was visiting in Bolivia, and they hadn't received all this information. When you are outside, you have the international media reporting in a much more . . . I guess crude way.

Where are your husband and his mother from?

My mother-in-law is from Ohio, but she's lived in Georgia for over thirty years now. I think in the South more than the North you understand the racial conflict, the interrelations, and the history.

Is there anything similar in Bolivian culture?

Oh, absolutely. We have very few Africans. We didn't have any slave trading or anything like that, mostly because there were Indigenous peoples there. The Spaniards conquered the Incan Empire, which was a belligerent empire with two ruling Incan brothers fighting over the death of their father, the king. It was a moment of weakness in the empire. But we have a huge mixture of races, from European to Indian and everything in between, just like here in New Orleans.

So, during Katrina where were you in your career?

Well, I'm an industrial engineer. In Bolivia you start university when you're nineteen or twenty, and you go into the career that you want to have. We don't have the major system, so I started studying industrial engineering when I was nineteen. By the time I was twenty-two I wanted hands-on experience because I didn't know what I wanted to do for my specialty. So, I started working for the poorest city in Bolivia, El Alto. It has over a million people who are mostly migrants from the countryside who came to El Alto near the capital city of La Paz to work.

Is it a slum?

No. It's neighborhoods, but it's very poor. The houses are made out of adobe bricks and lot of people have dirt floors, but in Bolivia homeownership is extremely important. So even the poorest people own their own houses. Everybody owns. It doesn't matter how big or small it is or how poor it is, usually people own their property.

So, you were from a middle-class background and were already conscious of helping other people at a fairly young age.

Yeah. When I was eighteen, I started with environmental engineering, and the dean made a rule that everybody had to have eighty hours a semester of social service or volunteering. I remember him saying that we needed to learn something about "reality." I used to go to the children's hospital in my hometown of Cochabamba and work with the children that were in the infection sector. In Bolivia people are so poor that they don't have money to pay for care. They don't know what to do. So, they abandon the child at the hospital because they're scared. That was really my first volunteer experience. That opened my eyes.

When I moved to La Paz, I switched to industrial engineering, and my teacher was the head of the city council in El Alto. I told him I wanted to work and that I was very inspired by the people in El Alto. The people are very hardworking. They have hard lives. So, I worked there for three years in the environmental department. We planted a million trees and set up greenhouses. I had many talks with the mayor. It was very interesting to see government and policy so close up and be a part of it so young. I asked why he ran to be the mayor of such a poor city, and he told me that when you are in a situation where things can't get any worse, you can provide solutions that people will notice.

How long did you stay there?

Three years. And after that I started working for an oil company. In our office in El Alto, we would review a lot of environmental and hazard mitigation plans for oil companies. We were very stringent on them, and one of the companies decided they wanted to have somebody running their planning that knew what the city wanted. They wanted to do the right thing, which was very strange for the evil oil companies. So, they offered me a job after I had left from working in El Alto. I was working with them for about two-and-a-half years until we moved away from Bolivia.

My boyfriend at the time and I got engaged. Then we left Bolivia. We had been together for several years, and I was worried about being married to a foreigner because the question of "Where do we go next?" always comes up.

Well, with your degree and your background you can be successful in a lot of different places.

That helped. That definitely helped. But we were only in places for six weeks to three months. So, it was hard to work. And when we started traveling, we had a schedule. When we were in Mexico City, I volunteered for Greenpeace. When we went to Colombia, I worked with his company. It has a foundation, and I worked with them on social indicators for moving back the people displaced by the guerrillas in the southern part of the country, the FARC.[4] It's the second-biggest migration in the world of people moved out of their lands because of war. The company has a foundation that helps resettle people in their lands, and that was interesting.

Most people who get married young are not thinking about coordinating volunteer activities with their trips around the world. They think, "I've got six weeks; I'm gonna sightsee." What in your background gave you this orientation? Your parents? Religion?

---

4. The Revolutionary Armed Forces of Colombia, also known as the FARC, fought the Colombian government in what the BBC called the "longest-running armed insurgency in the Western Hemisphere." BBC News, "Who Are the FARC?"

That's an interesting question. Honestly, I like to work. I don't like hanging out. Maybe I should hang out more. (*Laughter.*) I don't know what it is. I always had a lot of love for my grandparents. I grew up in a great family that had a lot of advantages, and that made it possible for them to send me to learn English and send me to a German school, and I think that work ethic is something you learn with education. My mother's a single mother and a feminist, and she's always worked. But to be honest, going to work in El Alto changed everything in me. It was really an eye-opening experience.

So, you were with the oil company for two-and-a-half years.

It was about six months in setting up the programs, and then the next two years I did mostly monitoring and reporting of anything that we were gonna do, like taking samples of the soil in the exploration fields. Then in the afternoons, I started tutoring children from the German school in science, math, chemistry. I liked that a lot.

So, even though you took a break from being as community oriented as when you worked with the city environment, you pulled yourself back into it.

Yeah. The name of the company's Petropack. Even there we had opened a couple of fuel storage facilities in El Alto. So, we did a lot of community organizing, making sure that everybody agrees, that people understand what we're doing there, and leading a little bit on social responsibility. I think they saw that as one of my advantages. I already felt comfortable in that area. I wasn't scared of going to work there. That was definitely something that was an advantage for them. and it's something I'm proud of.

What happened after the oil company?

Well, my husband got a job offer from the company and we left Bolivia. We lived in Mexico City, then Colombia, then London and Cameroon. In Cameroon, I taught physics at a college. That was an amazing experience too. And then we came to New Orleans for the last two months of the program. I had already gotten in touch with the previous director of Rebuilding Together, who used to be my neighbor, and now is a city councilwoman for our district, Kristin Palmer. And I told her, "I'm an engineer. I can help you with whatever you want. If you want me to file papers, I'll file papers. If you want me to look at your processes and tell a little advice on efficiency and bottlenecks, I can do that. I can do whatever you want." And we hit it off.

So, you looked into that before looking at a formal job-job?

We didn't even know that we were gonna stay in New Orleans, and everywhere we went, he would go to work. So, I'm not gonna just be sitting by myself. So, I got in touch, and she responded, "The minute you're available just knock on my door," and ever since then it's never stopped.

What did you start out doing?

Well, I wanted to do something that could fit my skills. So, for about the first six weeks I was in every department. I answered phones for the intake of homeowners that were calling looking for help, and I helped the people in finance file paperwork, but I was trying to map the process and asking questions, "What comes before this? And what's the next step?" Then I started working in the field and went to the warehouse. It was a big priority because it's the core of the organization, the field operations. I just started looking at the step-by-step process of all the different components of the organization. As I was doing that, Kristen and I would see each other on the porch every night and start talking about why is this being done like this. It was tough because nobody likes somebody new coming in to question what you're doing.

What was that like for you to be poking around in all these departments with no one really even knowing who you were?

It was hard, but to be honest, that was part of what I liked about it. Everybody knew I was a volunteer. So, you tend to trust. If I had been a hired consultant or if people knew I was being paid, I think that would be more touchy. It was fine, but it's always hard. If you're an outsider, and a foreigner, and a woman, and you're younger than the person you're asking, it definitely creates some tension. I think a lot of people were also worried that they would lose their jobs somehow if I gave a bad report about them.

In discussing what could be done better, some things I didn't understand about the American system were the bureaucracy and how we work with grants. This was really my first experience in nonprofit management.

How did nonprofit management feel different?

When you have a mission, everybody's here for a cause, and that's the best part of it. One of the things that struck me the most was that some people had the attitude that we're getting free money. So, it doesn't really matter how we account for it. I remember asking the supply manager at the time, "How do we know exactly how many materials go to the site? How many nails." And he said, "We don't need to track that. We're a nonprofit." I was kind of surprised by that. But that was the thought. We don't need to be perfect, because we're not generating a profit. When you're in a corporate environment, your goal as a company is to make money. That's what it is. Everybody's a piece of the puzzle, and everybody has a responsibility. You can have the cool responsibilities, or you can have the boring responsibilities, but everybody's part of the puzzle, and everybody's there to insure that, number one, the company doesn't lose money; hence, you want to have safety. I think sometimes what motivates corporations to follow the rules is the fact that they might be fined. But that's why we have systems in place as a government, to prevent those things and to force people to get compliant. I think in the nonprofit environment, the hardest thing for people to understand is where is the money coming from and how we should be the stewards of this money.

So, were people primarily results oriented, like "We had done work on this home or done work on this property"?

There are a lot of results-oriented people, but there are a lot of people that are.... Honestly, I had a person tell me that he was in the nonprofit because he didn't want a real job. He didn't want responsibility. It was the same person that told me he'd been there before me, and therefore he wasn't gonna do what I said.

What did you think about that?

Well, it's a normal attitude from a certain kind of person. You always have people that think that a nonprofit environment is easy. You don't have the big corporate hammer coming down. I think that's also kind of the result of the location of the recovery. You have a lot of dynamos obviously, but you also have people who want to hang out. New Orleans is famous for being the Big Easy, where life is nice and easy, and you don't have to do that much to have a good quality of life. So, I think it attracts a lot of those kinds of people too.

What year were you coming in?

2007, exactly two years after. I came after the second anniversary. When people told me, "Oh, you can volunteer. People are rebuilding," I was asking, "What are they rebuilding? Wasn't that two years ago? Why are they still rebuilding?" I definitely didn't understand the magnitude. And I didn't understand the extent of the problem. Until you work in a disaster recovery situation, you can't really grasp everything that the victims go through.

What did you see when you got here? I remember that when I came in '08 there were still properties where you could see the waterline, and you could still see debris even as you drove into the city.

Yes. I was shocked. I remember having the first tour thinking, "Where are all these people?" It was like all the neighborhoods were abandoned, and you wouldn't see a family in their house for blocks. That's when you start thinking, "How are they gonna send their children to school? How are they gonna get back? Where do you stay if you're gonna try to rebuild?" Everything was destroyed, so everything was affected. But there was an amazing outpour of volunteers.

Back then, we would have 150 every day with a lot of corporate support—A LOT of corporate support. Even until 2008, most of the support was from the private sector, from donations and volunteers coming down. We had many big sponsors. Hearst Magazines was one of our bigger ones. Fannie May and Freddie Mac. The NBA. You always have the first response. You just have all this money, but the people weren't here. It was really hard to find the people that wanted to come back. And even now it's still sometimes hard to figure out: "Do they really want to come back? Are they gonna come back? Or do they want you to rebuild their house because it's part of their personal healing process."

I want to step backward for a second.
What did you find after you finished
evaluating Rebuilding Together?
How did the processes look?

A lot of the issues were mostly about planning. It was very hard to plan, and there was a lot of chaos. For example, I couldn't believe that we couldn't get people to work for us. It was really hard because there were so many subs [subcontractors] flooding the city from out of town, and everybody was desperate to get their house built. You couldn't get a sub to work for you with conditions, timelines, and insurance. If you asked for that, they wouldn't work for you. The demand for workers was so high.

I remember also one of the things that was surprising was the volunteer coordinator on Friday afternoon asking the construction managers, "We have volunteers on Monday, and where are we gonna put them?" I asked, "Everybody knows what's the next step in the house. Why don't we just plan two weeks in advance?" You don't need to plan out the whole year. But nobody really wanted to commit to being accountable and a lot of it was, "These are old houses. The moment that you open the walls, you never know what you're gonna encounter." I think that in a nonprofit environment, everybody wants to save the world, but nobody wants to be responsible when things go wrong. Whereas in a corporate environment, if things go wrong, you get fired and that's just how it works. And here a lot of people feel like they're doing a favor to the organization to work here: "We're gracing you with our presence." A lot of people have that attitude because we pay less. Then when we get a funder, everything was done in a rush. It was more reactionary than a plan, but it was also because of the need. I mean, nobody had time to stop and think and evaluate.

Did people still feel overwhelmed at that time?

Oh my God, yeah! There was too much work. And that's the other thing when you're in a disaster recovery situation: a long-term view and a long-term commitment are critical. If you don't care about what happens in six months because you won't be here, you have a very different attitude.[5]

Does that work institutionally **and** *at a personal level?*

Oh, I think so.

Institutionally in terms of like how you develop the institution and personally in terms of how people take care of themselves?

Absolutely. Everybody wants to be the saint. Everybody wants to save the world. Nobody likes to carry a lot of responsibility. Nobody likes to be the one at fault for something going wrong. But inevitably something will go wrong. You have to have some sort of safeguards to prevent things from going wrong. But you also have to accept that things may go wrong. Like, for example, we got a huge donation of Chinese drywall from Habitat.[6] Today we have twenty-eight houses that we have to redo because of this mistake of taking the contaminated drywall. Of course, we weren't aware. And they weren't aware that the drywall was bad. Nobody's to blame, but who takes responsibility? We had to take responsibility for the homeowners.

Did you have a long-term timeline when you were looking at things from the onset?

You know during those first two months I was mostly focused on the sustainability of the organization. But I wasn't really committed to staying. I didn't even know where I was gonna go next.

So, you were thinking about sustainability as part of your professionalism?

Yeah. As an engineer, one of my teachers always used to say, "Engineers will never be forgiven for their mistakes because their mistakes are visual. You can see the mistakes. If the bridge falls down, everybody will be there to see your mistake, and you'll have to pay for your mistakes." You can't

5. In *Floodlines,* Casey Leigh, a volunteer coordinator with Common Ground, made a similar point regarding working with short-term volunteers. Flaherty et al., *Floodlines,* 100.
6. New Orleans Area Habitat for Humanity.

hide them. It's not like being a politician or even a doctor who can sew the body up and no one knows what happened. When you're in this profession, you can see what went wrong.

Do you think it helped you that you weren't thinking you would be here long term?

No. To be honest, as I started going through these things, the more I wanted to just be here. You fall in love. The hardest one was answering the phones to homeowners in need. Everybody was in FEMA trailers back then, and people were calling and crying. When you hear people that are in need, talking directly to you, and you see it every day, and you're in direct contact with the need . . . I think that changed my mind. I love the city. The architecture is beautiful. It's just a city that people love. And that is a major factor in disaster recovery. You better have a city that people like, or otherwise you might as well move and start from scratch somewhere else. But here . . . the souls of the people. I remember my first Mardi Gras. God. They had the floats with all these flooded houses. I was just not ready to joke about it, but there's something healing about being able to. I guess you have to laugh to not cry—whatever they say, you know?

Yeah. It's a very specific sense of humor.
It's very New Orleans.

Yes! And I think what captivates most people is the city as a whole and the people. It's just so special. Then you learn it was the levee failure and not Katrina that destroyed the city, and you just start wondering all these questions: "Why did they even build these levees in the first place? Who puts another body of water in the middle of your city that's already under sea level?" I really did fall in love with the city and with the mission of the organization. It's a perfect mission. You can't go wrong with "we're gonna help elderly, disabled people who owned their houses get back in their homes." These people have gone through life taking care of themselves, and now they were on a fixed income, in a bad situation through no fault of their own.

So, Rebuilding Together was around before Katrina and had historic preservation in its mission.

It was improving the quality of life of low-income homeowners through home repair and community revitalization. We would work in playgrounds and community centers, but we were mostly volunteer driven. We used to be called the Christmas in October organization. All our volunteers from local corporations and organizations would come together during October. We would have seven teams or eight teams that would help people maintain their houses.

How did you transition from being a
volunteer auditor to being where you are now?

Two things happened. One, I kept talking to Kristen: "What do you think about this? What do you think about that? Why are we not planning for the volunteers? If you know you have these volunteers and you know what houses you're working on, why do we not have a schedule set up to make sure that we are targeting our priorities?" Kristin was the director, and she managed the intake and the field part. She was in direct contact with all these staff. And she felt to really do the duties of a director—to fundraise, to talk about strategy, to plan long-term sustainability—she needed a field operations person. In December our company was supposed to tell us our permanent posting, and they asked my boyfriend, "What if you stayed in New Orleans?" I didn't even need to think about it. I was sold. He was a little disappointed, because back then you just didn't know if New Orleans was gonna make it or not. It was still a gamble. Now we know it made it. We know everything. People came back. The city's not dying. We have other issues, but we know we're back. In 2007, though, we didn't know if anything was gonna be back, and he was worried about his career and what was gonna happen.

I was a tourist. I had a tourist visa, and I was supposed to be here for only two months. That's when we had to start deciding, "Oh, what are we gonna do? I'm not a resident. I don't have a work permit." We thought we were going back to Latin America where we have treaties, and you can work in different countries. That posed a logistical situation. We were planning on getting married the next November, but we had to get it done so I could start my paperwork. The company, which is a British company and has offices worldwide, told my husband, "Well, you're an American and you're in your country. We shouldn't be processing your wife's paperwork." If they had sent us to China or to Brazil, they would have taken care of all that. But if you're in your native country, it doesn't count. That kind of sucked. So, I told Kristen, "You know, my paperwork situation is gonna take maybe six, eight months, but I'm not gonna sit at home doing nothing all day long. I will volunteer but I want the job of the director of field operations. If you like what I do by the time I get my green card, then you can hire me if you have the money." You know, a lot of things were in the air still. Nobody wants to commit to hiring more staff in this kind of growth, but it was a win-win situation because in the worst-case scenario, I wasn't costing the organization anything.

That was a gutsy move.

What was the other option? Sitting at home?

What would you think if someone walked in your office and said, "I'm gonna do this job for you for six months, and I'm gonna do it so well that when you get your funding, you'll want to hire me?"

I'd tell them, "Start tomorrow."

Really?

Yeah. Why not? You don't have anything to lose. By then we had established a bond and people started believing. I think people didn't really believe in me until when we did our Starbucks project. We had 5,000 volunteers. I was the main person organizing the logistics, and once that was successful, everybody was like, "Alright. We'll accept you. We're fine with the situation." In the beginning, nobody knew that I wasn't getting paid. And it was a new position. There were a lot of questions, "Why did this position not get opened to other people that were in the organization?" But I remember we had a warehouse manager who is an older Black guy. He's probably about fifty now. He told me, "I have two daughters, and if my daughters ever got in this situation, I would hope that somebody would support them. So, you can count on me for anything."

Were you able to make processes more efficient once you got to be field operations director?

It's always a work in progress. I think the biggest win of all my time here at Rebuilding Together, all these four years, has been putting into people's minds the fact that if you're doing something today, it doesn't mean you're doing it wrong, but it also doesn't mean we can't do it better, or it doesn't mean that we shouldn't explore other ways to do it. It's a constant process of implementing certain processes. Then you evaluate how you're doing. Sometimes you will implement something that doesn't work, and that's fine too. If you don't try, you'll never know. That was definitely the biggest win. We implemented a lot immediately as I started. I put together a volunteer calendar for the next two months. Some things were easy, and some things were harder, but I think if we hadn't had that transition, if we hadn't had the growth, the processes, and the policies that we have in place today, we couldn't be working with federal grants.

I talked to another organization that got a federal grant early in their development. They were happy about the funds they received, but they weren't prepared for all the detail work that was involved with it, and in some ways, it ended up making their situation worse.

Oh, yeah. It can bring you down. One of the things that I see that shocks me: everybody thinks that federal money is free money. "We're gonna give you a $3 million grant." No private funder says, "Here's $3 million, go ahead and spend it the way you want." Nobody gives you that level of support. You can find that the grant can be the tail wagging the organization because you're so bogged down with what do you need to do and setting everything up. Luckily, in 2008 we started receiving some money from the Salvation Army. and they had a process that was not as stringent but was very similar to a federal grant of qualifying the homeowner. Every funder wants to make sure that whoever is getting this money really needs it, especially the federal government. When the money is public, that gets extrapolated to the extreme. When we started with the Salvation Army, we adopted those things as our regular case management process.

⚜ ⚜ ⚜

AUGUST 21, 2013

I heard yesterday that you're starting your own business.

Oh, who told you that? (*Laughter.*) Well, I did open up a small consulting company when I left Rebuilding Together, and that's how I started working for Land Trust.[7]

How has the transition been?

Pretty seamless. Rebuilding Together and the Louisiana Land Trust had worked together. The Louisiana Land Trust is an organization that was created by the state legislature after Katrina to deal with the homes that were sold to the state. Homeowners as part of the Road Home Program had three options. Option one was to get money to rebuild your house. Option two was to sell your house to the state and relocate within Louisiana, and option three was to sell your house and go wherever you want. Between options two and three, 11,000 homes were sold to the state, and we are the ones that manage all those houses. About 8,000 or 9,000 were demolished. Rebuilding Together with our deconstruction program—where we would go into houses and salvage doors, windows, lumber, etc.—had a partnership with the Land Trust where they would let us go to the houses that they were gonna demolish and salvage all that stuff. So, I had a relationship with them, and when I left, literally the day that I left, they called me and said, "How would you like to be working for us?" I was like, "Well, first, I have to have surgery." I got my tonsils removed so I was out a whole month, and I told 'em, you know, "I'll call you in a month and we can talk. I'm not prepared right now. I just left."

I thought you left partially to
give yourself a little break.

Yes. When I got back in touch with them in January, they were very flexible. They were like, "How about if you just work for us part-time? And you can work your own hours." I started working for them just four hours a day, and that's when I started this little consulting business. Then in September of last year, the person that was in this director of properties position left and

7. Rivero at this time had become the property management and development director of the Louisiana Land Trust.

they offered me her job. By then I think I was kind of ready to go back. It's a lonely life when you don't work.

Right. So, what was going on with you as you ended your time at Rebuilding Together? Were you tired?

Yeah.

When you were still in Latin America and you worked with the president, you said you got a little burned out 'cause you worked Monday to Monday. How did this feel compared to that?

Yeah, and from five a.m. until whenever we were done. That was hard. That was really hard, but this is completely different. I think the hardest part at Rebuilding Together was being the head. Heavy lies the crown they say, and it's true. There were three things that if they would have been different maybe I would have stayed.

One of them was the instability with the city. The city owed us $1.5 million for a year's worth of work. We had a $2.5 million grant from the Housing Department that was supposed to be for one year. By the time the contract was signed, it was two-and-a-half years later. It was a community development block grant. They have their own housing program, and it was from the disaster recovery pot. Right when I took over at Rebuilding Together, the leadership at the city changed. They decided that they were gonna review and reevaluate every contract, but we were already halfway through that year of the grant, and we'd always had this money from the city for twenty-five years. It was a real partnership where everybody was happy. We were happy, and we were doing a lot of work for them. But when the new mayor came in, they stopped everything. Some organizations decided, "Until we have a signed contract, we're not moving. We're not moving a finger." But if you don't move a finger, you don't have any leverage to get your contract signed. It's an egg and a chicken situation. That was really hard. We had to fight a lot to get that contract signed, and we had a lot of money in the street. Also, when people owe you money, you can't work as fast. You have to prevent yourself from running out of money. All the money that we used to float the project was money that we could have received from the city.[8] We could have done double or triple what we were doing, but we didn't even have a signed contract. That was really hard. When they finally signed our contract, they handed me a $1.3 million check.[9]

It was a huge weight off my shoulders, but can you imagine the stress of a year-and-a-half of our CFO saying, "They're not going to sign this contract. We're not gonna get this money. What are we gonna do?" That was just the city. We had a $4 million contract with the state. By the time I left, they had paid us a whole million dollars.

One-quarter of what they owed you?

8. "Floating the project" means carrying debt for a project that is underway while awaiting reimbursement from a granting agency.

9. Several directors mentioned this problem, but I had difficulty determining how this money from the city fit into the more well-reported sources of government funding in the press. In an email exchange from January 2018, Rivero shared that RTNO had received $2.4 million from the city in a Community Development Block Grant (CDBG). She wrote,

The main issue is that the funds are reimbursed after they are spent by the grantee. There is a detailed and complex regulation around these funds, and if any of it is not done correctly, you don't get paid back by the funder.

First, the grantee submits project work-scopes and a budget to the funder, who must approve. Then, as you get the work done, every penny must be documented, and every nail properly procured. For instance, if you want to hire a plumber you need 3 quotes from different plumbers, and of course in order to get the quotes you have to write up a detailed work order with everything the job needs. If it turns out you need more work done on that plumbing job, there is more paperwork to be done, and then the funder must approve the change order.

In addition, CDBG funds have restrictions as to how much money can be used for "admin," which is up to 20%. That doesn't even begin to cover all the upfront "admin" work that needed to be done to take a homeowner from application to project approval, which generally lasted about one year from the time the person came to us to the point where we had the go ahead to work on their house.

Once the project was approved, you hire the contractors (following the bidding process described above), most of whom require 30% advance to start. As work progresses, you pay the contractor and prepare your "reimbursement package" to send to the funder. The funder must approve, inspect the property to ensure the work was done, then (if approved) they would order payment and you'd get a check within 1–2 months. The first reimbursements for us took about 6 months. This is in the midst of excellent relationships with Mayor, city council members, people at HUD, and State people in charge.

At the worst point, we were waiting on reimbursement of $1M from City and $1.2M from State. We actually once got a million-dollar check from the city—a reimbursement of work done for a whole year! We opened a champagne bottle that day.

Well no. They had already been paying us, but there was a mistake made on their part, and they had to stop. Until they reconciled everything, they stopped payments for the whole program, but we couldn't stop construction. I couldn't tell the staff, "Okay, since the state is taking a hiatus, everybody can go home for two months until we figure it out." You can't do that. You can't tell the homeowners, "We're just gonna stop rebuilding your house." You can't tell the volunteers, "Don't come." There are so many moving pieces, and that was really hard. They paid us. We had a signed contract with them. We had a good relationship, but it was still stressful because we had $2.5 million on the street. Then we discovered that Habitat had given us contaminated Chinese drywall for almost forty houses and that we had to rebuild them again.

How did the relationship with Habitat in regard to the drywall start?

My impression is they approached everybody. I was not in the director's position then. When I arrived in 2007, we were already using this drywall. I think after Katrina, Habitat thought they were gonna be building thousands and thousands of houses. So, they wanted all these materials and things, and the story that I heard was that somebody approached them and said, "Hey, we have this huge amount of drywall at some of the warehouses on the port." At the time, it was really hard to get materials. You know the Chinese drywall is throughout the South of the United States—in Florida, Alabama, Mississippi, Louisiana, everywhere—because there wasn't enough local production. So, they bought 120,000 sheets.[10]

10. In an interview, Jim Pate justified Habitat's response to the corrosive drywall as follows:

> We had no legal obligation whatsoever to repair and replace it. I want to say with the exception of One Build in Florida, I think we were the first builder anywhere, of any substance, who took it on and said, "We're gonna do it." And, one of the reasons we did it is because our families had no capacity to get a loan to do it themselves. They didn't have connections. They didn't have that kind of stuff. There was not and never has been any FEMA funding for it or anything. There's no pot of gold that says, "Here's the money for you to take that corrosive drywall out and fix it."
>
> Not only had nobody ever heard of it [corrosive drywall], there was no testing protocol. . . .
>
> As I said, unless I'm badly mistaken, we are one of the first and very few builders, home builders, who have gone in and addressed this issue. And because of the multi-

Did they sell it at reduced cost?

No, they gave it to us for free—120,000 sheets of drywall—and you use about 75 per house; so, you have sixteen hundred houses. They'd had it for a while. Then they realized, "We're never gonna use this." So, they started selling it out of their salvage store to anybody that wanted to buy it, and they started donating it to the nonprofits to rebuild for low-income homeowners. We would fill out a form with the homeowner's name, the address, etc., and we would pick up the drywall.

It was the same with everybody. They gave it to the Mennonites. They gave it to a pastor in the Lower Ninth Ward, and he distributed it on behalf of Habitat. When we discovered this, he called me and was like, "You're the only person that's willing to talk about it." Habitat kept denying it until the bitter end.

Is that where you first heard it?

We heard about it on the news about a year before, because Sean Payton [the coach for the New Orleans Saints football team] had it in his house.[11] We knew that our drywall was Chinese, but most drywall was Chinese, and not all Chinese drywall was bad—that's what everybody kept saying. It was saving us $1,000 per house, which is not a lot, but when you combine fifteen houses, that meant we could bring another family home. We were

---

jurisdiction litigation, I reiterate we didn't have any obligation to go do the work. We chose to do it 'cause we knew our families had no resources to do it. So what we did was take an assignment—any future claim against the drywall manufacturers—and we had that assigned to us, which is very dicey since one of the major ones is owned by the Chinese government. We figured probably it's gonna be all gone, but we chose to do it. There were also evidentiary requirements and everything else. In other words, you had to prove up your claim, and it had to be done house by house. It included things such as a sample of copper wiring, a sample of air conditioning, the coil from an air conditioner, two or three sockets from different places. But the kicker was you also had to take a photo of the back of every piece of sheet rock in the house that reflected the printing on who manufactured it. So we hired an environmental engineering firm that basically for a year-and-a-half, that's all they did."

11. Payton had used Chinese drywall to rebuild his home in Mandeville, Louisiana, which is on the north shore of Lake Pontchartrain, after Hurricane Katrina. The drywall deteriorated, causing electrical and HVAC systems to fail, as well as emitting a sulfurous (rotten eggs) smell that permeates the home. Hinton, "Chinese Drywall Concerns Investigated"; Granger, "Chinese Drywall Cases Settled."

saving every dime that we could. Our construction managers said that the quality wasn't as good, but nothing that's ever free is the best quality. I've never seen anybody give you a beautiful diamond ring that's free, right?

I remember about six months into being director that one of our construction managers calls me. He had bought drywall from Habitat for his house that he was rebuilding for his family. Later he tried to sell the house, and at the inspection, the inspector told him, "This house has Chinese drywall, and it has to be gutted." When he heard that, he called me and said, "Daniela, we have a big problem because I put this same drywall in all the houses that I rebuilt." So, we started testing, and the first house we tested was in Hollygrove.[12] I remember the first homeowner that we told. His house was completed. He was ready. He had his mattress already in the hallway and everything. The problem was that nobody knew exactly what to test for. That was the confusing part. During 2007, 2008, and 2009, the Habitat warehouse was shut down by the EPA. They came down in all these astronaut suits and tested everything, and then they reopened.

So that kind of implies that it's okay.

Yeah, and they sent everybody faxes saying, "Dear Partner, Rest assured, Habitat will continue using this drywall, blah-blah-blah, and you can too if you want." They were all reassuring everybody. They had boxes of this testing and were saying that everything was fine.

Did you guys get to see those test results?

Oh no. I'm an industrial engineer. I went through ten semesters of chemistry. That's what upset me the most, that I should have known to do something. But it never occurred to me that Habitat's gonna give us a product that's contaminated. I assumed they're not gonna lie like that. And it's not like something that you can hide. It's gonna come out. We tested this man's house. We took out the copper wires and saw that they were corroded. And our first question was, "What's the extent? How many houses do we have it in?" For the early houses, some of the records were lost. We had a lot of AmeriCorps and a lot of volunteers that would go pick it up. Everything wasn't as tight as it was later. We ended up having to test maybe like 200 houses.

12. A neighborhood in New Orleans's Seventeenth Ward.

*You guys had built 200 houses since
Katrina at that time?*

We probably had built more, but at the very beginning we weren't using this drywall. There was a point when we started using it, and we started going through the records, "Did we pay a drywall contractor? Did we pay for labor and materials or labor only?" You know, to try to narrow it down.

What a waste of money just to do that.

And time. Imagine the time and the stress of having to tell everybody throughout the organization. Imagine how that affected everybody morally to think, "We're gonna have to undo these perfectly looking houses. We already moved these people in. and now we're gonna move them out. How are we gonna . . . ? Who's gonna . . . ?" What volunteer can you tell, "Come gut this beautifully renovated house in the middle of this devastation." It was just impossible. That was huge. It was horrible. I think if the Chinese drywall wouldn't have been a factor, I wouldn't have been as exhausted and tired.

You all managed to do it without having to shut down?

Yeah, but that meant we had a lot of people in the queue that we couldn't help—people that had been waiting for our help for months or a year. We had to tell them, and that was hard to explain. Mentally it was really, really hard to make our intake staff and the case managers that were working with the people understand, "Okay, Mr. Lars comes first because we put that drywall in his house. Yes, he has a finished, completed house. Yes, we spent $60,000 on his house. But now we have to move him out. You're gonna have to work with him. I understand that you thought we were done." Then you have to tell these people that are in the queue they're gonna have to keep waiting. And all our resources have to go to solve this problem."

Is that one of the toughest things you ever had to do?

Yes, by far. Absolutely.

*It seems like with everything else you had done,
you could feel like it was positive and moving forward
in a certain way, but this was backward.*

Oh yeah. This was a huge setback. Absolutely. I was worried about this person, for example, who had it in his [own] house. He was promoted to the position I'd had, director of field operations. I was concerned: Is he gonna be able to be objective about this because he's going through it? His house got foreclosed. He ended up losing the house. He had to declare bankruptcy. He was going through all this personal stuff, but he was a lawyer. He helped, but it was really hard. There was a big debate on the board about whether we tell the homeowners or wait for them to come to us. Well, if you know you have a problem, you can't really not tell them.

Was the board concerned about liability?

Absolutely. The board. Our national organization. Everybody was concerned. "If they sue us, are we gonna lose it all? What are we gonna do? How are we gonna pay for this?" Don't forget at the time all our money was committed to other projects we had already started. This is not like we were not doing anything, and all of a sudden this happens. No. The wheels were in motion, and we were rebuilding all these houses. We have all this money out on the street, and now we have this huge problem.

Did it help to be part of a national organization?

Not really. The national organization was not very cooperative. As a matter of fact, when this happened. . . . (*She stops and sighs heavily.*) I took over at the end of 2009 and in August of 2010 it was the fifth anniversary of Katrina. We were preparing a huge event, rebuilding fifty houses in Gentilly. Well, we found out about all this in June of that year, and our insurance used to go through the national organization. So, obviously, they have to be informed and everything. Well, the response from them was, "Do not do anything until after this event." And I was telling them, "Well, we can't. It doesn't work like that." They were like, "This is gonna destroy us. It's not just you guys going down; it's everybody going down. Plus, if you go to the homeowner, you're basically accepting culpability." And I was like, "Yeah, but it's our fault! What do you want us to do?" Obviously, we didn't put this in knowing it was bad, but how can you not tell people? You would hear all these horror stories of people getting sick and not knowing what's going on. So, it was like, "How are you asking me to not to do anything until after the event?" Because for them we're not the priority.

What do you feel that you learned from that experience?

Well, I learned that nothing is ever really free. I can assure you that. That was my main lesson. But I felt that when you do the right thing, God helps you.

How do you think Habitat should have communicated this? Because it's clear that at a lot of levels due diligence wasn't done.

Oh, absolutely. But no, to be completely fair, it was such a new problem. I don't even know if they knew that they had a problem in the beginning, and like I said, the EPA came down, they closed them down. But then they let them reopen, you know?

That's a good point.

I don't think they were doing it on bad faith. However, all over the news there were homeowners that bought houses from Habitat saying that they had this Chinese drywall that was making them sick. They had to redo the whole Musicians' Village. They had to redo 120 houses there. But when I approached them, they completely denied it, and that was what upset me. Elizabeth Lyle, the number two person at Habitat, and I were friends. That's what upset me the most. We had a relationship, and we would go to lunch together. And I told her, "Elizabeth, something is wrong." And she was like, "Well, maybe it's not our drywall. Maybe you put some other drywall there." I was like, "No, Elizabeth. I am 100 percent sure that this is your drywall." And you know what she told me? "Maybe it's something wrong with the copper that you're installing." I mean, it was just excuses— ostriches sticking their heads in the sand.

Even though all this stuff was happening in Musicians' Village?[13]

Oh yeah, and then she told me, "No, those people are crazy." And it's true that sometimes you rebuild a house for somebody that's really difficult and

13. Musicians' Village was an area in the Upper Ninth Ward in which musicians Harry Connick Jr. and Branford Marsalis partnered to build more than seventy homes for musicians who had been forced to evacuate because of the hurricane. Ellis Marsalis Center, "About: Musicians' Village"; New Orleans Area Habitat for Humanity. "Musicians' Village."

they'll never leave you alone. I understand. That's also what upset me. In this friendship that we had, we would complain to each other about the difficult volunteer and the crazy homeowner. That's normal.

But that's almost taking advantage of that knowledge.

Absolutely. That was what upset me. She was very condescending and was like, "We don't have a problem." Then I went and told them. I was the one that told everyone. I called Zack from the St. Bernard project.[14] He was like a typical lawyer. He was like, "I don't know what you're talking about. We didn't take anything. We don't know anything." And I told him, "Look. I'm just letting you know that if you took Habitat drywall, it's all bad. You can do what you want with that information. I'm letting you know." I told the Mennonites. I called Thom Pepper.[15] I told everybody because I felt like we can't deny this. I think what Habitat should have done is accepted responsibility like the organization that they were supposed to be and paid for it. And then go to their insurance company and sue the supplier. But not put it on our shoulders.

Right. If it had been taken care of communally,
there might have been a way to come up with a trust
or an amount of money designated for that.

Absolutely. A strategy. And they had the money. That's what upset me the most. They had the money. But everybody manages their own organization, manages the risk differently. And everybody had a different level of morality too.

How is Habitat's relationship to other organizations
at this point?

I have no idea. We had to sue them. We had to enter the class action lawsuit against the manufacturer, and in between that you have to sue everybody that's related. We had to sue Habitat. We sued the manufacturer. We ended up not having to sue our insurance company. Our insurance would only pay out after each house had spent $25,000 on repairs. The new director was

14. Zack Rosenburg was the CEO and cofounder of the St. Bernard Project.
15. Thom Pepper was the executive director of Common Ground.

telling me about six months ago that they just got the first big insurance check for the Chinese drywall. Imagine, almost three years later. I think they gave him like $400,000 or something like that, but it was probably a $2 million, $3 million problem.

So that had to be tough for you, not just in terms of work but emotionally. I remember that you said, if you were still here after 2007, that meant that you were one of us. We were all in it together. This episode really violates that.

Yeah. It was really horrible. It was the worst experience I've had professionally, because of all the factors and the burden of meeting with the homeowners every week. We're talking about elderly people. All the people that we helped needed the help, you know? But they were very understanding. With everyone that would get upset, another one of them would call and be like, "Don't worry, baby. We know you got it. Don't worry." And, I was like, "I really wish I couldn't . . . that I didn't have to worry about. I really wish . . ." I really felt betrayed by Habitat. I felt horrible for our staff. And the remediation was horrible because it was almost impossible to make volunteers understand, "Yes, we're tearing up this house that's really nice and has been rebuilt."

Was it mostly college people still?

No, all kinds of volunteers. But everybody wants to come see the destroyed house that we're gonna bring back to life, right? Plus, people were scared, "What about the health? Is this gonna make us sick?" They had to wear a Tyvek suit, but the drywall is not toxic. It gives out a very low concentration of these hydrogen sulfite fumes. It takes years to even show the problem. So, for you to be there one week and have open windows, doors, it's not like you're in a gas chamber. But at the same time, if you don't know any better, how can I blame them for worrying about their health?

Let me take you back for a second. So, you talked about the difficulty of getting funds from city government and also through the state. How effective are those processes where money is coming from the federal government, and it's supposed

to be distributed to the state of Louisiana or New Orleans?
How effective are those processes of getting [money] from
funders to the folks on the ground doing the work?

It can be an effective process. It's not always horrible. The problem is that it's a reimbursement basis. You have to spend the money, and then you have to send them your paperwork and they go through it. Sometimes the regulations are extremely complex, you know: "You bought a pencil. Did this pencil really need to be bought?" Now you have a $100,000 reimbursement being held up for a 50-cent expense that they're not sure is eligible. You really need a good team of accountants to flow through that.

Is that why larger organizations
like Rebuilding Together and Habitat are, it seems to me,
more able to effectively get and spend money?

Absolutely.

I think Operation Helping Hands did pretty well,
but they had Catholic Charities behind them.

That's why they closed down. The Chinese drywall and the state grant shut them down because they had so much money out on the street.[16]

Yeah. I remember even four years ago they were
waiting for money to come.

Correct. The big advantage that Rebuilding Together had is we had been working with this money for over twenty years. Since the beginning of Rebuilding Together, we'd had a grant from the city. So, we knew the process, and we knew what kind of backup they needed. What really stopped us was our contract not getting signed when we had the mayoral change. If that hadn't happened, things would have flown more smoothly. But organizations that had never dealt with federal money, I can't imagine. . . . Some didn't even have an accountant on staff.

16. See Nolan, "Hurricane Relief Groups are Gutting"; Nolan, "Chinese Drywall Forces"; DeBerry, "Hope Takes a Hit"; Threlkeld, "A Job Well Done."

How do you think things could have been made better
for those smaller groups that wanted to start?
Or do you think that maybe smaller groups shouldn't
be doing this type of thing?

That's a big question, because it's all about capacity and knowledge. And managing bureaucracy is very difficult. For keeping track of what did you send and what are you waiting for, you really need a good team of accountants. When the government's giving you multimillion-dollar grants, people think, "Oh my God! We have this huge amount of free money. It's gonna be easy. It's gonna be great. We're getting millions of dollars." This is a huge misconception. There're so many strings attached. They don't understand that for every cent of those millions of dollars, you're gonna have to provide a backup, you're gonna have to show where it went, you're gonna have to show that it was proved, you're gonna have to show this and that, and blah-blah-blah-blah-blah-blah. Sometimes I think if you don't have the capacity, you're better off not taking the money.

So there needs to be some sort of auditing and
accountability process, but, at the same time,
how much money and hours have to be spent by
organizations to run and manage the grant
instead of doing the actual mission?

Correct, but it's on the government side too. Here at the Louisiana Land Trust, we're funded by the state. Sometimes we ask, "Are we going to spend $10,000 of lawyers and staff time to solve a $200 invoice? Or, are we just gonna let it go? Would we just rather not spend those $200?" We did that a lot at Rebuilding Together, but a big difference is that we had a lot of private funding too. Let's say funders would tell us, "We didn't approve tile to go in this room. We're not gonna pay for the tile. but we'll pay for how much it would have cost to do the wood floors." Okay, well that tile was $2,000. It's holding up $100,000 and it's just one invoice within a big batch of stuff. So. then we would just say, "Okay, make it ineligible and don't pay us for that."

Then we would use other money to cover that. But in that back and forth, they have so long to get back to you. So, then you have to solve the problem. Then they have to accept the solution to that problem. Then they have all this other time to move the thing to the next level. The bureaucracy is sad because so much more could be done if the money could flow freely. But at the same time, organizations have to have the knowledge of managing these grants. It's huge. It's what brings organizations down. If you don't know how to manage this, you're gonna go spend a million dollars, and you'll never get your money back. I think that happened a lot. With this state grant, we were the largest recipients, but St. Bernard Project and several small groups in the Non-Profit Rebuild Pilot Program also got money. The idea was, "Let's give the money to the nonprofits and see what they can do with this since, obviously, other things aren't working out."

What year was this?

This started in 2009 or maybe the beginning of 2010. The state is actually much easier to work with than the city, but they're watching every penny, and the devil is in the detail for these things. I knew of organizations that couldn't even put together a file for a homeowner. How are those people gonna keep track of all this paperwork, of all these invoices and things? One thing for example, with state money, you can't just go out and buy a sheet of drywall. You have to have three quotes and show what you're spending. That makes me feel good because it's my taxpayer money too, right? You don't want your tax money going to people that are buying the most expensive [items] or buying from their little friend, but that requires a huge amount of paperwork and record keeping. Then what happens is basically you stop doing the little work and start hiring out to contractors.

Is that a bad thing?

No. It's not a bad thing, but you're probably spending 30 to 35 percent more than you could spend if you were able to manage it in-house—if you were buying the materials yourself, if you were hiring an electrician, a plumber, instead of hiring a general contractor to do it. Every general contractor's giving you their 20 percent profit margin within the bill.

That's interesting, 'cause another director was saying that part of what they want to do is work with more contractors so that they don't have to do the work the contractor would do in terms of picking the best materials.

And then they could use their volunteers to give man-hours
to the things that volunteers can do. In other words, make
sure the contractor's doing like electricity or plumbing,
and use volunteers to do things like paint or carry stuff
from the truck to the home. But you're saying that there's
still a cost that built into that.

Oh yeah. The contractor's doing work, right? They're not a nonprofit. They're not gonna work for you at no profit. (*Laughter.*) Obviously, if the contractor's charging you $100, $20 of those $100 is his profit. The difference between Rebuilding Together and other organizations was they didn't have the capacity. They didn't have the staff. They didn't have a plumber and an electrician on staff like we did. Rebuilding Together had a general contractor's license. So, it's very different. We had the capacity, but at the same time it's kind of ironic. Because I say, "I want to rebuild this house." I bid it out and then you come back, and the best price is $100. I pay you $100, and you don't have to tell me what sheetrock you used, right? I could do it for $70 but I'd have to explain every single nail that I buy. Why I bought it. Where I bought it. What the other prices were.

What's your sense of what's going on with the city now?
I heard the phrase "post-Katrina" like a few times
in the news, and I saw it in the paper here.
So, is this the new normal now?

I feel like we're in a pretty good place, and I feel very hopeful. I think there's still a lot of issues, but these issues were there before Katrina. I think that the big, silver lining of Katrina has been that it gave a huge influx of funds, and a lot of this money is still being spent. How many times can you really rebuild your whole city, your infrastructure, your schools? I feel like it also made a lot of leadership emerge from the neighborhoods, from the grassroots. I feel like every day is better. I see the projects. I feel very hopeful about the future. The school system is getting better. It took shutting everything down. and that takes its toll too. Many times in places that I've been when you're trying to solve a problem you say, "What we need is just to fire everyone. We need to start brand-new." I feel like Katrina kind of provided that for the city and also brought in a huge influx of new people.

The population had been declining for a while before Katrina. It's not a post-Katrina issue. But I feel like it brought a lot of innovation, entrepreneurship, opportunity.

I think that money could have been managed much better. That momentum that the money generated could have been much bigger if it had been managed correctly. But at the same time, it's like being in the eye of the storm. It's very hard to see clearly what the next step is and all the consequences. I used to have a book of problems when I was a teenager: "We have problem 'A,' and these are the possible solutions. I want you to tell me five consequences that are gonna be negative about this solution." But it's really hard to, and until you implement "A," you don't really know what's gonna happen.

What would you feel like would have been more effective guidance? If you could go back and set up some sort of oversight, what do you think you would have liked it to be?

Well, when you have a disaster situation, you're spending public money, but we need some sort of waiver on how that money gets spent, at least in the very beginning. I think the key thing in a disaster recovery situation is how well you administer the early response. From there, things will either spiral up or down.

I'm not saying just open the floodgates, spend the money, and do whatever it takes, but it's too hard to spend this money, especially when you're in a situation where your city's empty, where you don't have schools, and where you don't have infrastructure. How are you even gonna bid out contracts to be able to spend this money? I think if I were king of the world, I think I would have a group of experts with experience on the ground. For example, we've gone to Newark to help with the Hurricane Sandy recovery and talked to people about how to manage these grants.

Okay, so with experience in disaster work?

Yeah, managing these monies and knowing what worked and what didn't work. We had Ed Blakely at the beginning, who was the disaster czar, the genius, and he turned out to be just another disaster in and of itself.[17] Now this

17. Mayor Ray Nagin appointed Ed Blakely as the executive director of recovery management in 2007. Blakely left in 2009 after what had been universally described as a disas-

is a little autocratic view of mine, but if I were able to do whatever I wanted, I would have a big set of people that could relocate to the city and manage the disaster. Don't hand it over to the city because the city's suffering. The city government, the municipal governments are suffering, you know?

They need someone to go to.

Correct. Their own people don't have houses. They are victims of the disasters. So, it's very hard and totally subjective. If you're the mayor and you live in neighborhood A, what neighborhood do you think that they're gonna put the focus on? If you're the one working on these recovery efforts, it's really hard to look objectively. I think there should be some sort of local and national team that can get meshed together and set up a plan, phase A: "We're gonna rebuild these ten schools in the next six months, and we're gonna bid it out immediately." Instead of having to write action plans. It just takes so long. For [Hurricane] Sandy, we were in New York in March of this year. Sandy hit last year in September. Seven months and they were just finishing their action plan.[18]

The problem is the process is too hard. The people that are working at city government don't have disaster relief experience. You have to train them. There's a learning curve. Now, of course, with Sandy, you don't have the same devastation that we had here. So, the urgency's not the same. People here just decided, "Okay, we're gonna put up our own street signs. We're not gonna wait," because you couldn't.

Eighty percent of the city was underwater.

Exactly. So, people just decided, "Okay, we're just gonna get it done." It was very grassroots, but it was also because of the situation. If you're not in a situation where everything is destroyed, people just move to another family member's house, or they rent, and then they just wait it out.

So, Phase 1 would be something along the lines of getting people who have experience in disaster relief together with

---

trous tenure in the job, during which he called the residents of New Orleans "buffoons." "Ed Blakely, Former New Orleans Recovery Chief"; Hammer, "Ed Blakely Lambastes New Orleans."

18. Hurricane Sandy hit in October 2012.

some members of the community and, say, you have a
budget that's already set for the whole process, but you
allocate some portion of it that's very flexible at the outset.

Yeah. Correct. Due to the priorities.

Because what you can do then is you can give people
hope faster.

Yeah. That's why I'm saying that the beginning is the key. Because if you don't show people who have been relocated that something is happening . . .

Families aren't gonna want to come back.

Exactly. They shut down the schools after Katrina. Power plants, your infrastructure, streets, lights, for example, all of that is important but it's not the number one priority. You need your schools, your hospitals. You need that done immediately. I'm not saying we're gonna rebuild every single school in the city in the first six months, because you also want long-term planning. You want to know who's coming back. It's a chicken-and-egg situation in the beginning, but I think if you had a team who could have a pot of money that can be spent in a more discretionary way . . .

With much less bureaucracy of filling out
multiple paperwork.

Correct, just get it done.

8. Motivation

THE MAKING OF A
LONG-TERM VOLUNTEER

I knew that I wanted to return to the city that made me fall in love
with service, no matter what. I'd only been here twice. I'd only
been here for two weeks total, but it just made that much of an
impact on me that I knew that this is the place that I wanted to
be, and I had to at least give it a try and see if I liked it or else I
would never know. I was definitely actively searching for a way
to get back. I also knew that there was still a lot of work to be
done, and I felt that I can't do a lot, but I can do my small part.

—Alyssa Provencio, volunteer coordinator with Rebuilding Together New Orleans

When I volunteered with Operation Helping Hands (OHH) during the
spring break of 2008, I was struck by what I saw around me. At OHH alone,
there were more than a dozen volunteer teams being led by people barely
older than the college students I had just been teaching the week before.
Each evening at the large communal dinners we shared, I saw Americans
from across the country breaking bread together and feeling good about
their contributions, however small, to the city's recovery. Moreover, the
apparent abundance of volunteers from other organizations crisscrossing
the city hinted at the immense scale of the efforts that were occurring all
around us.

Perhaps in that imperceptible way that the universe can guide you to
exactly where you need to be, what I was witness to at that time coincided
perfectly with my own long-held personal interests. As a scholar, I had
sought to understand what motivated ordinary people to become involved
in events that would later be seen as phenomena of historical importance—
particularly those phenomena pervaded by race and class. This question
led me to explore Americans' participation in early twentieth-century racial nationalist movements and the 1919 Chicago Race Riot, as well as the

efficacy of electoral politics for civil rights change in the mid-twentieth century. In college, I was a student leader, a volunteer in the Boys and Girls Clubs, and a congressional intern and was very active in the 1992 presidential campaign. Though I felt devoted to service, this activity decreased during graduate school and after my appointment as an assistant professor. It was not until after I earned tenure that I was able to resume my commitment to making a more tangible impact on the greater good by leading mission trips, working with unhoused persons, and distributing food to disadvantaged families in Chicago. Despite this work, I remained unsatisfied, and after witnessing the level of commitment I saw in New Orleans, I was drawn to it, wondering, "Who exactly are the people behind all of this? What has inspired them to put aside a good salary to spend months guiding college kids, retirees, and church groups in building and repainting homes in extreme heat and humidity?"

These questions sparked my interest in recording the experiences of the city's long-term volunteers, who differed from the much more numerous short-term volunteers like me who tended to come in stints of one week or shorter. That interest grew into a focused study and assessment, including research into the history and background of New Orleans itself, immersion into the scholarship of volunteerism, and analysis of the interviews my students and I conducted that are represented here. This study is the result of that work. Overall, it finds that long-term participants in New Orleans's recovery possessed attributes that aligned fairly consistently with those that scholarship shows to be predictive of volunteering. Most prominently, our interviewees uniformly possessed a history of activism or civic engagement before their commitment to New Orleans.

For example, during college Adrian Manriquez protested U.S. foreign policy by fighting for the closure of the School of Americas. After graduating, Caitlin Reilly "moved into an intentional community in a Presbyterian church on the Upper East Side of Manhattan to do a social justice internship with a homeless outreach program." Reilly's future supervisor at Bayou Rebirth, Colleen Morgan, began her career as an environmental reporter in Litchfield County, Connecticut, where she exposed ecological threats posed by real estate development. Jay Welch and Daniela Rivero both attempted to fight corruption and advance the causes of the less fortunate from the inside by working in local government. Lastly, it was long-standing spiritual beliefs that drew Fred Franke to leadership in his New Orleans church community and Robert Goodman to advocate for prison reform. Both men found themselves called to lead once again in the aftermath of Katrina.

Despite the compelling nature of these stories, they are not unique: the vast majority of participants in this study came to New Orleans with significant personal histories of giving to others. Their time spent giving aid to New Orleans represented just part of an ongoing narrative of service.

Thus, the experience of the participants in this study and in existing research demonstrates that volunteering within normal contexts largely predicts who will volunteer within the more extreme context of disaster recovery and who will commit to service for a long-term period. To better understand the attributes that our volunteers shared, we can begin by looking at what scholars generally agree are the individual characteristics that correlate with volunteering under regular circumstances. According to Wilson and Musick's integrated theory of volunteer work, which is perhaps the most frequently cited model for volunteer motivation, the typical volunteer is well educated, somewhat religious, married, employed, and a member of one or more civic organizations.[1] Although the data indicate that altruism correlates with volunteerism, Wilson and Musick argue that individuals can volunteer for both selfish and altruistic reasons: "Volunteers give their time freely for the benefit of others. This brief characterization does not deny that benefits may accrue to the donor; nor does it rule out altruistic motives. However, this definition does not require us to establish a 'return' on the gift or a 'right motive.'"[2]

This definition is a cornerstone in the intellectual foundation of this study. The subjects in this project could not be considered volunteers if a total absence of pay were a necessary condition. Although many started as unpaid volunteers, the work affected them so much that they transformed their lives to contribute to the recovery for the long term. Yet, none were independently wealthy people who could do work for free: most received at least minimal pay for their efforts. Indeed, as can be seen from several of this book's featured interviewees, the tension between the gratification

1. Dass-Brailsford et al., "Paying It Forward," 35; Michel, "Personal Responsibility," 633, 638.
2. Wilson and Musick, "Who Cares?" 695.

they found in the work and the struggles they faced in making ends meet was a common theme.

Returning to the integrated theory of volunteer work, Wilson and Musick argue that the likelihood of volunteering emerges from differences in human, social, and cultural capital. First, they propose that volunteer work is based on several premises. "Volunteer work," they argue, "is a productive activity." As such, a market exists for volunteer work, and some who do it can make the transition into paid labor. Volunteers, therefore, need certain qualifications—human capital—to be allowed to do the work. Markers of socioeconomic status, such as education and work experience, for instance, qualify people to volunteer and make them attractive to volunteer organizations.[3]

Wilson and Musick contend that "collective action" drives the next category—social capital—in that the decision to volunteer is influenced as much by "what other people are thinking and doing as by what you are thinking and doing." Therefore, having large social networks—through circles of friends, work associates, and membership in voluntary organizations—can expose and connect individuals to volunteer opportunities.[4]

Finally, Wilson and Musick claim that volunteerism correlates strongly to an individual's cultural capital or altruism. They write that the "volunteer-recipient relationship is an ethical one" and that volunteer work requires people to give their time to others. Although it is possible that some may use "ethical language" to mask selfish motives, "we have no right to dismiss as rationalizations of material interests, people's statements of commitment to ideas of justice, fairness, caring and social responsibility."[5]

Involvement in religion is typically one form of cultural capital and is one of the strongest predictors of volunteerism, just behind one's level of education. Still, unlike education, which correlates relatively directly with volunteerism, religion's association is more nuanced. Although scholars

3. Wilson and Musick, "Who Cares?" 695; St. John and Fuchs, "The Heartland Responds to Terror," 399.

4. Wilson and Musick, "Who Cares?" 695; St. John and Fuchs, "The Heartland Responds to Terror," 399.

5. Wilson and Musick, "Who Cares?" 695; St. John and Fuchs, "The Heartland Responds to Terror," 399.

agree that religion's predictive power also has to do with social capital—the connections and opportunity to volunteer through religious networks and organizations—they disagree about the extent to which the amount of cultural capital (i.e., intense religiosity) leads to the participation of the religious in volunteer efforts.[6] Whatever the case may be, it does appear that religion motivated high numbers of short-term volunteers to come to New Orleans and for many more people to donate to the cause. According to Vincanne Adams in *Markets of Sorrow,* more than $700 million and hundreds of thousands of volunteers came into New Orleans through religious organizations:

> Rates of church involvement in the recovery were unparalleled, with reported numbers that were beyond expectations. Within two years, 28,000 volunteers served under the recovery programs of the United Methodist Storm Recovery Center alone, which served more than 32,500 clients and brought in almost $30 million in in-kind donations. The United Methodist Committee on Relief raised a record $66.5 million in gifts and created an unprecedented consortium of volunteer groups called Katrina Aid Today. It also received funds that were managed by or funneled through FEMA, and which were originally donated by religious groups across the country. By the end of 2006, Katrina Aid Today had provided assistance to approximately 90,000 people. The more locally based Louisiana United Methodist Disaster Recovery Ministry stated that more than 40,000 volunteers had been hosted by 2010 and that over half of their volunteers had come back more than once.
>
> The Southern Baptists reposted almost 17,000 volunteers, gutted 600 homes, and provided reconstruction work for churches: it had cleaned out three, rebuilt another five, had fifteen under construction, and had eighteen still on its list waiting for assistance. Southern Baptists estimated that 30,000 Baptists had volunteered in the New Orleans area. Presbyterian Disaster Assistance (PDA) raised more than $20 million in donations and sponsored 31,350 volunteers who gave more than a million hours of service;

6. Dass-Brailsford et al., "Paying It Forward," 30; Garland et al., "Social Work with Religious Volunteers," 256; Lam, "As the Flocks Gather," 41, 405, 406, 411–412, 415, 420; Oesterle et al., "Volunteerism during the Transition to Adulthood," 1126–1128; St. John and Fuchs, "The Heartland Responds to Terror," 399, 411.

long-term volunteers gave another 70,520 hours of service. The PDA volunteers worked on 3,380 homes and completely rebuilt 565 homes.

Although their churches were possibly the most damaged, Catholics responded quickly to Katrina with at least $7 million in direct survival assistance to more than 700,000 people. It also established community centers to provide emergency assistance and set up a clinic in a downtown hotel to immunize, treat, and counsel first responders. Its 11,500 volunteers gutted 1,800 homes and organized a coalition of faith-based groups called Providence Community Housing with the goal of bringing back 20,000 displaced victims and by restoring and developing 7,000 homes over a five-year period.

Of what was reported from the top ten private charities involved in Katrina relief, six were faith-based, with the Salvation Army raising $336.0 million; Catholic Charities USA, $142.2 million; United Methodist Committee on Relief, $69.6 million; International Aid (a Christian Relief/ Mission organization), $50.5 million; Feed the Children (a Christian, nonprofit relief organization headquartered in Oklahoma City), $47.1 million; and Habitat for Humanity (with Baptist Crossroads), $82.0 million.[7]

Religion appears to have played a minor motivating role for those in this study, although scholarly arguments emphasizing the importance of volunteers connecting their service to their personal religious beliefs are illuminating.[8] Those rare participants who connected their work explicitly to a religious motivation, such as Fred Franke, articulated a Christian spirituality that called for action. Take, for example, the testimony of David Harms, who began his long tenure in relief work as a volunteer in the Houston Astrodome in 2005. The following summer, he went to Pass Christian, Mississippi, with Mennonite Disaster Services and then landed in New Orleans in October 2006. Within a year, he had become a volunteer coordinator with Operation Helping Hands, and at the time of his interview in 2011, he was a special projects coordinator with Catholic Charities, tasked with remediating homes contaminated by toxic drywall. When asked about

7. Adams, *Markets of Sorrow,* loc 2323–2336.
8. Garland et al., "Social Work with Religious Volunteers," 256.

his best memories of working in the recovery efforts, Harms told stories of seeing God working through the volunteers without their even knowing it was happening:

Well, one of my favorite stories was a house that we had been working on. This is one of the first houses that we rebuilt, and it was a bigger house, and so it took us a long time. I think we were probably working on it for about ten months altogether. And during the whole time that we were working on it, there was a tree that was growing out of the neighbor's yard that was kind of hanging precariously over the house. So, it seemed like at any time we might have a thunderstorm that brought the tree down and took part of the house with it. But it was growing up through this chain-link fence, and it was hanging over the house. It wasn't something that was going to be very easy to take out. and we didn't necessarily have funding for it—I mean we didn't have funding to hire an arborist to come in and take it out. And then in the last month of finishing up that project we got a group of volunteers from New Hampshire that included two retired Forestry Service workers that had spent their entire careers taking out trees with chainsaws, and they did a beautiful job of it. So, I think there were a number of different things like that where it was just clear that there was a greater power that was kind of directing some of the work that was happening rather than any of us on the staff.

And then Harms shared this story:

This was back in Mississippi, and it wasn't when I was there, but there was a story going around the circles at Mennonite Disaster Services. Apparently, they had been asked to put a roof on a house one day and had gotten the address wrong. And so, they went out and put a new roof on this other house, and it turned out that it was a man in a really desperate situation. He was coming back to his house and had planned to kill himself at his house. Then saw that he'd gotten a new roof, and it was sort of the infusion of hope that he needed.

I think they were both examples of things where it seemed like God was there helping us and multiplying our efforts. It really felt like we were doing the Lord's work and that there was an opportunity for us to be the hands and feet of Jesus by serving in a way that the community needed.[9]

Another relatively rare form of religious-oriented testimony was that of Robert Goodman in chapter 4. Recall that Goodman was an ex-offender who had educated himself in prison, where he also became an activist for prisoner rights. After his release from prison, he moved to Texas to rebuild his life and to advocate for criminal justice reform. Tragically in 2007, New Orleans police shot and killed his brother, who was unarmed and mentally disabled. Goodman subsequently returned to New Orleans, where he became the director of organizing with Safe Streets/Strong Communities, "a post-Katrina community-based group of people like him who have experienced harassment, discrimination, and brutality by the police and justice system."[10] Goodman frequently traced his work in New Orleans back to his time in prison and saw it as God preparing him for what was to come. Consider this bit of testimony that did not make it into the edited interview: "It's like I tell folks who praise or thank me for the things, 'Believe it or not, it's nothing but God because I ain't that smart.' I know He was in the mix of all of this 'cause everything I touch turns to gold. He was just saving me for this thing, you know?"[11]

Where Goodman cited God as the source of his accomplishments as an activist, pre- and post-Katrina, Fred Franke sought to use the devastation wrought by the storm as an opportunity to redeem Christianity in the eyes of Americans whom he perceived as decreasingly valuing the church as part of their lives. Franke began with an account of his redemption from a church full of "Phariseeism" to a small, diverse, broad-minded church—an experience he describes as "going from the storms into a quiet garden." His opening story, even the specific wording, foreshadows the remainder of his account. During his harrowing evacuation from New Orleans, Franke was once again transformed by God, whom he believes laid the task on him to rebuild church communities in the city, which he began only weeks after the storm. By the time Franke gave his interview in 2010, he had woven the

9. Harms, interview.
10. Voice of the Experienced, "Robert Goodman."
11. Goodman, interview.

"Phariseeism" he had experienced in his personal history into a broader picture of the decline in church membership across the United States, framing the work of Operation Nehemiah as a constructive and nonjudgmental way to bring people back to God.[12]

Despite the power of these religiously centered narratives and despite the presence of tens of thousands of short-term volunteers who came into New Orleans with religious organizations, religion did not emerge as a major motivating factor in this study of individuals engaged in *long-term* work. Contrast Goodman and Franke's testimony regarding their personal experiences to this observation about long-term volunteers in Operation Helping Hands by former OHH crew leader Adrian Manriquez: most long-term volunteers were "agnostic about" religion.[13] Manriquez's perception corresponds with scholarship that reveals a noticeable absence of religious motivation for most interviewees. Even though hundreds of thousands of short-term volunteers came to New Orleans through membership in religious networks, as shown by Lam's research,[14] Manriquez claimed that many of them came to New Orleans "to have a good time"; this matches the observations of many participants in this study, including Caitlin Reilly, Colleen Morgan, and Daniela Rivero. Finally, his assertion of an "agnostic" attitude among long-term staffers in volunteer organizations reflects scholarship's lack of consensus about the connection between religion and volunteering.[15]

Although this study does not find that religion was a prominent motivating factor for those who dedicated themselves to the recovery long term, many other traits of long-term volunteers noted in the scholarship do match their individual profiles. A desire to act out one's values, for example, which was found by a 1996 study to be the most important motivation for volunteering, was routinely expressed by the long-term volunteers.[16] The life histories of participants who were older than twenty-five

12. Franke, interview.
13. Manriquez, interview.
14. Lam, "As the Flocks Gather," 41, 405.
15. Lam, "As the Flocks Gather," 41, 406.
16. Garland et al., "Social Work with Religious Volunteers," 256; Oesterle et al., "Volunteerism during the Transition to Adulthood," 1144.

demonstrated that their work in New Orleans represented an acting out of values they had held long before the storm; for instance, Colleen Morgan came with a background in investigative and environmental journalism, Jay Welch had a long career in public interest law, and Daniela Rivero had extensive experience in community development.[17]

A close ally of Rivero, Kevin Fitzpatrick came to the work from a career in a helping profession, which was not uncommon for older volunteers. He shared that his background played a major role in his work in OHH, where he started as a volunteer coordinator and eventually became executive director. Before the storm, Fitzpatrick had been a teacher at New Orleans's Catholic De La Salle High School. With a degree in pastoral studies from Loyola University New Orleans, Fitzpatrick taught classes on conflict management, and these skills became very important in his OHH work. In response to a question about his toughest moments, Fitzpatrick indicated that he spent a significant amount of time dealing with internal difficulties:

Now what has hit home is we have seventeen long term volunteers and they're not perfect; some of them bring a lot of baggage. So far this year—you know, we think of years starting like academic years—so far this year, we haven't had too many problems, but we have a lot of people that had a lot of baggage. They couldn't live with each other, and they didn't really perform well at work, and I had to intervene a lot with that. And that's tough to help these young people become adults and maybe help them make the decision that they don't really belong with the program.[18]

In the same breath, Fitzpatrick also noted difficulties with OHH's Youth Builds program, funded by a Department of Labor grant. In this program, OHH taught construction skills to at-risk youth while providing them with resources to obtain their GED. Although Fitzpatrick expressed pride in the program, he noted that some of its participants, many of whom were people of color, had been caught stealing equipment from OHH and that these thefts led to significant racial tensions within OHH:

17. Morgan, interview, July 06, 2010.
18. Fitzpatrick, interview, November 20, 2011.

The Youth Builds Program, even though I described it pretty glowingly earlier, these are average kids. They've done some really horrible things. They've stolen a lot of property from our volunteers and that—that creates a lot of tension. Mostly they've stolen bikes, but they stole a car from one of our volunteers. So that doesn't help. I mean it's good that we're doing this with Youth Builds, but it carries a lot of risk too, and there's tension there between our staff and our long-term volunteers in the Youth Builds Program. We're working on trying to intermediate that, but it's not been easy.[19]

Elsewhere, Fitzpatrick, like other interviewees, indicated that long-term volunteers and staffers like himself were lucky if they received any training at all and that it was his background in pastoral management and conflict negotiation that allowed him to deal with these circumstances:[20]

Well, there's not a lot we can do like with stolen property, but we're working on relocating Youth Build to another location. So, they don't have access to tools anymore and they don't have access to our whole staging area, and they don't have much interaction with our volunteers. We've decided to reduce that from our volunteer program, which is really the heart of what we do. Fortunately, I wear a lot of different hats and I have some pretty good conflict management experience, so I've been able to deal with that and that's one of the other things, to try to deal with personnel issues when they come up. I do a lot of coaching. We have a lot of young adults on our team that have to deal with this directly, and I try not to rescue them. I just coach them and help them to deal with the long-term volunteers or wherever the conflict is. If it's their fight, then I usually just help them come up with a plan on how to deal with it.[21]

In contrast to older participants who came to the work with experience in community development, a helping field, or a profession, young adults who participated in this study did not fit into the integrated theory quite as well. The integrated model actually predicts a drop-off in volunteering

19. Fitzpatrick, interview, November 20, 2011.
20. Ross, interview; Ryan, interview.
21. Fitzpatrick, interview, November 20, 2011.

as young adults become preoccupied with the "social freedoms of the single and childless life." This study found the opposite: even though most of the young adult participants were single, not particularly religious, and had minimal work experience, their years in New Orleans marked a peak in their volunteerism, rather than a drop-off.[22] Nevertheless the young adults in this project did share several characteristics—such as a history of activism whether through service learning, personal activism, or legacy volunteering—that are linked to volunteering by other theories.

Scholars have found, for example, that volunteering runs in families—a phenomenon they call "legacy volunteering." Mustillo, Wilson, and Lynch write that parents act as role models and "pass on the socioeconomic resources needed to do volunteer work."[23] Several subjects in this study pointed to their parents' and sometimes their grandparents' activism and community orientation as being important to their development.[24] For example, Mike Ellis of Love Knows No Bounds recalled that his parents were active in the civil rights movement and protests against the Vietnam War.[25] We also saw this in the case of Caitlyn Reilly, whose parents met through community organizing in the Bronx in the 1970s; unlike other white activists who had worked in the Bronx in those years, they continued to make the Bronx their home.[26]

Moreover, Reilly's later transition into wetlands restoration in New Orleans is not surprising, given findings that volunteering is a "stable behavior" that continues from adolescence into young adulthood and that a form of volunteering that has been proven particularly powerful in stimulating civic engagement in young adulthood is service learning.[27] Service learning is "a form of experiential education in which students engage in activities that address human and community needs together with structured opportunities intentionally designed to promote student learning and development."[28] It is distinguished from other forms of experiential

22. Wilson, "Volunteering," 226.
23. Mustillo et al., "Legacy Volunteering," 66, 530.
24. Reilly, interview; Eustis, interview; Pate, interview.
25. Ellis, interview.
26. Reilly, interview; Eustis, interview.
27. Oesterle et al., "Volunteerism during the Transition to Adulthood," 1141, 144.
28. Armstrong, "Developmental Outcomes of Service-Learning," 1–10; Astin et al., "How Service Learning Affects Students," 144.

learning, such as volunteerism, community service, internships, and field education by its "intention to benefit the provider and the recipient of the service equally, as well as to ensure equal focus on both the service being provided and the learning that is occurring."[29]

Although some activists and intellectuals have questioned the efficacy of service learning, asking whether it merely allows privileged young people to patronize needy populations, studies have shown that it can have substantial positive effects in multiple areas, including academic performance, values development, self-efficacy, leadership, choice of a service career, and continued engagement in service after college.[30] Indeed, multiple project participants had service learning experiences that shaped their civic orientation and led to their long-term work in New Orleans.

Perhaps the volunteer who most exemplified the positive effects of service learning is Alyssa Provencio, a volunteer coordinator at Rebuilding Together New Orleans and a person whose experiences volunteering in New Orleans during her sophomore year of college led her to choose a career that would bring her back and enable her to become engaged in the post-Katrina recovery process. Provencio represents a large portion of the younger interviewees whose service learning experiences or involvement in social justice and leadership in college played a role in steering them toward New Orleans.

At the time of the storm, Provencio was a sophomore at Kansas State University living what she called a "normal" college life. As someone minoring in Leadership Department courses, she had already organized several projects, such as canned food drives and working with needy families. When the storm hit, Provencio and other Leadership students began planning an alternative spring break to help in the recovery effort. This was a life-changing moment for Provencio:

There was an alternative spring break group for the Kansas State Leadership Department. They do alternative spring breaks all over the country—you know, helping with Habitat for Humanity, serving food in homeless shelters. They usually pick three or four places to go each spring break as

29. Borden, "Impact of Service-Learning on Ethnocentrism," 172.
30. Astin et al., "How Service-Learning Affects Students," 144; Pompa, "Service Learning as Crucible," 68.

an alternative for people who want to do community service as opposed to taking a trip to Cancun and partying with your friends. After Hurricane Katrina hit and the relief effort started happening, we quickly got together a group of students. I was a part of our Leadership Department as a student, and they had this. . . . I mean, a lot of schools right now have alternative spring break programs.

So, we immediately began plans for sending a group of students down to New Orleans to assist with the relief effort, like a lot of people were doing. I don't think that when I originally signed up to volunteer here that I knew how much it was going to impact my life later and how much of a life-changing experience it really was going to be when I came here. I was a very involved student, you know? So, I wanted to get involved as much as possible.

I was helping coordinate the actual logistics of the trip and not really worried too much about the implications of what we were actually going to do. And then when I got here, that's kind of when it all hit home for me—the work we were doing, the people that we were helping, and just the vibrancy of the city.

After this trip, Provencio and four other students started a group called Building on Breaks. Although the alternative spring break program allowed students to choose from a range of places where they could volunteer during spring break, Provencio and her classmates wanted to establish an organization "specifically geared towards coming to New Orleans" throughout the academic year. They also wanted the volunteers they took to New Orleans to act as ambassadors, spreading awareness of what was happening in New Orleans to Kansas State and their home communities:

I think that for us it was a lot about, going home, telling your friends, telling your family, telling everybody that you can about what's going on here. The state of the city was still terrible, and it's been eight months out. And they're not getting the help that they need. They're not getting the support that they need. It's gonna be years and years and years before it's even close to what it was prior to. So, we would go around trying to get people involved to come down. We came up with our presentation, and we would go to anyone that would let us speak and give presentations on what we did there and try to recruit people for the next break. I served as the Secretary and the Recruitment Chair.[31]

This information strategy worked very well. During the following year, they took fifty students. In Provencio's last year as a student, Building on Breaks had more than 200 applicants and brought 75 students to engage in rebuilding efforts in New Orleans.[32]

The experience of volunteering in New Orleans was indeed life-changing for Provencio. Unlike many young adults in this project who came to New Orleans through a somewhat haphazard process, Provencio chose courses and early career opportunities that would best prepare her to do public service work in New Orleans. Within her major, hotel restaurant management, she focused on social event planning for philanthropic and fundraising events. After graduating, she tried to get back to New Orleans through Teach for America but was assigned to Phoenix. Four months in, she found Teach for America unsatisfying, and she took on a job as a volunteer coordinator in Phoenix while seeking opportunities to help in New Orleans:

I took a job as a volunteer coordinator, because I wanted to be able to share my love for public service with others, and it combines my event planning experience. I was there for a year and then as soon as I found a position here in New Orleans for a volunteer coordinator position. I knew that it was for me.

I knew that I wanted to return to the city that made me fall in love with service, no matter what. I'd only been here twice. I'd only been here for two weeks total, but it just made that much of an impact on me that I knew this is the place that I wanted to be, and I had to at least give it a try and see if I liked it or else I would never know. I was definitely actively searching for a way to get back. I also knew that there was still a lot of work to be done and I felt that I can't do a lot, but I can do my small part.

31. Provencio, interview.
32. Provencio, interview.

When asked what it was like for her having been in New Orleans as a "volunteer" and then getting a job as a volunteer coordinator, Provencio replied:

> It's kind of cool. Because the reason why I took my first volunteer coordinator position in Phoenix was because I wanted to share my love of public service with others. So, when I became a volunteer coordinator in New Orleans, not only was I able to share my love of public service with others and get them excited about coming here but also share my love of New Orleans. I am able to be like, "I was in your shoes. I was in college. I wanted to make a difference, and now I'm able to coordinate groups that are bringing people down for the first time." It's satisfying knowing that you're playing some small part in getting more people down here to help.[33]

Although somewhat unusual, Provencio's evolution from *participating* in an alternative spring break immersion to *organizing* an alternative break immersion—and to shifting the emphasis in her major and spending the early part of her career in community service—is just a more intentional version of the typical pathway of this study's young adult participants; it also reflects the documented positive effects of service learning.

Provencio's experience thus conforms to scholarly conclusions regarding the impacts of service learning, which has been found to have a strong association with choosing a service-oriented career—exactly her pathway. Indeed, studies demonstrate that this tendency is evident even when students had never considered a service-oriented career before their service learning experience.[34] In addition, scholars have found that service learning reduces ethnocentrism. Many interviewees discussed how their experiences changed their perceptions of others of different races and classes; Provencio shared how debriefings with her relatively diverse group of college students opened her eyes to the occurrence of racial microaggressions during her trips.[35]

33. Provencio, interview.
34. Niehaus et al., "Exploring the Role of Alternative Break," 134–148; Sax et al., "Long-Term Effects of Volunteerism," 187–202.
35. Borden, "Impact of Service-Learning on Ethnocentrism," 171–183; Sax et al., "Long-Term Effects of Volunteerism," 187–202.

Still, one must note the distinction between semester- or quarter-length learning projects and shorter, immersive, cocurricular service-learning experiences. Both forms of service learning have a positive influence, but immersive experiences have been found to be the most impactful, with the most powerful of all being those experiences organized by students and advised by learning professionals. Researchers hypothesize that it is the intense immersive quality of the experience that makes the difference.[36] Although writing about an academic service learning program, Lori Pompa intended for her analysis of the immersive experience working with a prison population to be broadly applicable: "This story is emblematic of what can happen when students experience the inspiration that occurs through a service-learning encounter. Intellectual understanding and analysis of issues combine with concern and passion for those issues propelling students to recognize their potential as change agents, ready to take the next step in addressing a particular dilemma."[37] This statement can just as easily have been applied to the young adult volunteers who participated in immersive, short-term experiences in New Orleans and then decided to become part of the long-term recovery.

Although several interviewees shared Provencio's service-learning background, others possessed a background in volunteering and civic activism that was not connected to their education. Take, for example, Daniel Maiuri, an AmeriCorps volunteer at RTNO, who explained why he decided to commit to volunteering in New Orleans:

> It kind of all started about two years ago you know after I graduated from college. I was volunteering in South Africa. I spent a year doing research for a nonprofit that represented children in court and meeting some of the young people who worked there as well. It really got my mind starting to think: there's so many problems in the world. There's so many things wrong, and I want to help. After I came back, I was thinking to myself: there's so many things within the U.S that I can do. It's kinda like . . . I don't know . . . "sexy" to say, "I went over to Africa to help these people, or I went to some other country." I have a lot of friends who've gone to South America to help.

36. Armstrong, "Developmental Outcomes of Service-Learning," 1–10; Beatty et al., "Effects of an Alternative Spring Break," 90–118.

37. Pompa, "Service Learning as Crucible," 74

That's all good, but I think sometimes we lose sight of the problems that we have here at home.

I was living in New York. The recession hit. and I was kind of looking for things to do. I just saw something on CNN. Anderson Cooper was talking about revisiting Katrina and not forgetting about what was going on. I had a couple of friends who had gone to Tulane, and it kinda came to mind that maybe this is something that the public has left off their radar. They still need people down there. I figured it's a neat place. I had never been to New Orleans before, and I thought I can use my talents and to come down and hopefully help out a little bit.[38]

We can see several strands of theory around volunteerism tying into Maiuri's narrative. Affirming the notion that volunteering begets volunteering, his determination to use the research skills that he developed in South Africa in an American context informed his decision to go to New Orleans.[39] His focus on fixing problems in the United States also relates to the finding that identifying with the people who need help is a motivator for volunteering, which I explore later.[40] Finally, the influence of his friends already working in New Orleans connects to Wilson and Musick's assertion that volunteer work involves collective action.[41]

In his interview, Maiuri emphasized the deeply personal roots of his desire to help others:

I guess part of it would come from my parents. I was raised you know, very religious. I'm not too much anymore, but I definitely think that instilled a lot in me about giving back to the community, service and helping other people. And I think it originally started by the ways that I volunteered and served before. They were very personal for me. They were things that I felt like directly affected my life.

The volunteer work that I originally started doing was with gay and lesbian organizations and organizations that were working with AIDS. I felt like that directly influenced me. Then I kind of got a broader worldview,

38. Maiuri, interview.
39. Oesterle et al., "Volunteerism during the Transition to Adulthood," 1126–1128.
40. Levine and Thompson, "Identity, Place, and Bystander Intervention," 230.
41. Wilson and Musick, "Who Cares?" 695.

partly from living abroad: just the idea that the human condition is every-body. So, the things that I don't think really affect me actually do affect me. I think I've learned a lot about that being down here. About how the con-ditions that we're all in and the things that we can do are things that affect me and other people. They're all connected. You can't really segregate the different aspects of it.[42]

Once again, we see that acting on one's values is a major motivator to vol-unteer.[43] In addition, Maiuri's perception that his volunteering deepened his capacity for empathy across human experiences conforms to scholars' assertions of the lasting impact that comes from cross-cultural interac-tions during volunteering.[44]

Although past volunteer experience helps account for why people like Maiuri volunteered in early adulthood, risk—defined as "the anticipated dangers whether legal, social, physical, financial and so forth of engaging in a particular type of work"—also helps explain why so many young adults were drawn to come and stay in New Orleans to help with the recovery. Wilson and Musick find that a notable exception to the pattern of declin-ing rates of volunteering for young adults is high-risk volunteering, which draws mainly young adults and has a very high burnout rate.[45] For those who came to New Orleans for the long term before 2008 when citywide house gutting was still occurring, the risk was real, and burnout was wide-spread. Of all the interviewees in this study, Adrian Manriquez laughingly expressed it in manner that captured a particular youthful zest: "Oh man. Being young and cavalier as I am, some of my favorite moments are doing really ridiculous things like hanging from rafters and narrowly escaping death to natural gas explosions several times."[46] Manriquez's laughter in-deed points to a cavalier attitude, but the risk was palpable. In the very earliest days, volunteers with Common Ground faced off against armed white vigilantes. Later, as volunteers fanned across the city gutting home

42. Maiuri, interview.
43. Garland et al., "Social Work with Religious Volunteers," 256.
44. Dass-Brailsford et al., "Paying It Forward," 35.
45. Wilson and Musick borrow heavily from Doug McAdam and Gregory Wiltfang. Wil-son, "Volunteering," 226; Wiltfang and McAdam, "Costs and Risks of Social Activism."
46. Manriquez, interview.

after decimated home, they experienced severe emotional distress and horrible working conditions. Over time the volunteer culture developed a kind of toxic masculinity that proved dangerous to female participants—an atmosphere that Scott Eustis called "exciting" but "chaotic."[47]

That chaos came with a price. A very small number of participants pointed to religion, family, and romantic relationships as a source of stress relief; unfortunately, most described a regrettable absence of constructive coping mechanisms; for instance, Scott Porot of OHH contended that this was an institutional failure. When asked whether he received support for the difficult issues he encountered in his volunteer experiences, he replied:

No. (*Laughter.*) At the time there was a Jesuit Relief coordinator. and they attempted to provide some reflection materials and those kinds of things, but in terms of addressing those issues, there really that was not something that people really worried about, to be quite honest, and maybe they should've. Especially for the younger volunteers. Conversations I've had with them have been really difficult. Some of them have really been challenged by this experience and are still sorting through what it means for them in their life. To know that they will never be the same because of the experience is something that would've been useful for them to sort through with someone or some type of structure, but it just wasn't there. Quite honestly, again it really just shows the lack of leadership in the not-for-profits on an overarching scale. If you had a structure in which people could go and say, "We really need to address this" then maybe it could've been addressed. But that structure wasn't in place even though people recognized that these kids were really stressed out. I don't think that structure was available to them. It just wasn't there. And the not-for-profits that were doing the rebuilding work themselves, to be quite honest, didn't have the time to worry about that unfortunately. They probably should have, for the well-being of their organizations, but hindsight's 20/20.[48]

You will also recall Colleen Morgan, Caitlin Reilly, and Adrian Manriquez describing the presence of alcohol, drugs, and partying among the younger

47. Manriquez, interview; Eustis, interview; Reilly, interview; Alverson, interview.
48. Porot, interview.

volunteers.[49] Although one could write off these behaviors as youthful excesses, in the context of the extraordinary stresses of post-Katrina New Orleans, they appear to be a sign of maladaptive self-soothing, as this anonymous interviewee relates:

> I was getting to a place where I could drive across the canal into the Lower Ninth and not feel the importance of what I was doing. I was still loving the city, but I was also getting worn down by volunteers. I was not feeling challenged in a positive way, by the work. And the other thing was that I was doing a lot of drinking. Then that relationship that I mentioned a few times ended. I started doing a lot of sleeping around. It's easy going to the Quarter and finding a bunch of women from out of town celebrating their birthday. It's pretty much like shooting fish in a barrel.

When asked whether sleeping around was a coping mechanism, this person answered, "Oh, I would; I would definitely say so. I would definitely say so. I just thought, it's time [for me] to start thinking about the next thing. So, I'm at seminary now in a rural backwater town."[50]

Indeed, one young adult female volunteer at one of the city's larger rebuilding organizations did not bring up stress as an issue during her interview, which took place in an office where one of the organization's top leaders was working. Afterward, however, as she and I visited some of the organization's rebuilding sites, she confided that having that leader in the room made her reluctant to admit that alcohol was the "primary" coping mechanism of the young adult volunteers; she even recalled an instance in which higher-ups supplied alcohol to a party.[51]

Jim Pate, executive director of Habitat for Humanity New Orleans, was aware of these tendencies, noting that the early volunteer scene attracted a lot of what he called "gutterpunks": transient young people with their "dad's credit card in their hip pocket" who just wanted a roof over their head and three meals a day. He cited this group as being particularly drawn to substance abuse—a description that dovetails with Reilly's

49. Morgan, interview, July 6, 2010; Reilly, interview; Manriquez, interview; Pate, interview.

50. Anonymous, interview.

51. Anonymous, interview.

testimony. Pate argued that Habitat had a much better understanding of "volunteer management" than the other large organizations involved in the rebuilding effort and that he was the only leader whose organization systematically attempted to address stress and burnout among volunteers.

During his interview, Pate said, "I've seen a lot of volunteers, the younger ones, talk about the stresses they went through. [They were] emotional. And I'm not talkin' about the ones who were here for a week. I mean the ones who tended to stay for three to six months. I noticed patterns—alcohol consumption, promiscuity, etc." He admitted that Habitat for Humanity was aware of these behaviors:

> Yeah, sure. We had some of those. Yeah. All of that. Well, our primary focus was to rebuild the city and to bring people who were displaced back, as much as possible. The Habitat volunteer tradition, certainly everywhere I've run, has involved AmeriCorps and what they call N-triple C's, which is a division of AmeriCorps. The best way to think of N-trips is they're like an AmeriCorps' S.W.A.T. team. AmeriCorps are typically an eleven- to twelvemonth commitment. It's actually based on hours. If somebody works a little more, they may knock it out in eleven months. N-trips are only in for six to ten weeks; right in the profile you're talkin' about. We had a regular briefing program that we had been giving to our N-trips and our AmeriCorps when they came pre-Katrina. A lot of that addresses the issues you're talking about, the stress of seeing the pain and the anguish of the members of the community. We tried to constantly offset that with a sense of purpose and a sense that you are helping these people tremendously.
>
> We solicited and received a donation of equipment for a fitness room. We set up a small area that we called a meditation room. There were no formal services. If there was a formal service, it was ad hoc by the Church of the Four-Leaf Clover and their volunteers. They'd say, "Well, let's all go to the medication room and have a little service." We didn't organize and run those. It was a place where if a group or an individual wanted to go in and meditate, there was a little sacred space set aside for that.
>
> We also, at times, had security and rules. We didn't try to govern what people did outside the camp, but we could certainly govern what they did inside the camp. And we could govern behavior. Last entry into the camp was 10 o'clock at night. If you showed up after 10, staggerin' blind drunk, you

didn't get in. I think creating structure and creating the right attitude has a tremendous amount to do with it.[52]

Although the danger of the work appeared to attract some, others came because they identified with the city of New Orleans. In their examination of the public response to the 1995 bombing of the Murrah Federal Building in Oklahoma City, St. John and Fuchs found that feeling a connection to the victims of a disaster tends to predict volunteering.[53] We witnessed this type of connection with Colleen Morgan, and it also occurred with Scott Eustis of Bayou Rebirth and the Gulf Restoration Network.

Eustis had a history of civic involvement dating back to his teen years as a member of the do-it-yourself movement. After earning a bachelor's degree in ecology, Eustis enrolled in a graduate program in Georgia. He explained that, as a native of New Orleans, he had witnessed numerous floods during his childhood and had long been worried about New Orleans's "destructive ecology." He had hoped that when the big one came, he would already be the owner of a large home and would have sufficient disposable income to provide refuge for his parents. Instead, he was still a graduate student researching a topic that, by his own admission, had limited practical use. Thus, the first thought that came into his mind when he saw coverage of the storm was that he "wasn't ready"—but he also knew immediately that he had to go back and assist.[54] Like many others, he went to the first organization that appeared to be making an impact, Common Ground, but he soon shifted to work at Bayou Rebirth, which seemed less tumultuous and whose work more closely aligned with his ideals.[55]

Nevertheless, few of the long-term volunteers interviewed for this project were native New Orleanians or former residents, and a significant portion did not have a cocurricular experience that had introduced them to the city. These volunteers, who were predominantly young, white, and not from the South, served populations who were largely older, African American, and very much Southern. If the scholarship is correct that volunteers need to share some salient identity with the people they are

52. Pate, interview.
53. St. John and Fuchs, "The Heartland Responds to Terror," 397.
54. Eustis, interview; Reilly, interview.
55. Eustis, interview; Reilly, interview.

helping, what factors related to identity motivated them to come?[56] Lacie Michel provides an answer, arguing that natural disasters destabilize "pre-disaster differences in social and economic status," leading people to act "sympathetically and sentimentally on the basis of human needs." In this situation, disaster-affected areas become the object of convergent behaviors in which a large-scale giving effort by surrounding communities and all levels of government focuses on one affected area.[57]

Along these lines, it appears that volunteers identified with New Orleanians as Americans, and they were particularly disappointed by the government's treatment of their fellow citizens. This stance arose directly in some interviewees' reactions to the televised storm coverage. When asked what really struck them by the initial coverage of the hurricane, several interviewees had similar reactions:

- Daniel Mauri: "I mean it was definitely just really shocking to see that this was something that was happening in the US."[58]
- Chris Hamsher, who created the Student Hurricane Network at the University of Minnesota to organize short-term trips to New Orleans and who came back to New Orleans as an attorney with Southeast Louisiana Legal Services: "Really I thought . . . this is my country and I want it back."[59]
- Adrian Manriquez: "I was pretty shocked that an American city could be flooding like that and that there wouldn't be relief coming for several days at a time."[60]

This identification of New Orleanians as fellow Americans suffering at the hands of a government that had failed them, coupled with Michel's contention that catastrophe can collapse pre-disaster differences, goes a long way toward explaining the motivation of so many to come to New Orleans and help a community seemingly so different from their own.

Gratifyingly for our participants, experiencing profound connections across class, culture, and race was a recurring theme. These experiences

56. Levine and Thompson, "Identity, Place, and Bystander Intervention," 230.
57. Michel, "Personal Responsibility," 634, 635.
58. Maiuri, interview.
59. Hamsher, interview.
60. Manriquez, interview.

appear to have enriched the volunteers' generalized yet powerful motivation to assist fellow Americans caught in an unimaginable catastrophe. Even without this convergence, though, it is likely that both the young adult and the older long-term volunteers would have still come in the thousands. With their personal histories of civic engagement—whether through the church, school, or careers in helping professions—or whether driven by religion, civic interest, or a family history of volunteering, the Americans who gave months of their lives to Katrina recovery were quite simply continuing a pattern of living in service to others. Although more experienced leaders like Daniela Rivero understood the limitations of their work, many newcomers arrived with visions to reshape the world—dreams that the reality of post-Katrina New Orleans would put to a severe test.

9. A Thousand Points of Light?

THE LIMITATIONS OF NONPROFITS IN ADDRESSING DISASTER RECOVERY

> Nothing is ever really free. I can assure you that.
>
> —Daniela Rivero, Rebuilding Together New Orleans

In 1989 President George H. W. Bush espoused classic neoliberal ideology when he accompanied his call to reduce Americans' dependence on public funds with an appeal for private citizens to channel their civic energy through community organizations that would spread across the country like "a thousand points of light." Just over fifteen years later, Americans' belief in volunteerism manifested itself in stunning fashion as some five hundred new charities emerged to meet New Orleans's recovery needs, bringing aid from 1.5 million private citizens to the city in the process.[1] Multiple scholars who have analyzed the Katrina catastrophe using a framework critical of neoliberalism have questioned the efficacy of this flood of volunteers.[2] Although Andy Horowitz casts doubt on the viability of this analytical approach, this study nevertheless agrees with Vincanne Adams's assessment that the explosion of new nonprofits "must be seen at least in part as a direct outcome of policy commitments to the basic philosophical assumption that the government should not be responsible for taking care of its needy citizens when the private sector can and should do this job better."[3]

1. Bush, "Inaugural Address of George Bush."

2. Arena, *Driven from New Orleans*, 58, 149, 153–157,183; Johnson, "Charming Accommodations," 189, 205, 218; Luft, "Beyond Disaster Exceptionalism," 97; Dixon, "Whose Choice?" 130–151; Strauss, "The 10 School Districts"; Clark, "Charter Schools In New Orleans"; Falk, "In New Orleans"; Hasselle, "What's Driving Better School Performance in New Orleans?"; Burris, "The Real Story of New Orleans and Its Charter Schools"; Lovell, "Reformers, Preservationists, Patients, and Planners," loc 2104.

3. Horowitz, *Katrina: A History*, loc 3368; Adams, *Markets of Sorrow*, loc 2203.

Given America's apparent continuing reliance on charitable organizations to address major social issues, this study asked its participants to evaluate the effectiveness of nonprofit labor to execute a recovery of this scale: in general, their testimony revealed significant inadequacies. Despite their dedication to rebuilding the city, interviewees noted serious inefficiencies in grant application processes, detrimental competition between recovery organizations for "numbers," safety concerns for volunteers who had no protections under the Occupational Safety and Health Administration, and the problematic workmanship of volunteers engaged in labor normally requiring professional competencies. Their testimony suggests that directing volunteer labor through hundreds of scattered charitable organizations is insufficient for the task of recovering from a catastrophe of this scale.

Before examining this testimony in detail, however, it is important to briefly consider storm recovery efforts predating the ascension of neoliberalism, thereby providing some basis for comparison. In 1965, the federal government responded slightly more effectively to Hurricane Betsy than it did to Hurricane Katrina. Betsy hit New Orleans on September 9, 1965, with an official wind speed of 125 mph. Approximately 500,000 people had already evacuated to safer places nearby, such as schools, military bases, and natural levees. When Betsy struck, it broke the Industrial Canal levee and flooded the Lower Ninth Ward. It also overtopped the lakefront levees. With a death toll of nearly eighty and damages of more than a billion dollars, Betsy was the deadliest and costliest hurricane in U.S. history to date.[4] Unlike Katrina, however, New Orleanians were not displaced to other locations across the country, and storm victims were kept out of their homes for only a week while the water receded and officials completed a search for bodies.[5] Meanwhile, writes Craig Colten and E. Sumpter, the federal government mounted an immediate response: "Red Cross volunteers and local federal agencies provided food and medical attention to the sheltered population. All hospitals remained operational. City and public utility crews began clearing and restoring basic utilities." Even though Colten and Sumter noted a "litany of suffering and damages" in later congressio-

4. Colten, "From Betsy to Katrina."
5. Reckdahl, "50 Years Ago, Hurricane Betsy."

nal testimony, they argue that a full review of the statements nevertheless revealed "the rapid pace of the initial response and early recovery."[6]

Although President Lyndon Johnson expedited the rescue process for storm victims, the urgency of the federal response lessened during the long-term recovery. In the Southeast Hurricane Disaster Relief Act of 1965—the so-called Betsy Bill—Congress allocated funds for individual Small Business Administration (SBA) loans and appropriated $70 million for farm and school recovery. Yet, only about one-quarter of New Orleans's poorest citizens qualified for the SBA loans. A Red Cross voucher program that gave $400 to $1,000 per family provided some help, but recipients could only spend the money on furniture, in one specific store, and on a single day. In the meantime, acute hunger struck, and the city stationed police at garbage dumps to prevent people from attempting to salvage spoiled food from discarded refrigerators. In the end, those who could not qualify for SBA loans received little more than a small pail and broom to clean their homes after returning to them from shelters. Just under a year later, flood victims petitioned New Orleans's City Council for help, asking for loan forgiveness and $10,000 grants to rebuild their homes.[7]

In response to the federal, state, and local governments' insufficient responses to Hurricane Betsy and, before that, to the Hurricane of 1915, citizens clamored for stronger government support for storm and flooding victims. Yet by the 2000s, the nation's political vocabulary had changed dramatically, and that cry from the previous century went unanswered. Neoliberal ideals so pervaded the political discourse of the early 2000s that even some Katrina survivors quickly skipped over questions of government responsibility and shifted almost immediately to notions of self-help and charitable organizing. Take, for example, these remarks by Katrina survivor Barb Johnson: "Once we got over the horror of watching President Bush ignore us while our governor and mayor locked themselves in a power struggle at our expense, we began to take care of business in the most efficient and cooperative way. Whoever was in the neighborhood cleaned up to ease the way for those who had yet to come. Neighbor by neighbor. Street by street. That didn't get a lot of press, but that's the way it was."[8]

6. Colten and Sumpter, "Social Memory and Resilience," 359.
7. Reckdahl, "50 Years Ago, Hurricane Betsy."
8. Antoine, *Voices Rising II*, 15.

In this study, Fred Franke's testimony reveals both the power and the invisibility of the neoliberal paradigm. Throughout his four interviews, Franke argued that government intervention in the recovery process should be limited to rebuilding infrastructure and keeping order. Meanwhile, he maintained that local forces on the ground, particularly churches, were much more suited to rebuild communities than the government—a position that is easy to understand after the federal government's failure to prevent the flooding, the city government's inability to stage an orderly evacuation, and the deadly slowness of both in organizing a rescue effort.

Indeed, Franke's seeming acceptance of neoliberalism is so deep that he appears to be speaking in a common-sense manner, rather than from the perspective of a particular political philosophy. For example, he noted that we are in "rough social times; they're gonna be cutting social services," and the church can fill that space. His conclusion that the church can be an important force for social good is honorable and admirable, but it does not follow any real logic. There is no reason to assume that social services will be cut unless one assumes that providing social services is not the appropriate role of the government.

Franke's testimony also demonstrates the power of neoliberal ideology to easily submerge evidence that contradicts its most basic premises. Take, for example, the unedited version of Franke's discussion of General Russel Honoré:

But, man, even at this point, with all the work, all these faith-based groups have done, from across the country as well as from local, they still don't get it. These guys should be allowed in right away with the police and fire department, setting up the home bases, the tractor trailer rigs are already on the way to bring emergency food supplies and water, and you saw the ineffectiveness of the federal government being able to do anything until Mr. Honoré got down here—I can't remember if he's a general or what he was. [He was a general.]

But he just cut through the junk. "People over there that need water—where's the water truck?" "It's right over there." He just cut through it. "Send it over there." "But we haven't got approval from above." "I'm the approval from above. Get it over there." Government's too big and each step of the way you go up, you got to get approved. Well, there's a lot of people, all the people can say no, but very few people can say yes. And in these kinds of situations, everything needs to be a yes. It all needs to be a yes because they need help right then. They need to be rescued out of the trees, off the rooftops?[9]

Franke characterizes FEMA's early efforts as ineffective—a perspective few observers would disagree with—and he asserts that faith-based and other volunteer groups should have been allowed to immediately enter New Orleans to administer aid. Yet, the person whom he cites as fixing the situation was Lieutenant General Russel Honoré, the commander of Joint Task Force Katrina, whom Franke does not quite seem to remember as a general, much less a representative of the government. Given that Franke is very sophisticated and well read, and that the general who sported camouflage fatigues, a black beret, aviator glasses, and a cigar was an unforgettable figure, it is surprising that he does not recall his military rank.[10]

One has to wonder what is happening here. In "What Makes Oral History Different," Alesandro Portelli writes that "memory is not a passive depository of facts, but an active process of creation of meanings."[11] One can thus speculate that the neoliberal narrative regarding the ineptitude of government was so powerful that it led Franke to disassociate Honoré's apparent status as a government agent from his effective leadership.[12]

Such an occurrence in the confusing period after Katrina was not unusual. Vincanne Adams described a similar phenomenon, noting how it was extraordinarily difficult for the average New Orleanian to realize that the much-despised Road Home program was run by a private multinational corporation, ICF International, rather than a government bureaucracy. Within that context, writes Adams, "It is easy to see how the merits

9. Franke, interview, July 16, 2010.
10. Boin et al., *Managing Hurricane Katrina,* loc 2671.
11. Portelli, "What Makes Oral History Different," 69.
12. Although they distinctly avoid any mention of neoliberalism, Arjen Boin, Christer Brown, and James Richardson discuss various powerful frames for understanding the crisis that emerged in the media including the frames: "Where is the government?" and "The military comes to the rescue." Corresponding with my argument regarding the perception of General Honoré, they argue that the military shone brightly as one of the few functioning institutions during the recovery and that this frame for understanding what occurred in the disaster remained powerful for more than a decade after the storm. Boin et al., *Managing Hurricane Katrina,* loc 3009.

of church and charity arrangements can fuel antipathy toward government programs and can heap praise on private-sector initiatives. Before lingering on the merits of such arrangements for too long, however, it is worth remembering that had federal relief funding gone directly to returning residents, it would probably have cost less for everyone and taken much less time for them to recover, whether or not the volunteer economy had arrived."[13]

In time, however, as the local media exposed ICF's negligence and the state of Louisiana sued the company for mismanaging recovery funds, one could surmise that most New Orleanians would no longer blame government bureaucracy for the program's failures.[14] Yet the drama between ICF and the state did not cause New Orleanians to question the neoliberal practice of handing off government responsibilities to private companies, as evidenced by the vast expansion of charter schools in the city. Even though scholars have documented the mixed results of charter schools in general and the adverse results for under-resourced New Orleans's families in particular, charter schools—long championed by neoliberals as providing parents democratic options through a free-market–style apparatus—now comprise 100 percent of New Orleans's elementary schools.[15] Given ICF's failure and the difficulties caused by charter schools for lower-income families, one has to wonder why more energy did not go into protests against neoliberal policies, such as the privatization of schools and a massive dependence on private citizens' charitable donations and volunteer labor, which amounted to a double tax because Americans' tax payments then went to private contractors.[16]

Perhaps a broader challenge to neoliberalism did not arise because the concept itself had little salience. In fact, only one of this project's participants—who were largely college educated and many of whom were pursuing advanced degrees—referred to neoliberalism as a concept. Adrian Manriquez was the only one to offer a multilayered critique of the nonprofit-led

13. Adams, *Markets of Sorrow,* 151.
14. "State Seeks $10M from ICF."
15. Dixon, "Whose Choice?" 130–151; Strauss, "The 10 School Districts"; Martin, "Charter Schools in New Orleans That Underperform"; Wells et al., "Defining Democracy in the Neoliberal Age," 338, 344–346.
16. Adams, *Markets of Sorrow,* loc 3238.

recovery process. In his interview, he tied the nonprofits' broad array of efforts to the slow distribution of Road Home money by ICF, criticizing the multinational for receiving a billion-dollar contract but failing to distribute any funds.[17]

Manriquez, who volunteered with Common Ground Relief and was later a staff leader with OHH, argued that outsourcing the recovery work to an inept private company led to the massive participation of nonprofits in the rebuilding effort. Yet, he claimed that this neoliberal critique was limited to his "political circles," rather than the volunteers and nonprofit staffers.[18] In contrast to Manriquez's focus on the root causes of the extensive involvement of nonprofits in the recovery process, most interviewees targeted their criticism at the various symptoms that arose from this circumstance.

Multiple interviewees, for instance, harshly criticized the nonprofit granting process. They argued that although their organizations tried to view individual clients holistically, grant limitations would not allow them to operate in that manner. In other words, even though most clients needed to have their entire home rebuilt, grants usually provided restricted funds for individual tasks like gutting, lead remediation, painting, and so on. Manriquez noted that the separate funding streams from multiple granting agencies made for a significant amount of redundant paperwork.

17. In 2006 ICF received a $725 million contract from the Blanco administration to distribute $7.9 billion in two Road Home Programs, one for homeowners and a smaller rental repair program. Louisianans criticized ICF's operations "as slow, unresponsive to applicants and weighed down by confusing and contradictory rules." The contract had not stipulated benchmarks against which to measure ICF's performance, however, and the state gave ICF until December 2006 to create those metrics. ICF failed to do so and received an extension. Finally, in 2007, the state negotiated some measures to assess ICF, and it fined ICF $1 million for missing those goals. After that, the two failed to negotiate any additional goals. Despite these considerable problems and to the dismay of the general public and state politicians, the Blanco administration increased the contract to $926 million in March 2008. Both the Blanco administration and ICF argued that expansion of the program required the additional funds. The expanded contract did not appear to result in improved services, however, and the state ended ICF's contract three months early when it awarded a contract—this one with benchmarks and timetables for delivery—to Hammerman and Grainger in April 2009. Hammer, "Blanco Administration Quietly Gave Raise to Road Home Operator"; "State Signs New Road Home Contract with HGI Catastrophe Services; "ICF's Oversight of Road Home Program Comes to an End."

18. Manriquez, interview.

Clients had to reapply for funds from every institution they contacted for assistance. In addition, they had to move physically from one agency's offices to another, which was particularly onerous because many were without transportation and the city's infrastructure was in shambles.[19] At the same time, nonprofits had no means of determining whether clients had applied for similar services from multiple organizations. As Leonard Penner, a retired contractor and community worker with Mennonite Disaster Services, noted, "You have so many cases and so many casework organizations were starting out. But there was no clearinghouse. You might have a fairly assertive client who might get to two or three organizations. But there was no one saying, 'Are you registered with someone else already?' It was a nightmare at first, just to get through the casework and to see that it was done correctly."[20] Situations such as these led several participants to recommend a common application for recovery funding and a central clearinghouse for nonprofit and government social services.

Various interviewees argued that the granting process, combined with the desperate nature of the work in its early days, led to severe inefficiencies in the application of resources. As Bethany Billman, a volunteer coordinator with OHH, argued:

> I think that the nature of this work is that you're just always very busy. People have wanted to all sit down at the same table and discuss ideas and share ideas, but I think one of the biggest reasons that didn't ever happen was because in a post-Katrina climate everyone's just working really long days, trying to focus on finishing the next house, and developing their own connections. So, if the money was coming in pretty steadily, if something's not broke, there's no reason to fix it.[21]

Moreover, Billman felt that the inevitable decline in foundation funding even further diminished the potential for communication: "I think that there are some really good rebuilding organizations, but people have been a little territorial in the past about money and ideas. Maybe they kind of keep their cards close to their chests because they need those grant dollars,

19. Manriquez, interview.
20. Penner, interview; Franke, interview, July 16, 2010; Billman, interview.
21. Billman, interview.

and if everybody starts sharing, their unique idea is not something that's maybe going to get a grant anymore."[22]

Perhaps because the various nonprofit organizations competed for limited pools of foundation money, many focused on showcasing their qualifications for grants and their suitability to get more funding by producing "numbers." Because it was up to individual groups, however, to determine their target geographic areas and target populations, the quest for numbers could lead to overlap and competition between organizations. Scott Eustis, who had experience with Bayou Rebirth and the Gulf Restoration Network, noted that these circumstances led to a lot of "drama."[23] Manriquez echoed Eustis when he argued that the competitive market nature of the grant application process could lead to organizations duplicating their efforts in one area (geographically or strategically) while leaving other areas of need untouched.[24]

Despite the apparent need to coordinate such a massive effort, the desperate circumstances of being involved in crisis work undermined attempts at coordination, leading interviewees to argue that planning needed to take place *before* the catastrophe occurred and to characterize such efforts after the fact as being a waste of time.[25] Multiple interviewees reported the existence of such coordinating meetings often without even being able to name them—a characteristic that indicated their irrelevance. Only one interviewee mentioned the meetings of the Greater New Orleans Disaster Recovery Partnership, where home-rebuilding nonprofits shared cases with others when a client's situation did not meet their criteria.[26] But even this single characterization was undermined by Fred Franke's discussion of his organization Project Nehemiah:

> Early on, we just dug in. We got to work doin' everything that was before our eyes that we could do. Didn't even think about hesitatin' on it. If people needed help, you just help. They were desperate. So, that's where my actions

22. Billman, interview.
23. Eustis, interview.
24. Manriquez, interview.
25. Pate, interview.
26. Greenhow, interview.

were. I heard about an organization called Greater New Orleans Disaster Relief Program, G.N.O.D.R.P.[27] I went to several of the meetings. They were talkin' about, "How can we coordinate this better? How can we do all of this? How can we function? How can we not be double-dippin' and tryin' to create something that is already goin' well? How can we collectively do all of this and save personnel, time, and money?" It was a great concept, but I got tired of the meetings. I knew they were going to be very beneficial, but I had too many people that needed help. I let one of my staff members go to keep an ear open, interject what she felt the direction of our organization was and how we might help. But that needed to be done beforehand. That's sort of like the theorist guys. They talk in theory about how a city ought to be built, but they sometimes overlook the people that are livin' in that city: "This will be good for them." Well, maybe not. Maybe that would be good for the way that they would envision a city, but it might not be good for the people that actually live in that city. We had a lot of that goin' on as well.

I see a lot of good that could be done in collective, and I believe collectives should do everything they can to work together because it can be very efficient. But we saw that some organizations got their funding only by what they said they were doin'. I'm not gonna mention an organization, but they asked for all our numbers, so we gave 'em all our numbers. We found out that they were usin' everyone's numbers that were in attendance and writin' grants' sayin', "This is what we're doin'." They weren't doin' anything. They were pullin' and pooling all these guys together for the better collective to go down the road together, but it seems strange that they were turning around and gettin' funds. I don't mind 'em gettin' funds. I mind 'em usin' our numbers.[28]

Franke's analysis is revealing. As with his incorrect recall of General Honoré, Franke cannot remember the correct name of the GNODRP, calling

27. Pronounced "no-drip."

28. In making this point, Franke joins many other interviewees in this project who argued that the nonprofit granting process, particularly foundations' desire for quantitative data to assess performance (i.e. numbers), can pervert the missions of nonprofits and foster unhealthy competition that makes their work less efficient within a disaster recovery context. For examples of this argument, see Berra et al., "To Render Ourselves Visible," 39–40; Adams, *Markets of Sorrow,* loc 2785–2807; Franke, interview, July 16, 2010.

it the "Greater New Orleans Disaster Relief Program," rather than the Greater New Orleans Disaster Recovery Partnership. Given his recollection of detailed data pertaining to own work, Christianity in the United States, and New Orleans topography, the fact that he forgot the organization's name may indicate its relative unimportance to his work.

The rest of his testimony is compelling, considering nonprofits' future involvement in disaster recovery and rebuilding efforts. First, Franke made it clear that he believed the coordination of nonprofits' recovery work was necessary, but he echoed Bethany Billman, who argued that the basic network to execute such an effort needs to be created *before* the demands of recovering from a catastrophe. Habitat for Humanity's executive director Jim Pate similarly argued for combining preplanning with building resistant infrastructure, allowing nonprofits to hit the ground immediately:

> The other thing I've been telling everybody I could ever have to talk to at the government level is you need to preplan and include your nonprofits. That includes almost every coastal place in the other parts of the country. They're doin' hardened emergency facilities. By that I mean they'll survive hurricane/tornado winds, flooding, elevated to whatever. But anywhere they had somethin' like that, go ahead and run some waterlines, sewage lines, electric overhead or underground. I prefer underground. And if you can do it right then, go ahead and put in little concrete pads.
>
> So, when your volunteers are comin' in, you just pop a trailer or in our case, we literally could have built a house, an adequate bunk bed type house in forty-eight to seventy-two hours and had housing for twelve to fourteen people.[29]

In addition to the urgency of present needs distracting from making coordinated efforts, multiple interviewees noted how the competitive process of getting "numbers" undermined effective coordination between groups. In the modern neoliberal context, nonprofits have increasingly operated on an outcomes-based competitive model that stimulates competition, not unlike that among for-profit businesses.[30] Yet testimony from

29. Pate, interview.
30. Adams, *Markets of Sorrow,* 153–169.

Franke and others indicates that this quantitative orientation fostered unhealthy competition between organizations and shifted nonprofits toward work that undermined their integrity, as indicated by this comment by former OHH volunteer coordinator and director Kevin Fitzpatrick:

> Volunteers show up. They want to work, most of 'em. They don't like to sit around and waste time or do jobs that are meaningless. One of my colleagues said that she would have 'em dig a ditch one day and then have the volunteers from another group fill in the ditch. They know you're just playing games with them to boost your numbers and they're not doing any work. So, you have to have meaningful work for 'em. You have to have an organization somewhere that they can feel like they're being used well.[31]

According to Scott Eustis, who worked both with Bayou Rebirth and the larger, established Gulf Restoration Network, only the big nonprofit organizations knew how to play the "game" of winning and administering grants well—a point made by scholars who have observed a trend of smaller organizations merging to become more competitive in the grant market.[32] Taking this critique a step further, one anonymous leader in the post-Katrina movement for criminal justice reform and a former resident of the St. Thomas Housing Development, dismissed nonprofits altogether, arguing that playing the 501c3 "game" rendered organizations unable to engage in radical, grassroots efforts:

> We're not in agreement with applying for the 501c3. Folks can't do what they really want to do in their heart of hearts because their work is being dictated by the 501c3 idea or concept. If I wanted to start a Black nationalist organization full of brothers who wanted to be self-empowered and believe in the idea of the red, black, and green, that would not be digested well. . . . We do not receive any funding as a result, but we believe that we want to create systems and institutions that we own and control for our community's sake.[33]

31. Fitzpatrick, interview, August 21, 2013.
32. Eustis, interview.
33. Anonymous, interview.

In trying to avoid the restrictions imposed by dependence on foundation grants, some organizations embraced the fee-based volunteer model with mixed results. Bayou Rebirth, for example, moved to the fee-based model after experiencing tremendous difficulties in trying to hold onto a large grant. When large numbers of Americans sought to help New Orleans, this model worked well. But when national attention shifted and the numbers of volunteers declined, it proved deficient. Bayou Rebirth experienced a decrease in volunteers and the money that came with them, but according to Scott Eustis, it could not return to the grant model because many foundations frowned on their past use of a volunteer fee-based model.

This model did not appear to be a problem, however, for Rebuilding Together New Orleans (RTNO), which provided volunteer experiences for a fee. Unlike Bayou Rebirth, Rebuilding Together had been in existence since 1988 and was a part of the Preservation Resource Center of New Orleans—a nonprofit founded in 1974 with more than a million-dollar budget.[34] By 2015—and perhaps because of the work undertaken after the storm—RTNO was "the largest home rehabilitation nonprofit organization in New Orleans, having completed more than 500 home repair and community revitalization projects since 2005."[35]

To the extent that organizations were not gaming for numbers, altruistic interactions did occur within the context of one-on-one relationships. Most project participants from home- rebuilding organizations and those from other nonprofits indicated that mission and funding limitations often rendered them unable to support those seeking assistance. However, they had well-developed relationships with other nonprofits that could sometimes provide clients the help they needed. As Amanda Murphy, a twenty-nine-year-old AmeriCorps volunteer with RTNO, described, "We never want to turn people away and make them believe that there is no hope or that there is nothing that can be done for them."[36]

Coordination also materialized in a dovetailing of resources. David Harms, first a long-term volunteer with Mennonite Disaster Services and then a volunteer coordinator with OHH, argued that New Orleans possessed a relational rather than transactional culture, which limited

34. "Preservation Resource Center."
35. Rebuilding Together New Orleans, "Rebuilding Together."
36. Murphy, interview; Maiuri, interview; Levin, interview.

the ability of out-of-town nonprofits to get things done. In such cases, it was common in his experience for Catholic Charities and OHH to assist nonprofits that did not have social connections or casework capacity to get things done in the city.[37] Interviewees indicated that the sharing of resources or volunteers provided benefits to both participating organizations by allowing each to count the results in their own "numbers." OHH, for example, was well known for loaning tools from its ample inventory to other rebuilding organizations.[38] Those organizations with more volunteers than projects often shared their people power with other organizations with more projects than volunteers.[39]

Nevertheless, developing deep partnerships with other nonprofits could invite more peril than support around mission. Colleen Morgan's story of Bayou Rebirth illustrates this point, as well as many of the vulnerabilities discussed thus far—from obtaining funding to generating revenue streams to depending on volunteer labor. I interviewed Morgan three times in 2010 and 2011. By the third interview, Morgan had gone full circle from the heady, sleepless nights of starting the organization to disillusionment to reflection. Her relaxed body language indicated that she was in a different place in her life than when we had met the year before. After some preliminary greetings and waiting for our coffee, she said in a subdued voice: "Students and whatnot call me up and say, 'I'm thinking about starting a nonprofit, and I'd love to talk to you.'"[40]

When heard rather than read, this second portion of the sentence is curious because, although Morgan is apparently a white-identified woman, she used a tone that sounded decidedly white, youthful, and entitled. She then continued in her normal voice, responding to this hypothetical query this way: "I'll take you out to dinner, and I'll convince you not to. Because the main thing you have to give when you're starting a nonprofit is about five years of your life."[41]

Unfortunately, I failed to follow up on the cues provided by Morgan's tone during the interview, and the exact meaning of her meta-message is

37. Harms, interview.
38. Manriquez, interview.
39. Franke, interview, July 16, 2019; Morgan, interview, July 15, 2010.
40. Morgan, interview, August 23, 2011.
41. Morgan, interview, August 23, 2011.

a mystery. Still, I was surprised by her lower level of intensity in the third interview compared to her earlier enthusiasm. I therefore asked, having in mind other interviewees who had pointed to downturns in donations and volunteers, whether the recession had hurt her organization. To which Morgan paused for a long time and responded, *"No, but that's what I say to people who ask, 'What happened?'"* She then told a very personal story of her organization's decline, making no mention of the broader framework in which she operated as being problematic, thereby implying that she, rather than the system, was the problem.[42]

When contextualized over the course of three interviews, these comments represented a conclusion to a narrative of struggle that she had begun to articulate many months earlier around the difficulties of administering a grant and engaging in continuous fundraising. In her first interview, Morgan began by focusing on her work to develop revenue streams for her nonprofit startup. At the time of that interview, Bayou Rebirth had little funding, and Morgan was struggling to keep things going with her small board of directors, a few interns, and occasional volunteers. In a regretful tone, she noted that she should have done more to keep up with grants and wished that she could have afforded to hire a grant writer.

At the outset, Morgan focused her efforts on writing as many grant proposals as she could, and her background as a journalist proved very helpful in that regard. Rather quickly, Morgan won a grant from the Gulf of Mexico Foundation (GMF) for $30,092: "In December of that year, I got an almost $10,000 check, and suddenly had the wherewithal to do a lot of work. It was fantastic, and I was way in over my head."[43] (*Laughter.*) Indeed, per its description on the GMF website, the project to be funded was very ambitious:

> This project will engage local students, community members and visiting volunteers in wetlands restoration through plantings. At the same time, two substantial areas within two wildlife refuges near New Orleans will be restored through plantings, which trap the soil and therefore reverse the ero-

42. In this way Morgan's testimony is reminiscent of Studs Terkel's subjects in *Hard Times* who, when discussing their experiences of the Great Depression, tended to form their stories on an individualistic and characterological basis, rather than examining the larger system within which they operated. Frisch, "Oral History and Hard Times."

43. Morgan, interview, July 15, 2010.

sion caused by hurricanes in recent years. Moreover, the project will train a cadre of youth to be restoration specialists by teaching them the techniques of water quality and habitat assessment as well as nurturing and growing out wetland plant species. . . .

The educational component of the project involves four sessions for each school: First, in the classroom, the students learn about causes of wetlands loss and methods of restoration. In their schoolyard they learn to propagate wetland plants and create a wetland plant pond where they grow out plants. Next, the students take two field trips to a local park with lagoons, where they learn why and how to test for water quality and then get a lesson in habitat assessment. Finally, the students bring their plants to the wetland planting site, assess water quality and habitat, and then plant.

The volunteer planting component will be ongoing but tied to the school program through student involvement. A local volunteer planting day will be held one Saturday each month, and plantings will be coordinated for visiting volunteer groups during the busy volunteer months of March and June. In the winter months the project will be focused on the education program, as it is not the best time of year to plant. The students in the spring will become involved during the grass-planting phase, bringing their plants and helping out at plantings during the summer as they take place. In the fall, the first group will mentor the new group of students.[44]

The grant-funded project began in January 2009, and Bayou Rebirth opened its doors three months later. The heavy burden of administering the grant quickly became apparent. Morgan soon realized that meeting all the grant's demands and running the programming that the grant was designed to support were too much for her and her small staff. Moreover, the administrative tasks associated with the grant were extremely time consuming, distracting Bayou Rebirth from its core mission of bringing attention to wetlands restoration and encouraging corporations to recognize their dependence on a healthy wetlands ecosystem. Aware that the grant would run out in December 2009, Morgan wrote more than two dozen grant applications that year, winning only a couple of small awards.[45] To Morgan, this process felt like time wasted relative to the mission.

44. "NOAA CRP Restoration Projects."
45. "NOAA CRP Restoration Projects."

Morgan's realization of the huge amount of time required to administer a large grant and to constantly apply for new ones led her to move away from the grant model toward a mixed revenue-generation model—one that included charging volunteers for their experience and collecting fees from educational programming. Morgan's relationships with larger nonprofits like Common Ground showed her that organizations sometimes had more volunteers than they had tasks at a given moment, and maintaining connections with a network of volunteer coordinators allowed her to "borrow" overflow volunteers to execute aspects of Bayou Rebirth's mission.

Revenue came in from elsewhere as well. The educational programming that Bayou Rebirth developed for the GMF grant increased Morgan's prominence, enabling her to charge speaker's fees for presentations on wetlands restoration. Bayou Rebirth created an adopt-a-plant program that, combined with some donations, paid for the staff. When things grew particularly tight, Morgan used her own money to cover expenses in the hope that more funds would come—and in the days when Americans were still mourning the devastation in Katrina, more money usually did. As all these activities constantly swirled and were reconfigured to support the mission, Morgan was at the center of it all: "I was a one-woman show for two years."[46]

While the taxing process of administering a large grant and applying for new funding led Morgan to lean into volunteer-derived income, this model ultimately proved as unreliable as grant funding. The 2010 British Petroleum oil spill revealed the instability of this form of revenue generation and imperiled Bayou Rebirth's work when it was needed more than ever. An insoluble problem arose when insurance companies refused to cover Bayou Rebirth's volunteers, citing the dangers of volunteers working in wetlands contaminated by a toxic oil spill. Thus, when Bayou Rebirth should have been expanding its campaign to demonstrate corporate America's dependence on and responsibility to the environment, it was unable to operate, losing volunteer-derived income and scrambling to secure insurance coverage.

Bayou Rebirth found itself in trouble. It did not have the staffing to ad-

46. Morgan, interview, July 15, 2010.

minister another major grant, and Morgan did not have the energy to take on grant writing again while running all the organization's operations. Morgan needed to find a solution by the fall, or the organization would have to shut down.

And so, Morgan sought a more formal partnership with Common Ground. Although the initial success of the partnership between the two organizations points to the adaptability of nonprofit organizations to conditions on the ground, its ultimate failure reveals how vulnerable nonprofits are to various short-term fluctuations, even if they are engaged in work that has long-term benefits for the communities they serve.[47]

Morgan's previous interactions with Common Ground, which went back to her graduate work on City Park in 2006, facilitated the expansion of that relationship when she came back to the city to found Bayou Rebirth; at that time, she characterized Common Ground's wetlands coordinator at as her "right arm." After the BP oil spill in 2010, Morgan met with Common Ground's operations director Thom Pepper, telling him that she did not know whether Bayou Rebirth would be able to survive. He responded, "Let's figure something out."

The two decided that Bayou Rebirth and Common Ground would jointly operate a wetlands mission. Bayou Rebirth would coordinate the planting sites, select the plants, and run the nursery in City Gardens, while Common Ground Relief would supply the trucks, provide volunteers, and cover the plantings under its liability insurance. The two nonprofits set up three neighborhood nurseries in blighted areas, including New Orleans East—a hard-hit community with a suburban feel that had long suffered from disinvestment and decay. Designed to improve the look of the communities, to engage the local population in ecology, and to use native plants to reduce flooding, the neighborhood nurseries synced with the missions of both organizations.

The partnership worked very well at first. The nurseries attracted volunteers and, through the volunteer fees, were financially self-sustainable. After paying for the volunteers' expenses and other overhead associated

47. In *Markets of Sorrow* Adams discusses the ways in which small private-sector volunteer organizations face a set of business-like pressures that often force them to merge with other larger organizations. Adams, *Markets of Sorrow*, 159.

with the nurseries, the two organizations split the proceeds. Bayou Rebirth made significantly less money than when the volunteers came directly through its doors, but the organization's administrative responsibilities decreased considerably. In fact, given Common Ground's stream of volunteers, supplies, and administrative structure, Morgan ultimately planned to hand the entire program over to Common Ground.

That remained her plan until a drought hit in 2011 and revealed the limits of altruism in their partnership. Fifty days of no rain scorched nine southern states, including Louisiana. According to the Southeast Regional Climate Center, southeast Louisiana averaged only 0.3 inches of rain in April compared to a normal rainfall of 4.44 inches. Then in May, the region averaged only 0.49 inches compared to a normal amount of 5.13 inches. Overall, the first five months of 2011 were among the driest in recorded history, and they combined with record-high temperatures. One manager of a commercial nursery indicated that its staff needed to water their plants almost 24 hours a day—literally quadrupling their water bill.[48] Presumably the Bayou Rebirth/Common Ground nurseries would face the same challenge, but unlike a commercial nursery they could not build the cost into their sales model to compensate.

While this natural phenomenon put the groups' community nurseries in great danger, operating within the nonprofit and volunteer context posed additional challenges. For example, the terrible spring weather cut the number of volunteers, a decline that usually did not occur until summer. A mismatch then occurred. Bayou Rebirth had a small staff who were trained to organize the work of volunteers, but with no volunteers, they had too little to do administratively. At the same time, however, it had the staggering responsibility of watering a thousand trees at three nursery locations across the city, which would require more hours of work than Morgan could pay her staff or anyone else to do. Morgan had hoped to recruit local volunteers. After all, the projects, which seeded the community with native plants, benefited the area's post-Katrina beautification efforts while drawing attention to the needs of the wetlands that had historically protected the region from the full impact of hurricanes. Nevertheless, res-

48. "Experts: Drought Could Continue"; "Drought Makes 2011 Second Driest Year on Record in Louisiana."

idents ignored Morgan's calls for aid even as the ponds dried up and the plants died. Morgan tried to take care of them on her own. As she put it, "So . . . in the end, it's me."[49]

The difficulties of maintaining the ponds triggered the deterioration of the relationship between the two organizations. Early that summer, Common Ground needed to renew its insurance but encountered resistance from insurance companies that cited the ponds as potentially dangerous to children and contended that the plantings were unsafe. At least, however, the insurance companies called Thom Pepper back, while totally ignoring Morgan's earlier pleas for insurance. Could it have been sexism that allowed him to make some headway? Or Common Ground's size and national prominence? Whatever the case may have been, tensions between the organizations mounted as Common Ground still had trouble getting affordable insurance; their relationship further disintegrated over accusations of the poor conditions of the ponds. Ultimately the two organizations parted ways in what Morgan called an ugly "divorce."

Despite Morgan blaming herself for the decline of Bayou Rebirth, the structural deficits that contributed to Bayou Rebirth's decline are apparent: the unsuitability of existing nonprofit funding models for disaster recovery and a lack of support for sustaining new nonprofit organizations. Bayou Rebirth's narrative arc points to an important analytical question regarding nonprofits acting in a disaster relief/recovery capacity: If the United States is going to continue to ask nonprofit, volunteer organizations to address fundamental local issues and needs in an emergency disaster context, should their funding be based on the standard nonprofit, grant-based funding model? How can enthusiastic and compassionate novices to the grant-writing process, under-resourced startups, and new organizations that do not know how to "play the game" possibly have the institutional infrastructure to meet long-term, complex needs, such as those generated by a Katrina-scaled event? Unfortunately, these questions cannot be answered by historical analysis alone.[50]

Two other concerns raised in Morgan's and other testimony is what I

49. Morgan, interview, August 23, 2011.

50. Like Bayou Rebirth, Project Nehemiah had won a government grant, but Franke found that the paperwork involved was not worth the trouble. The grant covered the work for rebuilding a single home, and Franke had to assign a full-time employee just to administer

broadly characterize as the lack of professional credentials of volunteers engaged in difficult work and the lack of regulation of the volunteer organizations generally. In some cases, volunteers working in unsafe conditions were injured. Scott Eustis relayed the story of doing a planting with Bayou Rebirth on a sandflat in June 2009 in 103-degree weather. The volunteers and crew leader had to take an airboat to the location, and when the airboat returned to get additional volunteers, it knocked over their water supply. Worsening matters, two airboats got stuck in low water. Eustis did not indicate how they ultimately extricated the boats and volunteers but called the whole affair a "disaster" and noted that Bayou Rebirth stopped doing plantings from late June through early August because of it.[51]

In gutting and home rebuilding, meanwhile, Adrian Manriquez laughed off "hanging from rafters and narrowly escaping death by natural gas." He also acknowledged the inefficiencies of volunteer labor, arguing that the lack of regulation for nonprofits had a range of outcomes from inefficiency to hazardous conditions. Claiming that nonprofits did not fall under OSHA, he indicated that volunteers signed waivers and then engaged in work that usually required licensure, creating dangerous situations.[52] Although Manriquez was the only interviewee to call out such risks explicitly, volunteer concerns sometimes came out as asides in their conversations, such as in an interview with Andrew Ryan, also of Operation Helping Hands, whose interviewer apologized for having a cough. Ryan was suffering from a cold at the time and had a cough as well. When asked about it, he very quickly said, "We breathe in some bad stuff. I'm hoping it's just a cough."[53] One can surmise that this concern must have been very near to the surface of his awareness for him to raise it so easily.[54]

---

the grant. For this reason, he decided not to seek another government grant. He did indicate that he would consider a foundation grant, but echoing Eustis's claim about knowing how to play the game, he felt writing the proposals was difficult, requiring exact buzzwords to be successful. He could have used a grant writer, but the grants they had won before did not allow any spending on hiring a professional writer, and they did not have sufficient funds to hire one. Franke, interview, July 16, 2010.

51. Eustis, interview.

52. Manriquez, interview.

53. Ryan, interview.

54. Ryan, interview.

Indeed, many interviewees found using volunteer labor to rebuild homes highly problematic.[55] Volunteer laborers, crew leaders, and even the leadership of the four largest rebuilding organizations all addressed the inefficiency of using volunteers. Caitlin Alverson, only six months into her stint as an AmeriCorps volunteer and still working as a volunteer crew leader, ran into homeowner frustrations with volunteer labor early on:

> I think it's a hard thing to do, to have unskilled laborers come into your house and work on it. I think it's hard to ask for that assistance, and it's also hard for the long-term volunteers out in the field to be micromanaging and making sure that things are coming out to a professional standard. I definitely think that sometimes it's hard on the homeowners. They're expecting a highly professional product, but they're not getting it. Then it's hard on the laborers because they're just learning. I think most of the time, homeowners are really grateful, but we definitely have had homeowners that are really frustrated with us.
>
> I did have one homeowner that I got pretty frustrated with . . . well no, I guess that's two. I had worked in the house for two months, and the homeowners came in for the walk-through. We did the walk-through with her. It took a solid hour and a half for her to thank us and that was like instigated by our project manager. It was surprising to me that it took that long just to get a thank you. After that was initiated, she seemed very grateful. That was unexpected, but understandable. In another instance, we had gone in to do insulation in a house, and it was impossible for us to insulate the entire attic because of the way the house was built. Half of the attic was inaccessible because the AC was done through the floors. We insulated half of the attic, and we told the homeowner the situation. Then she nearly had a heart attack. She was very upset and distraught and frustrated that we couldn't finish the attic. I probably should have been a little more sympathetic. It can be frustrating when you go in there and you give somebody an insulation job that's worth like $2,000, you do a good job, and they get mad at you because you can't do the whole thing.[56]

55. Greenhow, interview; Porot, interview; Fitzpatrick, interview, November 20, 2011; Ross, interview.
56. Alverson, interview.

Alverson's testimony highlights the difficulties that organization leaders faced in managing expectations both in volunteers, who often expressed irritation when clients appeared insufficiently grateful or deserving, and in clients, who expected the skills of volunteers to match those of contractors.

Crew leaders, tasked with managing short-term and newly arriving long-term volunteers, faced this difficulty daily. Take, for example, this highly complex reflection by crew leader Alex Lilly. Lilly correctly pointed to rampant contractor fraud as contributing to the demand for volunteer labor, yet she also wondered how the widespread use of volunteer labor affected professional builders. In addition, she expressed frustration around gender dynamics with "older men" in her volunteer work crews and with homeowners' expectations of professional workmanship:

> A couple of weeks ago, my friend was painting at a site and some construction guy was giving him trouble saying he hates volunteers 'cause they take work away from him. I've never really thought about that until he told us the story, but that does make a lot of sense. I can't blame them. We do take work away from them, but it's up to the homeowner how they want to do it. Volunteers are not going to screw them over, but I've come across plenty of homes where the homeowner is in our program because they were screwed over by a contractor. I think people are nervous about using contractors at this point because everyone's heard so many stories about people getting ripped off by them. And volunteers do it for free. They just have to pay for the materials. So, it's a lot cheaper for them. We don't do professional work, but we do the best we can, and it looks great when it's done. It doesn't look professional, but still looks great and the homeowners are happy with it.

Admitting that she did not guarantee the work of her volunteers, in contrast to that of licensed professionals' work, Lilly shared some instances when her volunteers performed substandard work:

> Yes. (*Laughter.*) I have [seen it] plenty of times, and it's very frustrating trying to explain to them that they're doing something wrong, especially when you have older people. They don't want to listen to you or at least most of the time they don't. When you have college kids, they listen to you. They think it's awesome that you can do all that, and they really want to learn. But I've

had crews of older men, especially that have had some experience just doin' work around their house. It's just hard to try to remind them that I have been doing this for quite a while. I don't consider myself a professional, but I do really good work, and I've had supervisors tell me that I do really good work. So that makes me feel good. But it's hard trying to get them to listen to you because they're older and they probably have had longer experience, but not the same experience that I have. Doing stuff around their homes is different from doing stuff for someone else that you don't know, because you need it to look good. If it doesn't look good in your home, that's your fault. But if it doesn't look good in someone else's home, that's your fault and that's not a good thing.[57]

All the top-level leaders interviewed for this project wrestled with the problem of volunteer labor. Operation Nehemiah's Fred Franke and Common Ground's Thom Pepper, for instance, each discussed using skill inventories for incoming volunteer groups to determine their most efficient deployment. Meanwhile, Jim Pate argued that Habitat for Humanity's dedicated professionals—with decades-old strategies for volunteer home building—gave them the capacity to engage in the work productively, but even he argued that ramping up that capacity at the outset of the recovery was a challenge. The tension regarding the appropriate blend of using professionals and volunteers always remained, as this extended reflection with OHH's last director, Kevin Fitzpatrick, illustrates:

This was one of the tough but valuable things we learned. I did some calculations on our expenses for volunteers. We did an assessment about whether we wanted to rebuild the houses that were contaminated with drywall with contractors or volunteers. We found it was just as expeditious, the same amount I should say, with contractors as the volunteers.

It was a big surprise. It wasn't a big surprise by the time I had done the math, but I started to sense that's where it was heading. That's one of the reasons I did the calculations. I was asked to consider doing the drywall houses with volunteers. I resisted at first, and then I was asked to do the math. When I did the math, I wasn't surprised, but I was surprised how

57. Lilly, interview.

close it was. It was within a dollar or two per square foot. The contractors were more than volunteers but only marginally. We've found that having high-volume numbers of unskilled volunteers is costly—you have to house them, you have to feed 'em, you have to insure them, and then you have to have a staff to work with them. It takes them a long time, so you have jobs open for a long time. They make mistakes. You have to go back and correct 'em. You have to have the right staff that can help them as opposed to a very small lean staff that can just go in, work with contractors, and keep them honest. If you give them enough volume of work, the contractors will keep the price down. But the flip side is we ran into the same problem with contractors that the homeowners ran into. They didn't always do good work. They were not always honest. We really had to be vigilant.[58]

The interview then progressed to a discussion about how to properly use volunteers, and Fitzpatrick, in a manner very similar to Common Ground's executive director Thom Pepper, argued that volunteers were most appropriate in so-called second-stage work:

We found that the contractors and volunteers were usually not a good match. The contractors were very impatient. Another issue we ran into was trying to build. It was ideal, but it didn't usually work out this way. We'd build a house up to a certain point and then bring the volunteers in to do the drywall and the painting and then bring the contractors in to do the finish work. Well, there's always the blame game. You know, it was never on time—the contractor would blame the volunteers, and the volunteer coordinator would say, you know, "The contractor wasn't ready." It was, it was very difficult to make that work.

At that stage in 2008, that was our management style. We had a way more organized process in 2009. We had another manager. His name was Russ. We'd do construction, and he was much better at organizing the worksites with the volunteers. Then we were much more selective about our contractors, and having several jobs open at once so that you had a place to put the volunteers in at any given moment. We were doing painting exte-

58. Fitzpatrick, interview, August 21, 2013.

riors, which was really helpful for us because it gave us a place to put over-flow volunteers. March would come and we would have hundreds of people, you know; by the time March was over, you had over a thousand-and-some volunteers, most of those would just go paint the exterior of houses. They wouldn't do anything inside a house. That helped a lot.

Fitzpatrick noted the importance of having staff who could work with both contractors and volunteers and who knew how to deploy volunteers most effectively, as well as smooth over tensions between the two:

> The contractors often don't have the soft skills for dealing with volunteers, and we had to have staff who did. We had a lot of long-term volunteers who came through AmeriCorps. Notre Dame would send a crew every summer. Plus, we had our own internal program that called on our own Catholic Charity volunteers. And we could never have done the program without them.
>
> They [long-term volunteers] were that intermediary. Our construc-tion manager would assign houses to each one of them, and they would get what they called their own house. So, Collin, Georgia, or whoever would have a house that they're responsible for usually from beginning to end. If we were assigning a new house, we would put one of the AmeriCorps in charge of it, there'd be a construction manager over her or him, they would see it through, and they would be on-site daily managing the volunteers. They would normally have another AmeriCorps volunteer with 'em —like a junior and a senior volunteer, along with the volunteers. They'd get trained if we were lucky.
>
> August/September, we would get them trained in the basic skillsets that they would need and then they would run the crews themselves. The St. Bernard Project uses that same model, and I think Rebuilding Together does to a degree. Without having them on site, we wouldn't have been able to get much done. They have their own kind of community 'cause many of them lived together. They would go out, and they would spend time together. They loved being in New Orleans. I'm still in touch with a lot of 'em through Facebook. I don't remember how many we ran through the program, well over 100 during the course of six/seven years.

Those are the volunteers we'd get to know well. They would stay any-where from three months to two/two-and-a-half years, and few of 'em ended up being hired on as staff.[59]

Fitzpatrick noted that RTNO and the St. Bernard Project used similar strategies, and Pepper of Common Ground also spelled out a somewhat intricate formula of using licensed contractors and high-volume numbers of volunteers.[60]

As if attempting to build homes with a volunteer workforce was not dif-ficult enough, multiple interviewees lamented the fact that most grants did not provide money for the work in advance or even in an ongoing manner. Instead, funders reimbursed rebuilding organizations only for fully com-pleted work after an arduous audit, essentially forcing the nonprofits to float the cost of their work without guarantee of being paid. This situa-tion was dire for nonprofits that did not have the resources to navigate the process, as described by Leonard Penner of Mennonite Disaster Services:

During our peak, we had from ten to twelve volunteer rebuilding organiza-tions in the city. The United Way director of New Orleans is a good friend of

59. Fitzpatrick, interview, August 21, 2013.

60. Thom Pepper began moving in this direction when he was charged with increasing the professionalization of Common Ground in 2007. Thinking back to the problems with volunteer labor after hurricanes in his home state of Florida, Pepper said in his interview:

Volunteers poured down there, but what had happened five/ten years after this storm is that people who had volunteers come in couldn't show how their houses had been put back together and it was affecting property values. Banks weren't interested in giving people a mortgage on a house where they didn't know the quality of the construction. And people who had rebuilt but hadn't hired contractors were being subjected to fines and demolition orders. So, I thought, "Well, if we're gonna do this rebuilding, I want to make sure that we don't put people in jeopardy." So, we partnered with a local general contractor in the fall of '07. And we made sure that as people came back to rebuild, they hired licensed general contractors to do the plumbing and the electrical work. And we limited our use of volunteers to framing, drywall installation and millwork installation. We might have organizations or companies that wanted to come down and volunteer with us. I mean, we put roofs on twenty houses/thirty houses when we had a big roofing company from Chicago come down a couple years. So, we had a certain expertise that could be done, but it was done by these licensed contractors. Luckily, we didn't have any exposure with the Chinese drywall, we haven't had anybody's house collapse, and we haven't had anybody hurt on the job. (*Laughter.*)

mine, and he said "that the volunteer organizations are literally driving the rebuilding." However, this is the important key: we needed the gap funding, whether it was state or federal funding. That was a very important component. I think we have a lot to learn there. In most disasters that are not this widespread, short-term funding, like what Red Cross or Salvation Army can provide, will usually rebuild. But New Orleans was so massive. We were warned ahead of time that the short-term funding was going to run out and we needed to be prepared for the longer haul. Those organizations like United Way and the better casework agencies were very busy writing grants, and that process takes longer to unfold. Those partnerships became very, very important to us.

State and national funding is very, very cumbersome. You have to have a really good organization to find your way through the maze. What we found is that those organizations that have good casework ability, good grant-writing ability and understand construction will be successful. Those who do not understand those three components turn into a disaster, because even the state organizations that often administer federal grant money get confused. They need help from the organization that is requesting the grant to understand the process.[61]

Penner's testimony points to the difficulties faced not only by nonprofits new to New Orleans but also by established organizations like OHH and RTNO.[62] RTNO executive director Daniela Rivero similarly described how the nonprofit was also forced into the precarious position of floating millions of dollars for ongoing projects on the promise of receiving grant money owed to them.[63]

Moreover, Rivero, like Thom Pepper and Jim Pate, frequently touched on the theme of organizational capacity in obtaining and administering grants. She was particularly concerned that small, startup nonprofits were unprepared to be good stewards of the funding they received.[64] RTNO be-

61. Penner, interview.
62. Porot, interview.
63. Rivero, interview, August 21, 2013.
64. Common Ground's Thom Pepper railed on this topic at length and with exceeding vociferousness. Perhaps that had to do with Common Ground's history. You may recall Caitlin Reilly's perception of expensive wastefulness in the early years of the Common Ground Collective. Pepper never admitted as much, but his taking on the role of executive director

gan its recovery work with greater administrative capacity than most new groups: it was part of a national organization that had been working with city grants for more than twenty years. In addition, Rivero entered disaster recovery work in New Orleans with significant corporate management and community organizing experience. Like Pate, she had to worry less about developing new capacities than about ramping up existing resources. While expressing frustration with the red tape associated with grant administration, Rivero indicated that these procedures nevertheless ensured that grant recipients complied with accounting standards.

Yet when Rivero started at RTNO, it had only recently begun to scale up its recovery work, and it had not fully embraced accounting standards that met the required federal level of stringency. Rivero wondered if this laxness stemmed from the attitude of some people she encountered in nonprofit work who associated efficiency with "real jobs" in the corporate world, which they explicitly sought to avoid.[65] Apparently, the problems associated with this character type played a prominent role in Rivero's set of leadership challenges; she discussed at length difficulties with working with staff who asserted that working in a nonprofit should be "easy." Rivero believed that people's desire to be in New Orleans, with its laid-back reputation, exacerbated these assumptions. From Rivero's perspective, volunteers and staff with this attitude, combined with the stresses and immediate needs of disaster recovery, created an environment that was not conducive to responsible long-term planning.[66]

These comments merged with those of Morgan, Franke, and others who pointed to the negative outcomes that resulted from being so caught up in immediate needs that long-term planning was overlooked.[67] Rivero went a step further when she noted that a lack of accountability in the context of receiving grant funding can ultimately destroy an organization:

---

at Common Ground was described in the media as an attempt to bring greater efficiency and business acumen to Common Ground's work, moving the group from its anarchist origins.

Reilly, interview; Pepper, interview; Pate, interview; Pope, "Common Ground Leader Thom Pepper."

65. Rivero, interview, August 24, 2011; Stiebler, interview; Pate, interview.

66. Rivero, interview, August 24, 2011.

67. Rivero, interview, August 24, 2011.

I think the biggest win of all my four years here at Rebuilding Together has been putting it into people's minds the fact that you're doing something today doesn't mean you're doing it wrong, but it also doesn't mean we can't do it better, or it doesn't mean that we shouldn't explore other ways to do it. It's a constant process of implementing certain processes. Then you evaluate how you're doing. Sometimes you will implement something that doesn't work and that's fine too. If you don't try, you'll never know. That was definitely the biggest win. We implemented a lot immediately as I started. I put together a volunteer calendar for the next two months. Some things were easy, and some things were harder, but I think if we hadn't had that transition, if we hadn't had the growth, the processes, and the policies that we have in place today, we couldn't be working with federal grants. We had the transition into the federal in 2008, and we got our first grant from the city since Katrina. We weren't used to environmental reviews and following regulations. Everything was, "Just get it done...

[All the work in grant management] can bring you down. One of the things that I see that shocks me: everybody thinks that federal money is free money. "We're gonna give you a $3 million grant." No private funder says, "Here's $3 million, go ahead and spend it the way you want it." Nobody gives you that level of support. You can find that the grant can be the tail wagging the organization because you're so bogged down with what do you need to do and setting everything up. Luckily, in 2008 we started receiving some money from the Salvation Army, and they had a process that was not as stringent but very similar to a federal grant of qualifying the homeowner. Every funder wants to make sure that whoever is getting this money really needs it, especially the federal government. When the money is public, that gets extrapolated to the extreme. When we started with the Salvation Army, we adopted those things as our regular case management.

Once you get to a higher standard, there's no reason to go backwards, and we realized that it was helping us screen homeowners better. At the beginning, we wouldn't tell homeowners, "We want to see your bank account. We want to see, this. We want to see that." People didn't have Road Home money yet. Every year of the recovery is different because the resources are different in every sense. The volunteers are different. The funding is different. The requirements that come with the funding is different. So, the opportunities are different.[68]

Despite Rivero's sophisticated understanding of so-called free money in the context of grants, she was still caught off-guard after receiving a major donation of drywall that was ultimately found to be contaminated; it forced a second rebuild of hundreds of homes across New Orleans. After the storm, large quantities of drywall had begun to arrive in the Gulf states. Habitat for Humanity in New Orleans received a large donation of drywall from Interior/Exterior Building Supply (INEX), which told the organization that National Gypsum had supplied the drywall and that National Gypsum only sold drywall in the United States. Based on this information, Habitat assumed that the drywall met U.S. safety standards.[69] According to executive director Pate, the donation exceeded their needs, and they let other rebuilding agencies, including RTNO and OHH, take as much as they needed.[70] As early as 2006, these and other organizations such as the Louisiana Methodist Conference, Lutheran Disaster Response, the Episcopal Diocese of Louisiana, and the St. Bernard Project began installing the drywall in homes across Orleans Parish.

Habitat's assumption regarding the safety of the drywall, however, proved tragically incorrect. Residents of rebuilt homes soon noticed deteriorating electrical appliances, failing HVAC systems, and corroded silverware; in some cases, they were experiencing health problems as well. Concern arose in the summer of 2009 when the media learned that New Orleans Saints' coach Sean Payton had to renovate his home, built in 2006, because of problems caused by the drywall.[71] According to Rivero, she and other directors of rebuilding nonprofits who had accepted donations from Habitat began to worry, but Habitat ignored their inquiries.[72] In fact, as late as June 2009, Habitat was still claiming that it had received no complaints. Ultimately Payton became the lead plaintiff in a suit against Knauff

68. Rivero, interview, August 24, 2011.

69. Reckdahl, "Chinese Drywall Concerns."

70. Pate, interview.

71. Armstrong, "Behind-the-Scenes Look"; DeBerry, "Hope Takes a Hit"; Gist, "For New Orleans Saints Coach"; "After Katrina in New Orleans"; Buchanan, "Lower Nine and Parts of Algiers Still Struggle."

72. Rivero, interview, August 21, 2013.

Plasterboard Tainjin, the Chinese company accused of manufacturing the drywall that was corroding home interiors and making people sick. It was only when news of this suit hit the media that Rivero, director of one of the top four rebuilding organizations in New Orleans, learned that all the drywall was certifiably defective. Although Rivero believes that other directors were similarly in the dark, I was unable to prove that they had the same experience. Nevertheless, many community members felt that Habitat took too long to recognize the scope of the problem and to commit itself to solve it. As one resident, whose home was being rebuilt for the second time, put it, "It's like there was a period when they went into corporate self-protection mode. I get that. But their name is Habitat for Humanity. I mean humanity is right in the name. They didn't own the problem until it was nailed to their heads."[73]

Although the contaminated drywall affected consumers across the southeast United States, its impact differed. Individuals like Payton, who had the means to construct a new home during these years, more than likely had the resources to rebuild and even sue INEX. Under-resourced New Orleanians who had stitched together Road Home money, insurance payments, and the support of charitable organizations simply did not have those resources, and once again, they had to turn for help to the nonprofits, which were themselves in a perilous position.

Ultimately, the city's largest nonprofit rebuilding organizations—Habitat for Humanity, OHH, and RTNO—took on the task of stripping the rebuilt houses down to the studs and installing new drywall at a cost of approximately $40,000 per home.[74] Rivero, who had managed the severe stresses associated with floating millions of dollars in credit while the city and state failed to reimburse promptly, indicated that remediating these homes took a heavy toll on RTNO and was her worst experience as an executive director: it was akin to "another Katrina."[75]

While RTNO survived, Operation Helping Hands, which had been in existence since 2005, had hosted more than 30,000 volunteers, had gutted 2,000 homes, and had painted or rebuilt 600, went under. The costs

73. Nolan, "Hurricane Relief Groups Are Gutting."
74. Pepper, interview.
75. Rivero, interview, August 21, 2013; McAllen, "Toxic Chinese Drywall Taxes Katrina Relief Groups."

associated with repairing homes damaged by the contaminated drywall were simply too great. Before the revelations, Catholic Charities had already determined to wind down the organization's work, but the drywall hastened the timeline, with OHH officials indicating that the organization could have otherwise continued serving the community for two more years or longer.[76]

The distribution of hazardous drywall throughout the post-Katrina home-rebuilding process reflected the use of a large cohort of uncoordinated nonprofit organizations to engage in widespread, long-term recovery work. Multiple interviewees at a range of levels spoke of the extent to which work was being executed with no centralized planning and oversight and with minimal observance of safety regulations, especially in the early days of the storm. At that time, there was no government inspection process for imported drywall. With the responsibility left to home inspectors during the buying process, this was essentially a case of "let the buyer beware."[77] But the people who received help from Habitat for Humanity, OHH, RTNO, and other agencies, however, were not "buyers." More often, they were among New Orleans's least economically empowered citizens, grasping for help in one of the largest disaster areas in American history. When reflecting on the drywall situation, Rivero used language parallel to her warning about using grant money to do nonprofit work: "Well, I learned that nothing is ever really free. I can assure you that."[78]

One can infer by her usage of parallel language that Rivero saw the large donation of drywall as a situation like that of an unprepared organization receiving a large grant; in this case, "the tail" of having to rebuild forty homes at $40,000 each threw RTNO severely off-course, while leading OHH to its demise.

76. Threlkeld, "A Job Well Done"; Nolan, "Chinese Drywall Forces."
77. Gromicko and Kenton, "Chinese Drywall"; U.S. Consumer Product Safety Commission, "Other Frequently Asked Questions."
78. Rivero, interview, August 21, 2013.

Conclusion
INTEGRATING NONPROFITS INTO
A BROAD RECOVERY EFFORT

> My hope is that when our generation is coming into political and societal
> roles it becomes a political question like for the generation before us
> with, "Where were you during Vietnam?" My hope is that "What did you
> do in response to Hurricane Katrina?" becomes a similar question for our
> generation, and it can kind of function to remind us that there are roles
> the government plays in our lives and that whenever there's a tragedy
> there are ways that we as individuals are responsible for responding too.
>
> **—David Harms, Mennonite Disaster Services**

Meteorologists called Hurricane Katrina a once-in-a-lifetime event. Yet almost fifteen years to the day that Katrina landed in 2005, Louisianans faced the possibility of being hit by two hurricanes simultaneously as Tropical Storms Laura and Marco bore down on them—a circumstance without precedence in "modern meteorological history."[1] On the West Coast, the second and third largest wildfires in California's history forced the evacuation of more than 136,000 people from their homes in a similarly unprecedented mega-event.[2] Meanwhile, the COVID-19 pandemic placed unparalleled stress on the U.S. economy, government, schools, hospitals, and charitable organizations. Clearly, it is only a matter of time before the United States experiences its next mega-event. With that in mind, our interviewees' suggestions to improve the charitable sector's participation in disaster recovery seem very timely. It may well be the exact right moment to examine and synthesize their ideas and allow them to guide us toward a more effective recovery process so that we are fully prepared when the next great catastrophe strikes.

It is important to recognize first what may be the most gratifying les-

1. CNN, "Marco Downgraded to a Tropical Storm."
2. Money, "'Significant Progress' as Weather Helps."

son emerging from the Katrina recovery period: a reaffirmation of the vast goodwill of the American people. Despite the country's deepening political and social divides, activists formed more than 500 new charities while over 1.5 million short-term volunteers arrived in New Orleans, providing over 100 million hours of volunteer labor across a broad range of activities from home rebuilding to wetlands restoration to legal advising. With the country moving away from viewing such work as a government responsibility, hundreds of mostly young adults rushed in to fill the void, transplanting themselves to the city to do long-term work. By any measure, these private citizens played a role—some would say the major role—in saving one of America's greatest cities.[3] As discussed in chapter 8, given New Orleans's uniqueness, the only single convergence factor that can account for the scale of this outreach is a shared sense of American identity.[4]

To some extent, the backgrounds of the volunteers we interviewed can provide insight into who in the private sector will answer the call for long-term aid and under what circumstances this aid will be given when the next mega-disaster arrives. As predicted by Wilson and Musick's integrated theory, these individuals will have characteristics associated with high rates of volunteering under regular conditions. As was the case among our participant volunteers, rather than being drawn to volunteerism for the first time by a single precipitating event, most will possess a history of activism, civic engagement, or volunteering long before the moment of tragedy. Although these characteristics can predict engagement by middle-aged and senior adults, they cannot be relied on to predict the involvement of young adults, who constituted most of the long-term volunteers in New Orleans. Indeed, the integrated theory predicts a drop in volunteering for young adults except for circumstances involving high risk, defined as "the anticipated dangers—whether legal, social, physical, financial and so forth—of engaging in a particular type of work."[5] Our volunteers confirmed this hypothesis by describing various forms of risk—ranging from

3. Threlkeld, "A Job Well Done."
4. In "Personal Responsibility and Volunteering after a Natural Disaster," Michel describes how natural disasters can lead to altruistic behaviors that override pre-disaster social differences and that can converge on political entities like states and the federal government. Michel, "Personal Responsibility," 634, 635.
5. Wiltfang and McAdam, "Costs and Risks of Social Activism," 989.

experiences of physical danger to extreme financial stresses to the work's extreme psychological toll as evidenced by frequent references to drug and alcohol usage as forms of stress relief. Thus, a higher perception of risk related to volunteer activities would likely draw larger numbers of young adults with backgrounds in volunteering and civic engagement to the next American catastrophe—mimicking the behavior we saw in New Orleans.

Our interviewee testimony reveals that volunteer goodwill and derring-do, even the derring-do of more than one million people, are still inadequate to meet the needs of a disaster zone.[6] New grassroots organizations quickly identified and articulated community needs, but lacking guidance or structural capacity, they struggled to sustain themselves over the long term.[7] Driven by the community's dire needs, unprepared young volunteers engaged in arduous, emotionally gut-wrenching, and occasionally physically dangerous labor for which they were often unprepared; executive directors meanwhile grappled with the contradictions inherent to using an untrained temporary labor force to do work that typically required professional skill. Even large established organizations like Habitat for Humanity, Rebuilding Together, and Catholic Charities struggled to expand capacity and could not coordinate a response to the toxic drywall fiasco.

To the extent that many in the United States remain committed to a neoliberal approach to disaster recovery that combines private contracting, the mobilization of charitable organizations, and the deployment of multitudes of volunteers, it is possible—even likely—that these dynamics could play out again. With this in mind, our interviewees offered several suggestions for improved performance. Their recommendations are significant because, in contrast to the haphazard way in which nonprofits grew and responded to the catastrophe, our interviewees advocated for an intentional integration of charitable organizations and volunteers into the recovery and rebuilding process. Their suggestions include enhanced and centralized communications; more flexible funding for early-stage recovery work, with gap funding for longer runway projects; preparatory work to increase the effectiveness of long- and short-term volunteers; and more deliberate engagement with the local population.

Interviewee suggestions on enhanced and centralized communications

6. Flaherty et al., *Floodlines,* 108.
7. Chandra and Acosta, *Role of Nongovernmental Organizations,* 3.

correspond to some extent with the strategies articulated in John Kania and Mark Kramer's influential 2011 theory, Collective Impact (CI), which proposes a holistic and intentional set of practices to execute large-scale social change, in contrast to what they call the "isolated impact" approach of most government agencies and individual nonprofits. Kania and Kramer identify five conditions for success: a common agenda, shared measurement systems, continuous communication, mutually reinforcing activities, and backbone support organizations.[8]

Given the theory's influence, it is not surprising that there have been several attempts to apply CI within a disaster recovery context.[9] Debashish Naik, for example, proposes applying CI principles to disaster recovery based on his observations of reconstruction in Odisha, India, after a super cyclone. Though a world away from New Orleans, Naik's observations about Odisha sound very much like those of our interviewees: although "large-scale rehabilitation and reconstruction require broad cross sector coordination," organizations involved in recovery focus on "isolated interventions." Naik appreciates the efforts of local and international charitable organizations, government, and international agencies but argues that these organizations persist in isolating their impact as a means of differentiating themselves in the competition for funding.[10]

Our interviewees' analyses of the recovery's shortcomings and their recommendations for more effective processes resonate with several elements of CI.[11] Foreshadowing Kania and Kramer's calls for mutually reinforcing activities and continuous communication, our interviewees' most common critique of the recovery effort was its lack of centralized coordination, direction, or authority to turn to for information. Take, for instance, this appraisal from Andrew Greenhow, a construction assistant with Project Homecoming:

> FEMA needs to know what Entergy needs. Entergy needs to know what FEMA needs. The Road Home needs to have it communicated to them

8. Kania and Kramer, "Collective Impact," 39–40.

9. "Hilton Prize Laureates Focus on Disaster Relief"; Brundiers, "Leveraging Disasters," 15–27; Naik, "A 'Collective Impact Framework.'"

10. Naik, "A 'Collective Impact Framework.'"

11. Kania and Kramer, "Collective Impact," 40.

that property taxes are not an acceptable way to shell out grants. I would suggest communication between the rebuild organizations and between the power companies, the water companies. The sewage and water boards frequently had absolutely no idea what Entergy was up to. None of them had a clue what FEMA wanted. And none of these people had any idea what my homeowners wanted.[12]

Poor communication was a significant issue that our interviewees felt was exacerbated by the federal and local governments working poorly with charitable organizations. Fred Franke, executive director of the small non-profit startup Operation Nehemiah, said, "We work with the city real well, but the city doesn't work real well with you." He went on to note, with some disappointment, that FEMA did nothing to develop the initial connections it had made with faith-based groups, despite the Bush administration's establishment of the Office of Faith-Based and Community Initiatives only four years prior.[13] Meanwhile, Emily Stiebler, a volunteer coordinator with the much larger rebuilding organization, Operation Helping Hands (OHH), indicated that she saw no substantive connections between OHH's efforts and local government. To the contrary, she explained, local government appeared indifferent to nonprofit rebuilding efforts. She asked why, for example, the city pooled applications for building permits and inspections from nonprofit organizations along with those from large commercial developers. This resulted in OHH having to hound the city to secure building permits and obtain inspections for "shovel-ready projects" in support of the most vulnerable victims of the storm.[14]

Many argued that this lack of communication not only hindered the nonprofit sector from coordinating with government agencies but also fostered an environment that discouraged the nonprofits from coordinating with each other.[15] Presaging Collective Impact's critique of the nonprofit sector's tendency to engage in "isolated impact," Mike Ellis of Love Knows No Bounds and Anna Tova Levin of Southeast Louisiana Legal Services, for instance, noted that the lack of coordination between nonprofit groups,

12. Greenhow, interview.
13. Fred Franke, interview, July 16, 2010.
14. Stiebler, interview.
15. Stiebler, interview; Ellis, interview; Silverman, interview.

combined with each one's narrow focus, resulted in confusion, redundant efforts, and significant gaps in addressing New Orleans's needs.[16] Ironically, although some interviewees saw gaps in meeting the city's needs, others, like volunteer coordinator Stiebler and OHH program director Kevin Fitz-patrick, noted occasional difficulties in finding work for volunteers: "Volunteers show up and most of 'em want to work. They don't like to sit around and waste time or do jobs that are meaningless. One of my colleagues said that she had volunteers dig a ditch one day and then would have the volunteers from another group fill in the ditch. She literally did this."[17]

To prevent the occurrence of such circumstances, Kania and Kramer advocate for communication and coordination to occur through a "back-bone support organization" using a "highly structured process that leads to effective decision making." Only executive directors Daniela Rivero, of RTNO, and James Pate, of Habitat for Humanity, expressed a similar idea: both noted that centralized guidance from nonlocal parties would have been ideal because local officials were themselves struggling to re-build their homes. Rivero went further when she very briefly considered the formation of a centralized group of recovery experts to direct activi-ties early in the recovery.[18] More commonly, our interviewees echoed the conclusions of a facilitated dialogue among forty-seven Louisiana NGO leaders led by Anita Chandra and Joie Acosta of the Rand Corporation. They concluded that local or state government could best fill the role of coordinating and integrating nonprofit efforts, as also articulated by Anna Levin of Southeast Louisiana Legal Services:[19]

I think that there needs to be a lot more communication between all of those groups, because without all of those groups communicating, there are groups duplicating effort. I think that's one of the biggest things, com-municating, so that you don't have three organizations all doing the exact

16. Anita Chandra and Joie Acosta analyzed testimony from a group of forty-seven lead-ers of NGOs involved in Katrina recovery and came to a similar conclusion. Chandra and Acosta, *Role of Nongovernmental Organizations,* 12; Ellis, interview; Levin, interview.

17. Fitzpatrick, interview, August 21, 2013.

18. Rivero, interview, August 21, 2013; Pate, interview.

19. Ellis, interview; Levin, interview; Stiebler, interview; Silverman, interview.

same thing. Instead have three different organizations doing three different things 'cause that is more effective. . . . I feel like you need to tell them in the event of a disaster, "These are the organizations that all need to communicate and here's what each organization's role will be." That sort of has to come from the state.[20]

Along these same lines, our interviewees argued that networks between charitable organizations and social/welfare agencies must be established long before disaster strikes.[21] Very few interviewees could even recollect such coordination during the recovery, making only brief references to the United Way, the Greater New Orleans Disaster Recovery Program, and the People's Hurricane Relief Fund. Indeed the omission of any references to these or any other organizational efforts by the rest of this project's interviewees indicates that such bodies had little impact on the experience of our volunteers operating in the field or leadership roles.[22] More frequently, they contended that the overwhelming urgency of addressing survivors' needs in the moment and the large inflows of money that allowed individual organizations to operate independently undermined collaboration.[23] Bethany Billman, a special projects manager with OHH, described this succinctly: "When there was lots of money in the beginning, no one talked. Since organizations increasingly compete for grants, they do not often share good ideas."[24]

As they reflected on this pattern, several interviewees advocated for communities with a high risk of disaster (like New Orleans) to create networks of nonprofits and government agencies *in preparation* for a disaster—a point noted emphatically by Fred Franke:[25]

20. Levin, interview.

21. A structured dialogue between forty-seven Louisiana NGOs involved in human recovery work in 2009 came to a similar conclusion, but with a greater emphasis on integrating NGOs with federal and state government agencies for the delivery of services. See Chandra and Acosta, *Role of Nongovernmental Organizations*, 10.

22. For a more exhaustive list of coalitions, see Gotham and Campanella, "Coupled Vulnerability and Resilience."

23. Ellis, interview.

24. Billman, interview.

25. Billman, interview; Franke, interview, July 16, 2010; Reilly, interview.

Now! Before the storm hits your area . . . whatever that storm of life is, get out there and find out who is doing it now! What groups are out there making an impact in your city? What are they doing? Find out and manufacture a database . . . an infrastructure of people that can help when something like this happens, because you're gonna need it. You're gonna be doing it anyway. You better coordinate how they're going to do that in the future rather than wait for the calamity to happen and then haphazardly try to find out who there is in town.[26]

More than just an emphatic assertion, Franke's statement complements arguments by his peers in this work across Louisiana.[27]

Despite this overlap, our interviewee's suggestions did not align with every strategy suggested by Collective Impact. In fact, their recommendations for closer work with the community correspond more closely to the principles espoused by Collective Impact's strongest critics. The authors of "Collaborating for Equity and Justice: Moving Beyond Collective Impact" argue that "Collective Impact fails to embrace advocacy and systems change as core strategies, retains a hierarchical approach to community engagement, and does not address the root causes and contexts of social problems." Moreover, they challenge large-scale change efforts to do more to involve and empower the grassroots.[28]

Resonating with these arguments, several interviewees advocated for relying on the local population as sources of information, as process leaders, and as key participants in the labor of recovery and rebuilding who should eventually be doing more of the work than volunteers as regional capacity returns.[29] Fred Franke, for example, critiqued theory-driven approaches to recovery created by individuals without a connection to the community they seek to assist, pushing instead for an emphasis on local contributions to planning:

A friend of mine from Kentucky wanted to come down here and plan a church. He and I have spoken probably a hundred times since Katrina. He's

26. Franke, interview, July 16, 2010.
27. Chandra and Acosta, *Role of Nongovernmental Organizations,* 10.
28. Wolff et al., "Collaborating for Equity and Justice."
29. Franke, interview, July 16, 2010; Caldwell, interview; Horton, interview.

been down here at least a half a dozen times. When I talk to him on occasion, he'd say, "Look, Fred. I got this great ministry plan worked up on the inner-city ministry and I'm gonna send it to ya." It's a great plan, but I'm lookin' at it and sayin', you know, "Wherever you decide to plan a church, this would work if that particular need was present." He said, "Well, what do you mean? Isn't that need present in most areas of New Orleans?" I said, "Sure it is." But, I said, "If you come down here and open your plan and say, 'This is the ministry that we're gonna be doin',' you might be missin' ministry in front of your face all day long."[30]

From a more secular perspective, Scott Porot, an AmeriCorps volunteer, crew leader, and a fellow with the Loyola University New Orleans Jesuit Fellowship Center, argued that state and federal government would have had a more accurate perception of recovery needs had they listened to and acted on input from the local population:

It would have been nice to have some very clear leadership citywide, at least, or state or nationwide. That wasn't there. Our motivator was really the homeowners we were working with at the time, as well as how we can best move the city forward. So, I think that the biggest learning experience was that you should always listen to the person on the ground. I think if they had really listened to the homeowners, volunteers and even the contractors and city councilmen that were on the ground, there would've been a lot less miscommunication. They would've been addressing the issues as they were instead of the issues as they saw them, which is not always the same thing.[31]

In the same vein of listening to people on the ground, Leonard Penner contended that Mennonite Disaster Services (MDS) was trying to determine how to serve New Orleans—but doing so by "walking alongside" the local people and implementing their agenda, rather than coming in as outsiders taking over. He described examples of such services, such as MDS's participation in community gardening programs and an initiative through which

30. Fred Franke, interview, July 16, 2010.
31. Porot, interview.

MDS sought to fill gaps in a local workforce training program by providing new funding and trainers.[32]

Common Ground executive director Thom Pepper most strongly articulated this theme of listening to people on the ground when he argued that the local population needs to replace outside volunteers and be intentionally integrated into recovery work as quickly as possible. Given Common Ground's prominence and dramatic transformation from a radical to a nonprofit organization, his observations merit consideration. Pepper argued that at the outset of a catastrophe, volunteer organizations could come into a disaster area and have a positive impact. He pointed to OHH's work with Plaquemines Parish during Hurricane Rita, which followed Katrina, as an example of the kind of volunteer response he would like to see: "Like when Operation Helping Hands came down to Plaquemines Parish and provided emergency assistance and everything else. Then boom! They were out. They were out in weeks. You have to have that initial impact. There are organizations that have the ability to come in here with tractor-trailers full of stuff. Even FEMA's much better organized than it was before."

Meanwhile, Pepper contended, while these initial efforts are occurring, attention needs to shift to integrating the local population into the work in two ways. First, he advocated for the incorporation of local contractors and volunteers through partnerships with charitable organizations that receive volunteers: local contractors know suppliers, they know how to get the best deals, they know the technical specifics of working in the area, and they have the ability to do the work requiring licensure and professional execution. Volunteers, meanwhile, can act as a low-skilled workforce to fill manual labor gaps until natives return.[33] Then, as the people come home, those survivors whose employment had been displaced by the disaster can be hired as part of the recovery effort, helping make it easier to phase out volunteers whose continued presence can become problematic: "The

32. Penner, interview.
33. There are several potential issues with this idea. The most glaring omission in Pepper's scenario is that of contractor fraud. As seen throughout our interviewees' testimony, rampant contractor fraud drained survivors' resources, particularly the elderly and those of little means, and increased the region's dependence on free volunteer labor. Moreover, Kevin Fitzpatrick, who as the executive director of Operation Helping Hands was Pepper's peer, argued that pairing contractors with volunteers proved problematic: "We found that

United Way created this not-for-profit rebuilding pilot program, and it's been a disaster. You can't give a kid a hammer and say, 'Go rebuild New Orleans.' You can't have everybody comin' in from wherever. You needed to connect with the local populace here. It had to be a public/private partnership with local contractors who knew who their suppliers were, where they could get the best deal, and where they could get labor cheaply."

When asked whether staff in disaster relief need to know how to use volunteers, Pepper replied:

They need to know that and to not let the volunteering spread willy-nilly into everything. Then there needs to be a second stage in which they are partnering with locals.

The thing here is that the rebuilding effort really sort of got underway at the time that the recession hit. There were people that were out of work, and there are still people that are out of work. What's so disheartening is that [the rebuilding effort] is not training local people and giving them that opportunity. We don't need a bunch of volunteers coming down here and becoming part of the problem. We had people that were coming in, even with us, who had problems of their own. I call 'em "disaster junkies."[34]

Pepper's views complemented Daniela Rivero and Kevin Fitzpatrick's reflections on the difficulties of managing volunteers who brought problematic personal characteristics to their work. And, despite numerous attempts I made to draw him out on this topic, this is one of the few times that Pepper came close to addressing the serious allegations made by several interviewees of a toxic climate within Common Ground in its early years. Pepper's descriptions of volunteer baggage and his interest in empowering local people's participation in the recovery to curtail the pres-

---

the contractors and volunteers were usually not a good match. The contractors were very impatient. [What] was ideal, but it didn't usually work out this way, [was to] build a house up to a certain point and then bring the volunteers in to do the drywall and the painting. Then bring the contractors in to do the finish work. Well, there's always the blame game. It was never on time. The contractor would blame the volunteers and the volunteer coordinator would say, you know, 'The contractor wasn't ready.' It was, it was very difficult to make that work." Fitzpatrick, interview, August 21, 2013.

34. Pepper, interview.

ence and influence of outside volunteers dovetail with analyses by scholars such as Jordan Flaherty and Rachel Luft.[35]

Moving away from Collective Impact and its critics, several of our interviewees at the leadership level stressed the importance of reducing bureaucracy and freeing up spending in the earliest stages of the recovery process.[36] Much of the bureaucracy to which they referred can be attributed to the Stafford Act, the legislative framework that determines how a disaster is declared and the subsequent distribution of aid.[37] Expressing his frustrations with the recovery work during its early years, James Pate spoke for several of his peers—both in this project and those in Chandra and Acosta's study—when he noted:

> Even people with FEMA in the state knew it was asinine, but that's what the Act said. I and many other people have commented on various flaws in the Stafford Act, which ties FEMA's hands in many respects on that kind of stuff. That is not to offer excuses for the extreme bureaucratic incompetence. Everybody down here was just goin' berserk—state, local, and national officials or working people like contractors—'cause something couldn't be done, and the decision was being made by somebody up a hierarchy in D.C.[38]

Pate and Daniela Rivero of RTNO advocated for a reframing of policy to one that would streamline the distribution of funds to local nonprofits

35. Flaherty et al., *Floodlines*, 94, 99 100; Luft, "Looking for Common Ground"; Luft, "Disaster Patriarchy," 2, 15, 16.

36. Provencio, interview; Billman, interview; Morgan, interview, July 15, 2010; Franke, interview, July 16, 2010; Rivero, interview, August 21, 2013.

37. "The Stafford Act authorizes the president to issue major disaster declarations that authorize federal agencies to provide assistance to states overwhelmed by disasters. Through executive orders, the President has delegated to [FEMA] . . . responsibility for administering the major provisions of the Stafford Act. Assistance authorized by the statute is available to individuals, families, state and local governments, and nonprofit organizations. Activities undertaken under authority of the Stafford Act are provided through funds appropriated to the Disaster Relief Fund (DRF). Federal assistance supported by DRF money is used by states, localities, and certain nonprofit organizations to provide mass care, restore damaged or destroyed facilities, clear debris, and aid individuals and families with uninsured needs, among other activities." Chandra and Acosta, *Role of Nongovernmental Organizations*, 4, 8, 9.

38. Pate, interview.

early in the recovery phase.[39] While acknowledging the importance of accountability in the stewardship of funds, Rivero and other interviewees also argued that using a reimbursement process to pay nonprofits for their work hindered their ability to address community needs nimbly.[40] Take, for example, this assessment of federal funding by Rivero, whose organization had the advantage of a large accounting team:

> Well, it can be an effective process. It's not always horrible. The problem is that it's on a reimbursement basis. You have to spend the money and then you have to send them your paperwork, and they have to go through it. The regulations are extremely complex. You bought a pencil. The government may ask, "Did this pencil really need to be bought?" Then you have a $100,000 reimbursement being held up for a 50-cent expense that they're not sure is eligible under this program. So, you really need a good team of accountants to be able to flow through that.[41]

Rivero and several others from larger organizations, such as Leonard Penner of Mennonite Disaster Services and Kevin Fitzpatrick of OHH, contended that this lengthy process exposed rebuilding agencies to high debt while they awaited repayment from the city, state, or local government, even as they continued to expend funds in response to community needs. To remedy this situation, Penner, Fitzpatrick, and Emily Stiebler argued that after the big international organizations like the Red Cross and United Way draw down their emergency response to a disaster, locally established organizations like OHH and RTNO should be eligible to receive direct "gap-funding." This would allow them to seamlessly take up the work without taking on debt—another suggestion that dovetails with conclusions generated in the facilitated dialogue led by Chandra and Acosta of forty-seven Louisiana NGO leaders.[42]

39. Pate, interview; Rivero, interview, August 21, 2013.
40. Reilly, interview; Daniela Rivero, interview, August 23, 2011; Rivero, interview, August 21, 2013; Pepper, interview; Alverson, interview; Manriquez, interview; Franke, interview, July 16, 2010.
41. Rivero, interview, August 21, 2013.
42. Stiebler, interview; Rivero, interview, August 21, 2013; Penner, interview; Fitzpatrick, interview, August 21, 2013.

Finally, our interviewees addressed the topic of how to enhance the mobilization of volunteers. They advocated for prescreening potential long-term volunteers to ensure they had the basic life skills to live in community in a disaster area, setting expectations for the work for long- and short-term volunteers before their arrival, and centering short-term volunteers' experience on learning, rather than completing a project. Although a handful of our interviewees noted having received training, most indicated that they were trained on the job—or, as one participant put it, they were "thrown to the wolves."[43] Take, for example, this point made by Scott Porot, which addresses both the lack of technical preparation needed to lead construction and the absence of training in managing conflict and emotional distress:

> We literally had two weeks of construction experience before we were leading crews. You're talking about people between the age of eighteen to twenty-four with two weeks' experience going out leading crews on how to hang drywall. And they totally trust you. Because you have this brand name. But as far as the emotional context, there really is no training whatsoever. That's something that I think could be improved upon. There really is no sense of what you do in those situations. I hate to sound like a bad action movie, but you really have to rely on your gut feeling and your natural instincts and maybe turn to your superiors to kind of address it, but really no one was really trained for those situations. You just address them as a person, and sometimes that means not addressing them because you're just not able to do so. I think the two weeks of construction experience kind of speaks to how the not-for-profits were so strapped to get people out and working. There was really a very limited amount of time to get people back in their homes before people really started considering not coming back because it's just not financially realistic. So, you have to really work under the crunch. They just wanted to get us out in the field as quickly as possible. I think sometimes that's a great decision, but they really could've provided us with better preparation for other things.[44]

43. Furst, interview; Greenhow, interview; Maiuri, interview; Porot, interview; Billman, interview; Alverson, interview; Ryan, interview.
44. Porot, interview.

Bethany Billman, a volunteer coordinator with OHH, recounted a similar experience:

When I was a long-term rebuilding volunteer, I mean, I came down here, I had like zero experience in construction. I think I'd like maybe painted a room once before that, so it was a lot of learning as I went, and a lot of the training was trial by fire. I didn't come during a time when they had any formalized training. That happened during a different time during the year. So, I got assigned to a site and I was just responsible for managing that site. I started out doing exterior paint for houses. That's a program that we provided for homeowners for free. These were busy times for us, and I was managing thirty volunteers. So, it was about learning really quickly how to manage volunteers and keep them happy and keep them busy and also finish painting a house, which I had never done before.[45]

Whereas several lower-level interviewees noted their lack of training as a problem, the leaders of large organizations such as Common Ground, OHH, and RTNO focused more on how long-term volunteers with "baggage" or poor coping skills could become a problem.[46] As described by Pepper:

I got a call from this guy in Switzerland, they were sending a crew down to Haiti. And I said, "You're gonna need to get volunteers who want to come down here and help." They'll come in and, it'll take 'em a couple days to acclimate. Then they'll work really well, and all of a sudden, they're gonna drop off. When they drop off, you need to be able to get them back on a plane and get them out of here because they start sucking up the resources that you need to help the population.[47]

Perhaps hearkening back to early experiences within Common Ground that have been documented by scholars and activists such as Rachel Luft, Jordan Flaherty, and Scott Crow, Pepper continued, "That's why directors

45. Billman, interview.
46. Fitzpatrick, interview, November 20, 2008; Pepper, interview.
47. Pepper, interview.

and management at these not-for-profits really need to be on top of their volunteers, because you can have, you can have a couple of crazy volunteers who will destroy your organization."[48] Having such volunteers around will cause "everybody to leave. They'll be like, 'Poof—I'm out of here.' The executive director's not taking care of this guy who's like smokin' weed like a madman, he's paranoid schizophrenic, and he chases everybody off. And all of a sudden, in a week, your organization's destroyed? It could easily happen."[49]

Despite the strong articulation of this theme at the leadership level, it was only Pepper who offered any remedy to improve long-term volunteer preparation, and even he dedicated only a short amount of time to discussing this idea compared to the lengthy period he spent discussing the problem. Nevertheless, Pepper advocated for paying close attention to the cycle of volunteer productivity and then deploying and removing volunteers accordingly. He also recommended there be a prescreening process. Pointing to the high stress levels associated with the work, Pepper noted that Common Ground's application materials unambiguously asked questions regarding basic life skills in areas such as hygiene and care for one's home—believing that such questions would facilitate the ability to screen out applicants whose presence would create more problems than they solved.[50]

While concern around long-term volunteers ranked high among these three executive leaders, there was also widespread concern around short-term volunteers, which warrants mentioning the relatively small set of suggested solutions that arose from the interviews.[51] Pepper indicated that he began seeing difficulties with short-term volunteers when increasingly large numbers came for alternative spring breaks, starting, by his estimation, in 2009—by which time the work was firmly focused on reconstruction.[52] By its nature, reconstruction requires more skill than

48. Flaherty, *No More Heroes*, 59–74; Luft, "Looking for Common Ground"; Crow, *Black Flags and Windmills*, 166–167.

49. Pepper, interview.

50. Pepper, interview.

51. Berglund, interview; Billman, interview; Greenhow, interview; Lilly, interview; Pepper, interview; Porot, interview; Stiebler, interview; Maiuri, interview; Ross, interview; Ryan, interview.

52. Porot, interview; Harms, interview; Billman, interview.

gutting. Yet short-term volunteers usually came for only a week, and much time would be lost in training them while combating their tendencies to want to spend several days partying.[53] Consequently, Common Ground implemented a prearrival process that began by sending mass emails describing their long-range projects to their college partners and indicating what skills Common Ground expected short-term volunteers to have on arrival: "This is what we expect of you. Please don't lie to us. [You can] go volunteer somewhere else. But these are what our expectations are of you as a volunteer or a potential volunteer." Pepper added, "That scares people. And that's great because we hardly have any problems whatsoever."[54]

Positioned lower in their organization's hierarchy than Pepper, worksite leader Caitlin Alverson and special projects manager Bethany Billman—both of OHH—suggested setting clear expectations for short-term volunteers and framing the volunteer experience as a teaching and reflective experience.[55] Alverson said, "As far as the volunteer groups, I think there was a gap between what these people were coming down here expecting to do and what they were actually doing. I think giving them clear expectations would increase a more positive experience. Then also being willing to teach, I think a lot of the times the project supersedes the importance of teaching volunteers."[56]

Similarly, Billman noted the difficulty of managing volunteers who came to New Orleans after 2008 expecting to gut a house when the much more painstaking labor of rebuilding would be their experience. She also expressed frustration with volunteers' preoccupation with touring the Ninth Ward, given the city's broad array of complex issues. Advocating for a holistic approach that went beyond just completing a project, Billman continued:

I think that reflection should be part of any volunteer experience, any rebuilding organization. Weeks are hectic, but I think that taking time to reflect on the experience, especially if you are a volunteer that comes to New Orleans for a week to work, is essential. Once you've worked here or

53. Maiuri, interview; Pepper, interview; Ryan, interview.
54. Pepper, interview.
55. Alverson, interview; Billman, interview.
56. Alverson, interview.

anyplace that's been hit by a disaster of that magnitude, you have to think about what's happened and about what that means for you and for others and how you fit into the big picture.[57]

Alverson and Billman's suggestions bring me back to my own experience, when my group was caught off-guard by our interactions with our first homeowner—a survivor who had been struggling to rebuild for nearly three years and whose excitement at having a chance to pick the paint color stalled our work by several hours. We could have benefited from the kind of intention that Billman and our interviewees called for, and only good fortune granted us a wise twenty-something crew leader who put our work into the bigger picture. Beyond this anecdotal instance of disorganization and a lack of empathy by one naïve, albeit well-intentioned, group of short-term volunteers, it is difficult to ignore the alarming patterns evidenced across our interviewees' testimony: the inefficiencies associated with using volunteer rather than professional labor; the uneven deployment of volunteer labor across the city; the lack of support given to volunteer startups that engaged in missions with value beyond the catastrophe, such as wetlands restoration and criminal justice reform; the unnecessary and socially costly competition between charitable agencies fostered by the competition for grants; and the seeming inability to coordinate efforts between government and charitable relief agencies from the earliest days of the recovery.

When the next mega-disaster occurs, we will likely call on the goodwill of the American people for aid once again. But how can we achieve better results and a more responsible stewardship of their time and resources than we saw after Katrina? What have we learned and synthesized from our interviewees' testimony?

Their experience and testimony point clearly to two answers. First, a much better result would be achieved by an intentional integration of the charitable sectors into the recovery, with the government acting as a more directive or coordinating force in contrast to the almost laissez-faire approach toward the participation of the nonprofit sector that occurred after the storm. Second, within volunteer organizations themselves, improved

57. Billman, interview.

outcomes would result from resisting the admittedly immense pressures of the catastrophe by bringing in outside assistance in a planful manner; the haphazard way in which aid and volunteers came to New Orleans fostered challenging, sometimes dangerous, internal group dynamics and difficult relationships with the local community—as attested to by our interviewees and documented by scholars like Luft, Flaherty, and others. Instead, charitable organizations would benefit from developing a more thoughtful approach to recruiting, training, and strategically deploying volunteers in a manner that ultimately results in empowering the local population seeking to regain its footing after an experience of immeasurable suffering.

BIBLIOGRAPHY

Books and Book Chapters

Adams, Thomas Jensen. "The Political Economy of Invisibility in Twenty-First-Century New Orleans: Security, Hospitality, and the Post Disaster City." In *Hurricane Katrina in Transatlantic Perspective,* edited by Romain Huret and Randy Sparks, loc 2548–2888. Baton Rouge: Louisiana State University Press, 2014. Kindle.

Adams, Vincanne. *Markets of Sorrow, Labors of Faith: New Orleans in the Wake of Katrina.* Durham, NC: Duke University Press, 2013. Kindle.

Adya, Meera, Monica K. Miller, Julie Singer, Rebecca M. Thomas, and Joshua B. Padilla. "Cultural Differences in Perceptions of the Government and the Legal System: Hurricane Katrina Highlights What Has Been There All Along." In *Racing the Storm: Racial Implications and Lessons Learned from Hurricane Katrina,* edited by Hillary Potter, loc 1394–2141. Lanham, MD: Lexington Books, 2007. Kindle.

Antoine, Rebecca. *Voices Rising: Stories from the Katrina Narrative Project.* New Orleans: University of New Orleans Press, 2008. Kindle.

——— . *Voices Rising II: More Stories from the Katrina Narrative Project.* New Orleans: University of New Orleans Press, 2010. Kindle.

Arena, John. *Driven from New Orleans: How Nonprofits Betray Public Housing and Promote Privatization.* Minneapolis: University of Minnesota Press, 2012.

Armstrong, J. P. "Developmental Outcomes of Service-Learning Pedagogies." *Journal for Civic Commitment* 8 (2006): 1–10.

Benham, Roger. "The Birth of the Clinic." In *What Lies Beneath: Katrina, Race, and the State of the Nation,* edited by South End Press Collective, 70–80. Cambridge, MA: South End Press, 2007.

Berra, Alisa, Mayaba Leibenthal, and Incite! Women of Color against Violence. "To Render Ourselves Visible: Women of Color Organizing and Hurricane Katrina." In *What Lies Beneath: Katrina, Race, and the State of the Nation,* edited by South End Press Collective, 31–47. Cambridge, MA: South End Press, 2007.

Blakely, Edward J. *My Storm: Managing the Recovery of New Orleans in the Wake of Katrina.* Philadelphia: University of Pennsylvania Press, 2012.

Boin, Arjen, Christer Brown, and James A. Richardson. *Managing Hurricane Katrina: Lessons from a Megacrisis.* Baton Rouge: Louisiana State University Press, 2019.

Boyden, James. "'Wilt Thou Judge the Bloody City? Yea, Thou Shalt Show Her All Her Abominations': Hurricane Katrina as a Providential Catastrophe." In *Hurricane Katrina in Transatlantic Perspective,* edited by Romain Huret and Randy Sparks, loc 1386–1634. Baton Rouge: Louisiana State University Press, 2014. Kindle.

Brinkley, Douglas. *The Great Deluge: Hurricane Katrina, New Orleans, and the Mississippi Gulf Coast.* New York: Morrow, 2006.

Brown, Tiffany. "Wade in the Water." In *What Lies Beneath: Katrina, Race, and the State of the Nation,* edited by South End Press Collective, 48–54. Cambridge, MA: South End Press, 2007.

Camp, Jordan. "Two Centuries of Paradox: The Geography of New Orleans's African American Population, from Antebellum to Postdiluvian Times." In *Hurricane Katrina in Transatlantic Perspective,* edited by Romain Huret and Randy Sparks, loc 180–693. Baton Rouge: Louisiana State University Press, 2014. Kindle.

——. "We Know This Place:' Neoliberal Racial Regimes and the Katrina Circumstance." In *In the Wake of Hurricane Katrina: New Paradigms and Social Visions,* edited by Clyde Adrian Woods, 267–292. Baltimore: Johns Hopkins University Press, 2010.

Carter, Mandy. "Southerners on New Ground: Our Lesbian, Gay, Bisexual and Transgender Community." In *What Lies Beneath: Katrina, Race, and the State of the Nation,* edited by South End Press Collective, 54–64. Cambridge, MA: South End Press, 2007.

Chandra, Anita, and Joie Acosta. *The Role of Nongovernmental Organizations in Long-Term Human Recovery after Disaster: Reflections from Louisiana Four Years after Hurricane Katrina.* Santa Monica: Rand Corporation, 2009.

Cole, Angela P., Terri Adams-Fuller, O. Jackson Cole, Arie Kruglanski, and Angela Glymph. "Making Sense of a Hurricane: Social Identity and Attribution Explanations of Race-Related Differences in Katrina Disaster Response." In *Racing the Storm: Racial Implications and Lessons Learned from Hurricane Katrina,* edited by Hillary Potter, loc 148–668. Lanham, MD: Lexington Books, 2007. Kindle.

Cotton, Allison M. "Stipulations: A Typology of Citizenship in the United States after Katrina." In *Racing the Storm: Racial Implications and Lessons Learned from Hurricane Katrina,* edited by Hillary Potter, loc 3502–3791. Lanham, MD: Lexington Books, 2007. Kindle.

Crow, Scott. *Black Flags and Windmills: Hope, Anarchy, and the Common Ground Collective.* Oakland: PM Press, 2011. Kindle.

David, Emmanuel. "Emergent Behavior and Groups in Postdisaster New Orleans: Notes on Practices of Organized Resistance." In *Learning from Catastrophe: Quick Response Research in the Wake of Hurricane Katrina,* edited by the National Hazards Center, 235–261. Boulder, CO: Institute of Behavioral Science, University of Colorado, 2006.

——. *Women of the Storm: Civic Activism after Hurricane Katrina.* Urbana: University of Illinois Press, 2017.

Diamond, Andrew. "Naturalizing Disaster Neoliberalism, Cultural Racism, and Depoliticization in the Era of Katrina." In *Hurricane Katrina in Transatlantic Perspective,* edited by Romain Huret and Randy Sparks, loc 1652–2068. Baton Rouge: Louisiana State University Press, 2014. Kindle.

Dixon, Adrienne. "Whose Choice? A Critical Race Perspective on Charter Schools." In *The Neoliberal Deluge: Hurricane Katrina, Late Capitalism, and the Remaking of New Orleans,* edited by Cedric Johnson, loc 2096–2363. Minneapolis: University of Minnesota Press, 2011.

Dyson, Michael Eric. *Come Hell or High Water: Hurricane Katrina and the Color of Disaster.* New York: Basic Books, 2007.

Flaherty, Jordan. "Corporate Reconstruction and Grassroots Resistance." In *What Lies Beneath: Katrina, Race, and the State of the Nation,* edited by South End Press Collective, 101–120. Cambridge, MA: South End Press, 2007.

——. *No More Heroes: Grassroots Challenges to the Savior Mentality.* Chico, CA: AK Press, 2016.

Flaherty, Jordan, Amy Goodman, and Tracie Washington. *Floodlines: Community and Resistance from Katrina to the Jena Six.* Chicago: Haymarket Books, 2010.

Ford, Kristina. *The Trouble with City Planning: What New Orleans Can Teach Us.* New Haven, CT: Yale University Press, 2010.

Frisch, Michael "Oral History and Hard Times: A Review Essay," In *The Oral History Reader,* 3rd ed., edited by Robert Perks and Alistair Thompson, 29–37. London: Routledge, 1998.

Gelbspan, Ross. "Nature Fights Back." In *What Lies Beneath: Katrina, Race, and the State of the Nation,* edited by South End Press Collective, 15–26. Cambridge, MA: South End Press, 2007.

Gotham, Kevin. *Authentic New Orleans: Tourism, Culture, and Race in the Big Easy.* New York: NYU Press, 2007.

Hartnell, Anna. "Katrina Tourism and a Tale of Two Cities: Visualizing Race and Class in New Orleans." In *In the Wake of Hurricane Katrina: New Paradigms and Social Visions,* edited by Clyde Woods, 297–322. Baltimore: Johns Hopkins University Press, 2010.

Hilderbrand, Sue, Scott Crow, and Lisa Fithian. "Common Ground Relief." In *What Lies Beneath: Katrina, Race, and the State of the Nation,* edited by South End Press Collective, 81–100. Cambridge, MA: South End Press, 2007.

Horigan, Kate Parker. *Consuming Katrina: Public Disaster and Personal Narrative.* Jackson: University Press of Mississippi, 2018.

Horowitz, Andy. *Katrina: A History, 1915–2015.* Cambridge, MA: Harvard University Press, 2020.

Huret, Romain. "Explaining the Unexplainable: Hurricane Katrina, FEMA, and the Bush Administration." In *Hurricane Katrina in Transatlantic Perspective,* edited by Romain Huret and Randy Sparks, loc 704–950. Baton Rouge: Louisiana State University Press, 2014. Kindle.

Jabari, Johari. "On Conjuring Mahalia: Mahalia Jackson, New Orleans, and the Sanctified Swing." In *In the Wake of Hurricane Katrina: New Paradigms and Social Visions,* edited by Clyde Woods, 223-244. Baltimore: Johns Hopkins University Press, 2010.

James, Joy. "Political Literacy and Voice." In *What Lies Beneath: Katrina, Race, and the State of the Nation,* edited by South End Press Collective, 157–166. Cambridge, MA: South End Press, 2007.

Johnson, Cedric. "Charming Accommodations: Progressive Urbanism Meets Privatization in Brad Pitt's Make It Right Foundation." In *The Neoliberal Deluge: Hurricane Katrina, Late Capitalism, and the Remaking of New Orleans,* edited by Cedric Johnson, loc 2776-3222. Minneapolis: University of Minnesota Press, 2011.

——. "Obama's Katrina." In *The Neoliberal Deluge: Hurricane Katrina, Late Capitalism, and the Remaking of New Orleans,* edited by Cedric Johnson, loc 20-121. Minneapolis: University of Minnesota Press, 2011.

Kempf, Jenn. "Picturing the Catastrophe News Photographs in the First Weeks after Katrina." In *Hurricane Katrina in Transatlantic Perspective,* edited by Romain Huret and Randy Sparks, loc 957-1380. Baton Rouge: Louisiana State University Press, 2014. Kindle.

Kennedy, Elizabeth Lapovsky. "Oral History and the Construction of a Pre-Stonewall Lesbian History." In *The Oral History Reader,* 3rd ed., edited by Robert Perks and Alistair Thompson, 344–356. London: Routledge, 1998.

Kish, Zeni. "'My FEMA People': Hip-Hop as Disaster Recovery in the Katrina Diaspora." In *In the Wake of Hurricane Katrina: New Paradigms and Social Visions,* edited by Clyde Woods, 245-266. Baltimore: Johns Hopkins University Press, 2010.

Klein, Naomi. *The Shock Doctrine: The Rise of Disaster Capitalism.* New York: Metropolitan Books, 2007.

Lapham, Lewis H. "Slum Clearance." In *What Lies Beneath: Katrina, Race, and the State of the Nation,* edited by South End Press Collective, 7–14. Cambridge, MA: South End Press, 2007.

Le Menestrel, Sara. "Memory Lives in New Orleans: The Process and Politics of Commemoration." In *Hurricane Katrina in Transatlantic Perspective,* edited by Romain Huret and Randy Sparks, loc 3296–3780. Baton Rouge: Louisiana State University Press, 2014. Kindle.

Lovell, Anne M. "Reformers, Preservationists, Patients, and Planners: Embodied Histories and Charitable Populism in the Post-Disaster Controversy over a Public Hospital." In *Hurricane Katrina in Transatlantic Perspective,* edited by Romain Huret and Randy Sparks, loc 2071–2535. Baton Rouge: Louisiana State University Press, 2014. Kindle.

Lummis, Trevor. "Structure and Validity in Oral Evidence." In *The Oral History Reader,* 3rd ed., edited by Robert Perks and Alistair Thompson, 273–283. London: Routledge, 1998.

Miles, Michelle, and Duke W. Austin. "The Color(s) of Crisis: How Race, Rumor, and Collective Memory Shape the Legacy of Katrina." In *Racing the Storm: Racial Implications and Lessons Learned from Hurricane Katrina,* edited by Hillary Potter, loc 668–1061. Lanham, MD: Lexington Books, 2007. Kindle.

Moore, Leonard N. *Black Rage in New Orleans: Police Brutality and African American Activism from World War II to Hurricane Katrina.* Baton Rouge: Louisiana State University Press, 2010.

Naik, Debashish. "A 'Collective Impact Framework' to Improve Output and Outcomes in Disaster Reconstruction Programs." In *Managing Humanitarian Logistics,* edited by B. S Sahay, Sumeet Gupta, and Vinod Chandra Menon, 141–151. New Delhi: Springer (India) Private Limited, 2015.

Neville, Charmaine. "How We Survived the Flood." In *What Lies Beneath: Katrina, Race, and the State of the Nation,* edited by South End Press Collective, 28–30. Cambridge, MA: South End Press, 2007.

Penner, D'Ann, and Keith C. Ferdinand. *Overcoming Katrina: African American Voices from the Crescent City and Beyond.* New York: Palgrave McMillan, 2009.

Perks, Robert, and Alistair. Thomson. *The Oral History Reader,* 3rd ed. London: Routledge, 1998.

Piven, Frances Fox. *Challenging Authority: How Ordinary People Change America.* Blue Ridge Summit, PA: Rowman & Littlefield, 2006.

Portelli, Alessandro. "What Makes Oral History Different." In *The Oral History Reader,* 3rd ed., edited by Robert Perks and Alistair Thompson, 63–74. London: Routledge, 1998.

Porter, Eric. "Jazz and Revival." In *In the Wake of Hurricane Katrina: New Paradigms and Social Visions,* edited by Clyde Woods, 167–188. Baltimore: Johns Hopkins University Press, 2010.

Potter, Hillary. "Reframing Crime in a Disaster." In *Racing the Storm: Racial Implications and Lessons Learned from Hurricane Katrina,* edited by Hillary Potter, loc 1068–1372. Lanham, MD: Lexington Books, 2007. Kindle.

Powell, Lawrence N. *The Accidental City: Improvising New Orleans.* Cambridge, MA: Harvard University Press, 2012.

Raeburn, Bruce Boyd. "Faith, Hip-Hop and Charity: Brass Band Morphology in Post-Katrina New Orleans." In *Hurricane Katrina in Transatlantic Perspective,* edited by Romain Huret and Randy Sparks, loc 2909–3277. Baton Rouge: Louisiana State University Press, 2014. Kindle.

Rahim, Malik. "This is Criminal." In *What Lies Beneath: Katrina, Race, and the State of the Nation,* 65–68. Cambridge, MA: South End Press, 2007.

Rathke, Wade. *The Battle for the Ninth Ward: ACORN Rebuilding New Orleans, and the Lessons of Disaster.* New Orleans: Social Policy Press, 2011. Kindle.

Reifer, Tom. "Blown Away: U.S. Militarism and Hurricane Katrina." In *Racing the Storm: Racial Implications and Lessons Learned from Hurricane Katrina,* edited by Hillary Potter, loc 4379–5062. Lanham, MD: Lexington Books, 2007. Kindle.

Rivlin, Gary. *Katrina: After the Flood.* New York: Simon & Schuster, 2015. Kindle.

Rodriguez, Dylan. "The Meaning of 'Disaster' under the Dominance of White Life." In *What Lies Beneath: Katrina, Race, and the State of the Nation,* edited by South End Press Collective, 134–156. Cambridge, MA: South End Press, 2007.

Rogers, Kim Lacy. *Righteous Lives: Narratives of the New Orleans Civil Rights Movement.* New York: NYU Press. 1993.

Russel, Chris, and Lavin, Chad. "From Tipping Point to Meta-Crisis: Management, Media, and Hurricane Katrina." In *The Neoliberal Deluge: Hurricane Katrina, Late Capitalism, and the Remaking of New Orleans,* edited by Cedric Johnson, 566–624. Minneapolis: University of Minnesota Press, 2011.

Salaam, Kalamu Ya. "Below the Water Line." In *What Lies Beneath: Katrina, Race, and the State of the Nation,* edited by South End Press Collective, ix–xvii. Cambridge, MA: South End Press, 2007.

Schneider, Aaron. *Renew Orleans? Globalized Development and Worker Resistance after Katrina,* Vol. 27. Minneapolis: University of Minnesota Press, 2018. Kindle.

Sexton, Jared. "The Obscurity of Black Suffering." In *What Lies Beneath: Katrina, Race, and the State of the Nation,* edited by South End Press Collective, 120–132. Cambridge, MA: South End Press, 2007.

South End Press Collective. "Up from the Depths." In *What Lies Beneath: Katrina, Race, and the State of the Nation,* vii–viii. Cambridge, MA: South End Press, South End Press, 2007.

——. *What Lies Beneath: Katrina, Race, and the State of the Nation.* Cambridge, MA: South End Press, 2007.

Sparks, Randi. "Why Mardi Gras Matters." In *Hurricane Katrina in Transatlan-*

tic Perspective, edited by Romain Huret and Randy Sparks, loc 3797–4234. Baton Rouge: Louisiana State University Press, 2014. Kindle.

Sterett, M. Susan, and Jennifer A. Reich. "Prayer and Social Welfare in the Wake of Katrina: Race and Volunteerism in Disaster Response." In *Racing the Storm: Racial Implications and Lessons Learned from Hurricane Katrina,* edited by Hillary Potter, loc 2984–3430. Lanham, MD: Lexington Books, 2007. Kindle.

Storr, Nona Martin, Emily Chamlee-Wright, and Virgil Henry, editors. *How We Came Back: Voices from Post-Katrina.* Arlington, VA: Mercatus Center at George Mason University, 2015.

Street, Paul. *Racial Oppression in the Global Metropolis.* Lanham, MD: Rowman & Littlefield, 2007.

Thomas, Lynell. "'Roots Run Deep Here': The Construction of Black New Orleans in Post-Katrina Tourism Narratives." In *In the Wake of Hurricane Katrina: New Paradigms and Social Visions,* edited by Clyde Woods, 323–342. Baltimore: Johns Hopkins University Press, 2010.

Trujillo-Pagan, Nicole. "From the Gateway to the Americas' to the 'Chocolate City': The Racialization of Latinos in New Orleans." In *Racing the Storm: Racial Implications and Lessons Learned from Hurricane Katrina,* edited by Hillary Potter, loc 2104–2523. Lanham, MD: Lexington Books, 2007. Kindle.

University of Colorado Boulder Natural Hazards Center. *Learning from Catastrophe: Quick Response Research in the Wake of Hurricane Katrina.* Boulder: Institute of Behavioral Science, University of Colorado at Boulder, 2006.

Van Heerden, Ivor Ll., and Mike Bryan. *The Storm: What Went Wrong and Why during Hurricane Katrina: The Inside Story from One Louisiana Scientist.* New York: Viking, 2006.

Wessman, Nancy Kay Sullivan. *Katrina Mississippi: Voices from Ground Zero.* Oxford, MS: Nautilus Publishing, 2015.

Woldoff, Rachael A., and Brian J. Gerber. "Protect or Neglect? Social Structure, Decision Making, and the Risk of Living African American Places in New Orleans." In *Racing the Storm: Racial Implications and Lessons Learned from Hurricane Katrina,* edited by Hillary Potter, loc 3739–4365. Lanham, MD: Lexington Books, 2007. Kindle.

Woodmansee, Jaye. "On the Run." In *Voices Rising II: More Stories from the Katrina Narrative Project,* edited by Rebecca Antoine, loc 1314–1438. New Orleans: University of New Orleans Press, 2010. Kindle.

Woods, Clyde Adrian. "Les Miserables of New Orleans: Trap Economics and the Asset Stripping Blues, Part 1." In *In the Wake of Hurricane Katrina: New Paradigms and Social Visions,* edited by Clyde Adrian Woods, 343–370. Baltimore: Johns Hopkins University Press, 2010.

——. "The Politics of Reproductive Violence: An Interview with Shana Griffin by Clyde Woods." In *In the Wake of Hurricane Katrina: New Paradigms and Social Visions,* edited by Clyde Adrian Woods, 157–166. Baltimore: Johns Hopkins University Press, 2010.

——, ed. *In the Wake of Hurricane Katrina: New Paradigms and Social Visions.* Baltimore: Johns Hopkins University Press, 2010.

Wooten, Tom. *We Shall Not Be Moved: Rebuilding Home in the Wake of Katrina.* Boston: Beacon Press, 2012.

Journal Articles

Aalbers, Manuel B. "Do Maps Make Geography? Part 2: Post-Katrina New Orleans, Post-Foreclosure Cleveland and Neoliberal Urbanism." *ACME* 13, no. 4 (2014): 557–582.

Beatty, Stephanie Hayne, Ken N. Meadows, Richard SwamiNathan, and Catherine Mulvihill. "The Effects of an Alternative Spring Break Program on Student Development." *Journal of Higher Education Outreach and Engagement* 20, no. 3 (2016): 90–119.

Borden, A. W. "The Impact of Service-Learning on Ethnocentrism in an Intercultural Communication Course." *Journal of Experiential Education* 30, no. 2 (2007): 171–183.

Brundiers, Katja. "Leveraging Disasters for Sustainable Development." *Environment: Science and Policy for Sustainable Development* 62, no. 1 (2020): 15–27.

Campanella, Richard. "An Ethnic Geography of New Orleans." *Journal of American History* 94, no. 3 (2007): 704–715.

Colten, Craig, and E. Sumpter. "Social Memory and Resilience in New Orleans." *Natural Hazards* 48, no. 3 (2009): 355–364.

Cone, Cynthia Abbott, and Andrea Myhre. "Community-Supported Agriculture: A Sustainable Alternative to Industrial Agriculture?" *Human Organization* 59, no. 2 (2000): 187–197.

Dass-Brailsford, Priscilla, Rebecca Thomley, and Alejandra Hurtado de Mendoza. "Paying It Forward: The Transformative Aspects of Volunteering after Hurricane Katrina." *Traumatology* 17, no. 1 (2011): 29–40.

DeVore, Donald E. "Water in Sacred Places: Rebuilding New Orleans Black Churches as Sites of Community Empowerment." *Journal of American History* 94, no. 3 (2007): 762–769.

Dreier, Peter. "Katrina and Power in America." *Urban Affairs Review* 41, no. 4 (2006): 528–549.

Duncan, J. Michael, Thomas L. Brandon, Stephen G. Wright, and Noah Vroman. "Stability of I-Walls in New Orleans during Hurricane Katrina: Performance of Geo-Systems during Hurricane Katrina." *Journal of Geotechnical and Geoenvironmental Engineering* 134, no. 5 (2008): 681–691.

Garland, Diana R., D. M. Myers, and Terry A. Wolfer. "Social Work with Religious Volunteers." *Social Work* 53, no. 3(2008): 255–265.

Glaser, Barney G. "The Constant Comparative Method of Qualitative Analysis." *Social Problems* 12, no. 4 (1965): 436–45.

Gotham, Kevin, and Richard Campanella. "Coupled Vulnerability and Resilience: The Dynamics of Cross Scale Interactions in Post-Katrina New Orleans." *Ecology and Society* 16, no. 3 (2011): 12–28.

Griffin, Shana, and Clyde Woods. "The Politics of Reproductive Violence." *American Quarterly* 61, no. 3 (2009): 583–591.

Harvey, Daina Cheyenne. "Gimme a Pigfoot and a Bottle of Beer: Food as Cultural Performance in the Aftermath of Hurricane Katrina." *Symbolic Interaction* 40, no. 4 (2017): 498–522.

Kania, John and Mark Kramer. "Collective Impact." *Stanford Social Innovation Review* 9, no. 1 (2011): 36–41.

Lam, Pui-Yan. "As the Flocks Gather: How Religion Affects Voluntary Association Participation." *Journal of the Scientific Study of Religion* 41, no. 3 (2002): 405–422.

Levine, Mark, and Kirstien Thompson. "Identity, Place, and Bystander Intervention: Social Categories and Helping after Natural Disasters." *Journal of Social Psychology* 144, no. 3 (2004): 229–245.

"LSBA Recognizes Legal Professionals, Law Students for Pro Bono Service." *Louisiana Bar Journal* 64, no 2 (August/September 2016): 136–137.

Luft, Rachel E. "Beyond Disaster Exceptionalism: Social Movement Developments in New Orleans after Hurricane Katrina." *American Quarterly* 61, no. 3 (2009): 499–527.

———. "Looking for Common Ground: Relief Work in Post-Katrina New Orleans as an American Parable of Race and Gender Violence." *NWSA Journal* 20, no. 3 (2008): 5–31.

———. "Racialized Disaster Patriarchy: An Intersectional Model for Understanding Disaster Ten Years after Hurricane Katrina." *Feminist Formations* 28, no. 2 (2016): 1–26.

Michel, Lacie M. "Personal Responsibility and Volunteering after a Natural Disaster: The Case of Hurricane Katrina." *Sociological Spectrum* 27, no. 6 (2007): 633–652.

Morrish, William R. "After the Storm: Rebuilding Cities upon Reflexive Infrastructure." *Social Research* 75, no. 3 (2008): 993–1014.

Mustillo, Sarah, John Wilson, and Scott M. Lynch. "Legacy Volunteering: A Test of Two Theories of Intergenerational Transmission." *Journal of Marriage and Family* 66, no. 2 (2004): 530–541.

Niehaus, Elizabeth, and Karen Kurotsuchi Inkelas. "Exploring the Role of Alternative Break Programs in Students' Career Development." *Journal of Student Affairs Research and Practice* 52, no. 2 (2015):134–148.

Oesterle, Sabrina, Monica Kirkpatrick, and Jeylan T. Mortimer. "Volunteerism during the Transition to Adulthood: A Life Course Perspective." *Social Forces* 82, no. 3 (2004): 1123–1149.

Olshansky, Robert B., Laurie A. Johnson, Jedidiah Horne, and Brendan Nee. "Longer View: Planning for the Rebuilding of New Orleans." *Journal of the American Planning Association* 74, no. 3 (2008): 273–287.

Pompa, Lori. "Service-Learning as Crucible: Reflections on Immersion, Context, Power, and Transformation." *Michigan Journal of Community Service Learning* 9, no. 1 (2002): 67-76.

Rodríguez, Havidán, Joseph Trainor, and Enrico L. Quarantelli. "Rising to the Challenges of a Catastrophe: The Emergent and Prosocial Behavior following Hurricane Katrina." *Annals of the American Academy of Political and Social Science* 604, no. 1 (2006): 82–101.

Sax, Linda J. Alexander W. Astin, and Juan Avalos. "Long-Term Effects of Volunteerism during the Undergraduate Years." *Review of Higher Education* 22, no. 2 (1999): 187–202.

St. John, Craig, and Jessie Fuchs. "The Heartland Responds to Terror: Volunteering after the Bombing of the Murrah Federal Building." *Social Science Quarterly* 83, no. 2, 397–415.

Vander Putten, Jim, and Amanda L. Nolen. "Comparing Results from Constant Comparative and Computer Software Methods: A Reflection about Qualitative Data Analysis." *Journal of Ethnographic & Qualitative Research* 5, no. 2 (2010): 99–112.

Wells, Amy Stuart, Julie Slayton, and Janelle Scott. "Defining Democracy in the Neoliberal Age: Charter School Reform and Educational Consumption." *American Educational Research Journal* 39, no. 2 (2002): 337–361.

Wilson, John. "Volunteering." *Annual Review of Sociology* 26 (2000): 215–240.

Wilson, John, and M. Musick. "Who Cares? Toward an Integrated Theory of Volunteer Work." *American Sociological Review* 62, no. 5 (1997): 694–713.

Wiltfang, Gregory L., and Doug McAdam. "The Costs and Risks of Social Activism: A Study of Sanctuary Movement Activism." *Social Forces* 69, no. 4 (June 1991): 989, 990, 994, 996.

Dissertation

Newton, Huey Percy. "War against the Panthers: A Study of Repression in America." ProQuest Dissertations Publishing, 1980.

Film and Video

Greater New Orleans Roundtable. *10 Years after Katrina: "Resilience," "Recovery," and "Reality."* Filmed August 2015, New Orleans. Video. https://vimeo.com/137311942.

Dantas, Luisa, and Bob Tannen. *Land of Opportunity.* New Day Films, 2010.

Holm, Rasmus. *Welcome to New Orleans.* Danish Broadcasting Corporation, 2006.

Lee, Spike. *If God is Willing and Da' Creek Won't Rise.* Home Box Office, 2010.

———. *When the Levees Broke: Part 4.* Home Box Office, 2006.

Lessin, Tia, and Carl Deal. *Trouble the Water.* Zeitgeist Films, 2008.

Interviews

All the interviews are digital recordings in the possession of the author, San Diego, California.

Alverson, Caitlin. Interview by Andrew Raffaele and Griffin Waterman, November 11, 2011.

Berglund, Hannah. Interview by Sidar Sahin and Jaqueline Torres, November 16, 2011.

Billman, Bethany. Interview by Catherine Crosse, Eric Jankowski, and Sierra Heavener, November 17, 2011.

Caldwell, Robert Jr. Interview by Marisol Rivera and Eric A. Schuster, December 5, 2011.

Ellis, Mike. Interview by Christopher Manning, October 28, 2010.

Eustis, Scott. Interview by Christopher Manning, August 10, 2010.

Fitzpatrick, Kevin. Interview by Caitlin Appel, Amber Kappel, and Candice Jones, November 20, 2011.

Fitzpatrick, Kevin. Interview by Christopher Manning, August 21, 2013.

Franke, Fred. Interview by Christopher Manning, July 8, 2010, and July 16, 2010.

Furst, Amanda. Interview by Melissa D'Lando, William Ippen, Eliot Pope, and Jeffrey Wing, October 22, 2010.

Goodman, Robert. Interview by Christopher Manning, August 20, 2013.

Greenhow, Andrew. Interview by Chris Manning, October 22, 2009.

Hamsher, Christopher. Interview by Brooke Wibracht, Paige Halpern, Anna Zawadzka, and Therese Embrey, October 28, 2010.

Harms, David. Interview by Anne E. Cullen and Rachel Boyle, November 10, 2011.

Horton, Robert "Kool Black." Interview by Mary Lind, La Wanna Daniel, and Joaquin Stephenson, November 18, 2013.

Levin, Anna. Interview by Konstandina Argyropoulos, Andrew Altpeter, Elizabeth Loch, and Kelsey Walsh, October 28, 2010.

Lilly, Alex. Interview by Kirby Pringle, Matthew Wehrmann, and Rebecca Redinger, November 21, 2011.

Manriquez, Adrian. Interview by Indre Jurksaitis, Elizabeth (Liz) Quinn, and Kristen Chaulk, November 08, 2009.

Maiuri, Daniel. Interview by Devin Hunter and Megan Stout, November 8, 2009.

Morgan, Colleen. Interview by Christopher Manning, July 6, 2010, July 15, 2010, and August 23, 2011

Murphy, Amanda. Interview by April Braden and Peter Thoma, November 8, 2009.

Pate, James W. Interview by Christopher Manning, August 21, 2013.

Penner, Leonard. Interview by Dan Ott and Rachel Ramirez, November 11, 2011.

Pepper, Thom. Interview by Christopher Manning, August 20, 2013.

Porot, Scott. Interview by W. Reilly McClure and Kimberly Medema, November 9, 2009.

Provencio, Alyssa. Interview by Christopher Manning, November 22, 2009.

Reilly, Caitlin. Interview by Christopher Manning, August 2011.

Rivero, Daniela. Interview by Christopher Manning, August 24, 2011, and August 21, 2013.

Ross, Vince Fiedler. Interview by Emma Bonanomi, Sarah Doherty, and Sarah Stephens, November 18, 2008.

Ryan, Andrew. Interview by Oliver Miller, Rochelle Caruthers, and Charlie Wilkins, November 17, 200.

Silverman, Whitney. Interview by Melinda Leonard, Elyssa Northey, and Pam Utsunomiya, October 18, 2010.

Stiebler, Emily. Interview by Christopher Manning, August 25, 2011.

Online Sources

Advancement Project, National Immigration Law Center, and the New Orleans Worker Justice Coalition. 2006. "And Injustice for All: Workers' Lives in the Reconstruction of New Orleans." Accessed March 3, 2020. http://nowcrj.org/wp-content/uploads/2010/03/and-injustice-for-all.pdf.

"After Katrina in New Orleans." ABA Journal. Accessed September 18, 2019. http://www.abajournal.com/gallery/neworleans2012/534.

Ailsworth, Ronald. "Remembering Althea Francois, Beloved Louisiana Black Panther, Prison Abolitionist, 'Pillar in our Struggle,'" *San Francisco Bay View*, March 12, 2010. https://sfbayview.com/2010/03/remembering-althea-francois-beloved-louisiana-black-panther-prison-abolitionist-pillar-in-our-struggle/.

Amadeo, Kimberly. "Hurricane Katrina: Facts, Damage and Costs." The Balance.
Accessed August 6, 2020. https://www.thebalance.com/hurricane-katrina
-facts-damage-and-economic-effects-3306023.

Angola 3 News. "Join Us in Helping to Send Sister Althea on Her Journey
Home." *Angola 3 News,* December 28, 2009. http://angola3news.blogspot
.com/2009/12/althea-francois-memorial-fundraiser.html.

Armstrong, Jennifer. "A Behind-the-Scenes Look at a Day in the Life of New
Orleans Saints Coach Sean Payton." Nola.com, August 13, 2009. http://www
.nola.com/saints/index.ssf/2009/08/coach_sean_payton_is_the_new_o
.html.

Associated Press. "$2,000 Debit Cards for Katrina Victims." NBC News. Last
modified September 8, 2005. http://www.nbcnews.com/id/9241177/ns
/us_news-katrina_the_long_road_back/t/debit-cards-katrina-victims
/#.XBv3ZC2ZOu4.

———. "Consulting Company Targeted in Katrina Blame." NBC News. Last
modified January 30, 2007. https://www.nbcnews.com/id/wbna16892323.

———. "FEMA to Give Families $2,000 on Debit Cards." *Seattle Times,* Septem-
ber 8, 2005. https://www.seattletimes.com/nation-world/fema-to-give
-families-2000-on-debit-cards/.

Astin, Lori J. Vogelsang, Elaine K. Ikeda, and Jennifer A. Yee. "How Service-
Learning Effects Students." *Higher Education* (2000): 144. https://digital
commons.unomaha.edu/slcehighered/144/.

Austin Informant Working Group. "Statement From Texas Anarchists," *Indy
Media,* January 1, 2009. http://www.indymedia.org/pt/2008/12/918526
.shtml.

Babcock, Jay. "Common Ground Co-Founder Is FBI Informant." *Arthur,*
January 15, 2009. https://arthurmag.com/2009/01/15/common-ground-co
-founder-is-fbi-informant/comment-page-1/.

BBC News. "Who Are the FARC?" Last modified November 24, 2016. https://
www.bbc.com/news/world-latin-america-36605769.

"Brandon Darby." Wikipedia. Accessed May 25, 2018. https://en.wikipedia.org
/wiki/Brandon_Darby.

Buchanan, Susan. "Lower Nine and Parts of Algiers Still Struggle to Rebuild
after Katrina." *Louisiana Weekly.* Last modified July 27, 2015. http://www
.louisianaweekly.com/lower-nine-and-parts-of-algiers-still-struggle-to
-rebuild-after-katrina/.

Burris, Carol. "The Real Story of New Orleans and Its Charter Schools."
Washington Post, September 4, 2018. https://www.washingtonpost.com
/education/2018/09/04/real-story-new-orleans-its-charter-schools/.

Bush, George H. W. 1989. "Inaugural Address of George Bush." Yale Law School,

Lillian Goldman Law Library, Avalon Project. Accessed September 9, 2021. https://avalon.law.yale.edu/20th_century/bush.asp.

City of New Orleans. "NOPD Consent Decree." New Orleans Police Department. Accessed July 16, 2020. https://nola.gov/nopd/nopd-consent-decree/.

Clark, Jess. "Charter Schools in New Orleans That Underperform Will Be Closed." NPR. Last modified September 3, 2019. https://www.npr.org/2019 /09/03/756976619/charter-schools-in-new-orleans-that-underperform -will-be-closed.

CNN. "FEMA to Give Katrina Victims Debit Cards." CNN. Last modified September 7, 2005. https://money.cnn.com/2005/09/07/news/fema/index. htm.

———. "Marco Downgraded to a Tropical Storm as 'Unprecedented' Back-To-Back Threats Target Louisiana." CNN. Last modified August 24, 2020. https://www.cnn.com/2020/08/23/weather/marco-laura-gulf-coast -weather-forecast-sunday/index.html.

Colten, Craig E. "From Betsy to Katrina: Shifting Policies, Lingering Vulnerabilities." Presented at the April 2006 MaGrann Research Conference. Accessed October 23, 2019. http://magrann-conference.rutgers.edu/2006/_papers /colten.pdf.

Critical Resistance. "Critical Resistance" Accessed July 15, 2020. http:// criticalresistance.org.

Cunningham, Wayne. "Q&A with Scott Crow." *Austin Chronicle,* August 28, 2015. https://www.austinchronicle.com/news/2015-08-28/qa-with-scott -crow/.

DeBerry, Jarvis. "Hope Takes a Hit from Toxic Drywall." Nola.com, September 11, 2011. http://www.nola.com/opinions/index.ssf/2011/09/hope_takes _a_hit_from_toxic_dr.html.

Deep South Center for Environmental Justice. "Monique Harden ESQ." Accessed July 15, 2020. https://www.dscej.org/our-story/our-team /monique-harden-esq.

"Drought Makes 2011 Second Driest Year on Record in Louisiana." Nola.com, February 2, 2019. http://www.nola.com/weather/index.ssf/2011/06 /drought_makes_2011_second-drie.html.

Eaton, Leslie, and Joseph B. Treaster. "Insurance Woes for Hurricane Katrina Victims." *New York Times,* September 2, 2007. https://www.nytimes.com /2007/09/02/business/worldbusiness/02iht-orleans.4.7353442.html.

"Ed Blakely, Former New Orleans Recovery Chief, Offers Australians Advice on Rebuilding." Nola.com, January 15, 2011. https://www.nola.com/news /politics/article_92b5196a-7ad5-5b91-be95-4b82cbfd2c16.html.

Ellis Marsalis Center. "About: Musicians' Village." Accessed July 23, 2020. https://www.ellismarsaliscenter.org/musicians-village.

"Experts: Drought Could Continue in Southern US." New Orleans City Business. Last modified April 26, 2011. http://neworleanscitybusiness.com/blog/2011 /04/26/experts-drought-could-continue-in-southern-u-s/.

Falk, Mallory. "In New Orleans, the Scramble for the Right Fit." NPR. Last modified April 6, 2015. https://www.npr.org/sections/ed/2015/04/06 /391024998/in-new-orleans-the-scramble-for-the-right-fit.

FEMA. "More Than $2.3 Billion in Expedited FEMA Aid Already Delivered to Hurricane Victims." Last modified October 2, 2005. https://www.fema.gov /news-release/2005/10/02/more-23-billion-expedited-fema-aid-already -delivered-hurricane-katrina.

———. "Nearly $690 Million in Assistance Helping More than 330,000 Families Displaced by Katrina." Last modified September 20, 2005. https://www.fema .gov/news-release/2005/09/10/nearly-690-million-assistance-helping -more-330000-families-displaced-katrina.

Friedman, Lisa. "Ten Years after Deepwater Horizon, US is Still Vulnerable to Catastrophic Spills." *New York Times,* April 19, 2020. https://www.nytimes. com/2020/04/19/climate/deepwater-horizon-anniversary.html.

Fussel, Elizabeth. 2005. "Leaving New Orleans: Social Stratification, Networks, and Hurricane Evacuation." *items: Insights from the Social Sciences.* Accessed May 22, 2020. https://items.ssrc.org/understanding-katrina /leaving-new-orleans-social-stratification-networks-and-hurricane -evacuation/.

Gist, Karen Taylor. "For New Orleans Saints Coach Sean Payton Chinese Drywall Crisis Kicks off Custom Home Redesign." Nola.com, September 4, 2010. https://www.nola.com/entertainment_life/home_garden/article _43a65152-9975-53e6-9fb8-5c56be05f7e0.html.

Glass, Ira, Thanh Tan, and My Thuan Tran. "Turncoat." *This American Life.* Last modified May 22, 2009. https://www.thisamericanlife.org/381/turncoat.

Glen, Stephanie. "Snowball Sampling: Definition, Advantages and Disadvan-tages." StatisticsHowTo.com. Accessed August 16, 2020. https://www .statisticshowto.com/snowball-sampling/.

Government Accountability Office. "Testimony before the Senate Committee on Homeland Security and Governmental Affairs. Expedited Assistance for Victims of Hurricanes Katrina and Rita." Last modified February 13, 2006, https://www.gao.gov/new.items/d06403t.pdf.

Granger, Chris. "Chinese Drywall Cases Settled in Louisiana: Big Award Granted in Florida." *Times-Picayune,* June 18, 2010. http://www.nola.com /crime/index.ssf/2010/06/chinese_drywall_cases_settled.html.

Griffin, Shana, and Joanna Dubinsky. "An Unfragmented Movement: Interview with Shana Griffin." New Orleans Independent Media Center. January 6, 2006. http://neworleans.indymedia.org/news/2006/01/6740.php.

Gromicko, Nick, and Kenton Shepard. "Chinese Drywall." International Association of Certified Home Inspectors. Accessed July 21, 2017. https://www.nachi.org/chinese-drywall.htm.

Guillod, Stephanie. "The First US Social Forum." Project South. Accessed July 15, 2020. https://projectsouth.org/wp-content/uploads/2012/05/USSF_report.pdf.

Hammer, David. "Blanco Administration Quietly Gave Raise to Road Home Operator." Nola.com, March 13, 2008. https://www.nola.com/news/article_978f3794-ba10-5a21-8103-995e381389e0.html.

——. "Ed Blakely Lambastes New Orleans, Saying Its Residents Are Racist, Lazy." Nola.com, November 2, 2009. https://www.nola.com/news/politics/article_6033f858-885f-5135-ac74-d112c5b99203.html.

——. "Examining Post-Katrina Road Home Program." *The Advocate*, August 23, 2015. http://www.theadvocate.com/baton_rouge/news/article_f9763ca5-42ba-5a62-9935-c5f7ca94a7c4.html.

——. "ICF's Oversight of Road Home Program Comes to an End." Nola.com, June 11, 2009. https://www.nola.com/news/article_ca8aa72c-cb96-50df-9909-83aa560588d4.html.

——. "State Signs New Road Home Contract with HGI Catastrophe Services." Nola.com, April 30, 2009. https://www.nola.com/news/article_20082c96-0e2b-5507-93de-71fbab6365af.html.

Harkinson, Josh. "How a Radical Leftist Became the FBI's BFF." *Mother Jones*, September/October. https://www.motherjones.com/politics/2011/07/brandon-darby-anarchist-fbi-terrorism/.

Hasselle, Della. "What's Driving Better School Performance in New Orleans? Tulane Researchers Say It's School Closures." Nola.com, August 20, 2019. https://www.nola.com/news/education/article_f2fbbc40-c35b-11e9-a03d-9ba3203b0bb1.html.

"Hilton Prize Laureates Focus on Disaster Relief, Recovery, and Resiliency in the Wake of Nepal Earthquake." PR Newswire. Accessed January 1, 2021. https://www.prnewswire.com/news-releases/hilton-prize-laureates-focus-on-disaster-relief-recovery-and-resiliency-in-the-wake-of-nepal-earthquake-300077814.html.

Hing, Juliane. "New Orleans Activists Want Feds to Get Real about NOPD Misconduct." *Colorlines*, April 22, 2010. https://www.colorlines.com/articles/new-orleans-activists-want-feds-get-real-about-nopd-misconduct.

Hinton, Matthew. "Chinese Drywall Concerns Investigated by Habitat for Humanity." *Times-Picayune*, June 19, 2010. http://www.nola.com/business/index.ssf/2010/06/chinese_drywall_concerns_inves.html.

"Hurricane Betsy Was, for Its Time, the Costliest and Deadliest Hurricane in U.S. History." Devastating Disasters: Devastating Disasters That Happened

in the Past. Accessed August 2, 2019. https://devastatingdisasters.com
/hurricane-betsy-september-9-1965/.

Johnson, Cedric. "Working the Reserve Army. Proletarianization in Revanchist
New Orleans." nonsite.org. Last modified September 4, 2015. http://nonsite
.org/article/working-the-reserve-army.

Jones, Pamela C. "Contingent Valuation." *Encyclopedia Britannica*. Last
modified December 5, 2018. https://www.britannica.com/topic/contingent
-valuation.

Kamenitz, Eliot. "Far More than 10 Blessings: An Editorial." *Times-Picayune*,
November 6, 2009. https://www.nola.com/opinions/article_e1e6d8df-3d10
-54fd-b44d-a1063fca4647.html.

Kerley, David. "Katrina Victims, Insurance Companies in Wind vs. Water
Dispute," ABC News. Last modified December 21, 2005. https://abcnews.go
.com/WNT/story?id=1430568.

Langenhennig, Susan. "Rebuilding Together New Orleans Becomes an Independent Nonprofit." Preservation Resource Center of New Orleans. Last
modified February 1, 2020. https://prcno.org/rebuilding-together-becomes
-independent-nonprofit/.

LaRose, Greg. "St. Bernard Project Has a New Home, New Name, Broader
Mission," Nola.com, May 25, 2016. https://www.nola.com/news/business
/article_45032ed4-648c-5ebe-9b46-a4b243bfc9a5.html.

Lee, Lauren. "New Orleans after Katrina: This Non-Profit Is Still Helping the
City Rebuild 15 Years Later." CNN. Last modified September 1, 2020. https://
www.cnn.com/2020/08/29/us/new-orleans-after-katrina-15-years-iyw
-trnd/index.html.

Louisiana Justice Institute. "Rest in Peace Althea Francois." Last modified
December 29, 2009. http://louisianajusticeinstitute.blogspot.com/2009/12
/rest-in-peace-althea-francois.html.

Maggi, Laura. "Trial to Decide Whether Barge Broke Industrial Canal Floodwall
during Katrina Begins." *Times-Picayune*, June 22, 2010. https://www.nola
.com/news/crime_police/article_77c03069-5291-5a1f-ad7e-e7b44075817c
.html.

Making Contact. "The Road to Detroit: US Social Forum 2010." Making Contact.
Last modified May 18, 2010. https://www.radioproject.org/2010/05/the-road
-to-detroit-us-social-forum-2010/.

Martin, Rachel. "Charter Schools in New Orleans That Underperform Will be
Closed." NPR. Last modified September 3, 2019. https://www.npr.org/2019
/09/03/756976619/charter-schools-in-new-orleans-that-underperform
-will-be-closed.

McAllen, Tiffany. "Toxic Chinese Drywall Taxes Katrina Relief Groups."
Religion News Service, April 27, 2011, https://religionnews.com/2011/04/27
/toxic-chinese-drywall-taxes-katrina-relief-groups/.

McCarthy, Brendan. "Common Ground Official Was a Federal Informant, Lawsuit Says." Nola.com, November 16, 2018. https://www.nola.com/politics/index.ssf/2011/11/common_ground_official_was_a_f.html.

Miller, Mike. "Sandra Bullock Donates Big to New Orleans High School in the Name of Her Late Mom." *People,* April 12, 2018. https://people.com/movies/sandra-bullock-warren-easton-high-school-donation-mother/.

Money, Luke. "'Significant Progress' as Weather Helps in Battle against Historic Northern California Wildfires," *LA Times,* August 26, 2020. https://www.latimes.com/california/story/2020-08-26/california-fires-burn-more-than-1-600-structures-but-total-losses-could-top-3-000-officials-say.

Mowbray, Rebecca. "Actress Sandra Bullock Purchases Home in New Orleans' Garden District." *Times-Picayune,* September 2, 2009. https://www.nola.com/news/business/article_7260f0f6-097c-579c-b229-a804af9f2692.html.

Moynihan, Colin. "Activist Unmasks Himself as Federal Informant in G.O.P. Convention Case." *New York Times,* January 4, 2009. https://www.nytimes.com/2009/01/05/us/05informant.html.

Murphy, Paul, and Mike Perlstein. "Ex-New Orleans Mayor Ray Nagin Sentenced to 10 Years." *USA Today,* July 9, 2014. https://www.usatoday.com/story/news/nation/2014/07/09/ray-nagin-new-orleans-mayor-sentencing/12397415/.

New Orleans Area Habitat for Humanity. "Musicians' Village." Last accessed July 23, 2020. http://www.habitat-nola.org/musicians-village/.

New Orleans Office of the Independent Police Monitor. "Hurricane Katrina: The Remaining Legacy." Accessed July 31, 2020. https://tbinternet.ohchr.org/Treaties/CAT/Shared%20Documents/USA/INT_CAT_CSS_USA_18551_E.pdf.

"NOAA CRP Restoration Projects." Accessed April 17, 2017. http://www.gulfmex.org/archive/crp/8005.html.

Nolan, Bruce. "Chinese Drywall Forces Hurricane Katrina Rebuilding Group to Premature End." Nola.com. Last modified September 8, 2011. http://www.nola.com/religion/index.ssf/2011/09/chinese_drywall_forces_katrina.html.

———. "Hurricane Relief Groups are Gutting, Rebuilding Homes Found with Chinese Drywall." Nola.com. Last modified April 11, 2011. http://www.nola.com/katrina/index.ssf/2011/04/hurricane_relief_groups_are_gu.html.

Pallardy, Richard. "Deepwater Horizon Oil Spill." Britannica. Last modified April 13, 2020. https://www.britannica.com/event/Deepwater-Horizon-oil-spill.

People's Institute for Survival and Beyond. "Dr. Kimberly Richards. Core Trainer and Organizer." Accessed July 15, 2020. https://www.pisab.org/dt_team/dr-kimberley-richards/.

Pope, John. "Common Ground Leader Thom Pepper Leaves a Legacy of Service to Adopted City; Memorial Set for February." Nola.com, December 23, 2019. https://www.nola.com/news/article_d6d1029c-1deb-11ea-ac96 -83af4fd529b7.html.

Powell, Alien. "Algiers Man Dies in Standoff after Firing on Cops outside His House." Nola.com, May 11, 2006. https://www.nola.com/news/crime_police /article_84b24b22-c313-59e3-9fb9-675f01cc17bf.html.

"Preservation Resource Center." Wikipedia. Accessed March 10, 2017. https:// en.wikipedia.org/wiki/Preservation_Resource_Center.

ProBono Project. "The Man of the Moment: Linton Carney." Last modified June 2, 2016. http://probono-no.org/news-highlights3/man-of-the-moment -linton-carney.

Quarantelli, E.L. "Catastrophes Are Different from Disasters: Implications for Crisis Planning and Managing Drawn from Katrina." *items: Insights from the Social Sciences.* June 11, 2006. https://items.ssrc.org/understanding-katrina /catastrophes-are-different-from-disasters-some-implications-for-crisis -planning-and-managing-drawn-from-katrina/.

Rebuilding Together New Orleans. "About Us." Accessed October 5, 2022. https://rebuildingtogether.org/about-us.

———. "Neighborhood Revitalization in Orleans Parish." Accessed May 15, 2020. https://www.rtno.org/about-rtno/.

———. "Rebuilding Together New Orleans." Accessed March 20, 2017. http:// www.rtno.org/about-us/.

"Rebuilding Together New Orleans Completes 500 Homes since Hurricane Katrina." *Uptown Messenger.* Last modified October 12, 2015. https:// uptownmessenger.com/2015/10/rebuilding-together-new-orleans -completes-500-homes-since-hurricane-katrina/.

Reckdahl, Katy. "50 Years Ago, Hurricane Betsy Offered a Foretaste of Katrina's Destruction." *The Advocate,* September 13, 2015. https://www.theadvocate .com/baton_rouge/news/article_85e3a80e-0f6d-5016-b89e-16bdcccd1286 .html.

———. "Chinese Drywall Concerns Investigated by Habitat for Humanity." Nola.com, June 18, 2010. http://www.nola.com/business/index.ssf/2010/06 /chinese_drywall_concerns_inves.html.

Reed, Adolph. "Three Tremes." nonsite.org. Last modified October 26, 2015. http://nonsite.org/editorial/three-tremes#.

Sahadi, Jeanne. "The New Bankruptcy Law and You." CNN. Last modified October 17, 2005. http://money.cnn.com/2005/10/17/pf/debt/bankruptcy _law/.

Saint Bernard Project USA. "About Us." SBPUSA.org. Accessed May 15, 2020, https://sbpusa.org/index.php?p=about-us.

Southeast Louisiana Legal Services. "Katrina Stories from our Staff and Supporters: Laura Tuggle, SLLS Executive Director." Accessed October 28,

2017. https://slls.org/support/item.6364-Katrina_Stories_from_Our_Staff _and_Our_Supporters.

———. "Southeast Louisiana Legal Services." Accessed July 31, 2020. https://slls .org.

"State Seeks $10M from ICF for Road Home Mistakes." *New Orleans City Business.* Last modified December 22, 2011. https://neworleanscitybusiness .com/blog/2011/12/22/state-seeks-10m-from-icf-for-road-home-mistakes/.

Statistics How To. "Snowball Sampling: Definition, Advantages and Disadvan- tages." Accessed August 16, 2020. https://www.statisticshowto.com /snowball-sampling/.

Strauss, Valerie. "The 10 School Districts with the Most Charter School Students." *Washington Post,* December 11, 2013. https://www.washington post.com/news/answer-sheet/wp/2013/12/11/the-10-school-districts-with -the-most-charter-school-students/?utm_term=.dbfcc38d848b.

Threlkeld, Scott. "A Job Well Done Helping Us Rebuild: An Editorial." *Times- Picayune,* January 10, 2012. http://www.nola.com/opinions/index.ssf/2012 /01/a_job_well_done_helping_us_reb.html.

Tulane School of Architecture. "After Hurricane Katrina, Most of the City's Public Housing Projects Were Demolished despite Protests from Residents and the Preservation Community." Accessed August 4, 2021. https ://architecture.tulane.edu/preservation-project/timeline-entry/1427.

U.S. Attorney's Office. "Former New Orleans Mayor C. Ray Nagin Sentenced for Conspiracy, Bribery, Honest Services Wire Fraud, Money Laundering, and Tax Violations." July 9, 2014. https://www.fbi.gov/contact-us/field-offices /neworleans/news/press-releases/former-new-orleans-mayor-c.-ray -nagin-sentenced-for-conspiracy-bribery-honest-services-wire-fraud -money-laundering-and-tax-violations.

U.S. Consumer Product Safety Commission. "Other Frequently Asked Ques- tions." Accessed July 21, 2017. https://www.cpsc.gov/content/Other -Frequently-Asked-Questions.

U.S. Geological Survey. "Louisiana's Changing Coastal Wetlands." Last modified July 12, 2017. https://www.usgs.gov/news/national-news-release/usgs -louisianas-rate-coastal-wetland-loss-continues-slow.

USSF Book Committee. "The United States Social Forum: Perspectives of a Movement." United States Social Forum. Accessed July 15, 2020. http://wiki .ussocialforum.net/images/e/ee/USSF_Perspectives_of_a_Movement_Book .pdf.

Voice of the Experienced. "Robert Goodman." Accessed October 17, 2019. https://www.vote-nola.org/robert-goodman.html.

———. "Norris Henderson." Accessed July 15, 2020. https://www.voiceofthe experienced.org/hendersonbio.

Winkler-Schmit, David. "Brandon Darby-FBI Informant and Common Ground Co-Founder." *The Advocate,* January 25, 2009. https://www.theadvocate.com/gambit/new_orleans/news/article_07f899ab-e630-524d-8291-974aaeb10c79.html.

Wolff, Tom, Meredith Minkler, Susan M. Wolfe, Bill Berkowitz, Linda Bowen, Frances Dunn Butterfoss, and K. S. Lee. "Collaborating for Equity and Justice: Moving beyond Collective Impact." *Nonprofit Quarterly,* January 9, 2017. https://nonprofitquarterly.org/collaborating-equity-justice-moving-beyond-collective-impact/.

INDEX

www.ingramcontent.com/pod-product-compliance
Lightning Source LLC
Chambersburg PA
CBHW020829270326
41928CB00006B/464